Off the
Beaten Path®

arizona

Help Us Keep This Guide Up to Date

Every effort has been made by the author and editors to make this guide as accurate and useful as possible. However, many changes can occur after a guide is published—establishments close, phone numbers change, hiking trails are rerouted, facilities come under new management, etc.

We would love to hear from you concerning your experiences with this guide and how you feel it could be improved and be kept up to date. While we may not be able to respond to all comments and suggestions, we'll take them to heart, and we'll make certain to share them with the author. Please send your comments and suggestions to the following address:

The Globe Pequot Press
Reader Response/Editorial Department
P.O. Box 480
Guilford, CT 06437

Or you may e-mail us at: editorial@GlobePequot.com

Thanks for your input, and happy travels!

INSIDERS' GUIDE®

OFF THE BEATEN PATH® SERIES

Off the Beaten Path®

SIXTH EDITION

arizona

A GUIDE TO UNIQUE PLACES

CARRIE MINER

INSIDERS' GUIDE®

GUILFORD, CONNECTICUT
AN IMPRINT OF THE GLOBE PEQUOT PRESS

The prices, rates, and hours listed in this guidebook
were confirmed at press time. We recommend,
however, that you call establishments to obtain
current information before traveling.

INSIDERS' GUIDE®

Text design by Linda Loiewski
Maps created by Equator Graphics © Morris Book Publishing, LLC
Illustrations by Carole Drong
Spot photography throughout © Daryl Benson/Masterfile

ISSN 1540-1197
ISBN-13: 978-0-7627-4195-3
ISBN-10: 0-7627-4195-3

Manufactured in the United States of America
Sixth Edition/First Printing

This book is dedicated to those adventurers in life who seek out new experiences by taking the road less traveled.

Page

NORTHERN
ARIZONA

Chinle

Bullhead
City   Kingman   Williams   Flagstaff   Winslow

WESTERN

ARIZONA   Holbrook

Sedona
Camp Verde   Show Low

Lake Havasu
City   Prescott   Payson   Pinetop-
Lakeside

Wickenburg   EASTERN

ARIZONA

Phoenix

CENTRAL
ARIZONA

Safford

Casa Grande

Yuma

SOUTHERN   Tucson   Willcox
ARIZONA

Tombstone

Sierra Vista

Nogales   Bisbee

N

Contents

Introduction ix

Northern Arizona 1

Western Arizona 33

Eastern Arizona 59

Central Arizona 87

Southern Arizona 121

Indexes 159

    General 159

    Museums and Sights 165

    Bed-and-Breakfast Inns, Lodges, Motels, and Guest Ranches . . . 166

    Restaurants, Cafes, and Other Eateries 167

About the Author 171

Introduction

Arizona is perhaps best known as the home of one of the world's most gorgeous gorges, the Grand Canyon. It has also gained a well-deserved reputation as a prime winter playground for snowbirds seeking sunshine and pampering. Indeed, it is all that—plus so much more.

Veer off the interstate highways or the main drags of Arizona's diverse communities, and you'll find hidden treasures that the Sunday travel sections often overlook. From secluded inlets on massive Lake Powell and stunning swimming holes in little-traveled regions of the Grand Canyon to an annual jousting fest in the desert and a folklore preserve tucked into a wildlife-rich canyon, Arizona holds more curiosities than any weeklong vacation itinerary could even begin to include (there's even skiing!).

Far from a cultural desert, Arizona has just about any arts-related diversion visitors might wish to enjoy, including Broadway-style shows; resident symphony, ballet, and theatrical companies; and venues for rock concerts and jazz jams. Add to this a generous supply of top-notch museums—showcasing Native American heritage, contemporary fine art, lifestyles of long-gone civilizations, and the flora and fauna of the enigmatic Sonoran Desert—and you'll quickly discover that there is infinitely more here than is often believed.

Sports fans will find their nirvana in the nation's fifth largest state, with professional teams wearing the uniforms of nearly every league imaginable—from the NBA's Phoenix Suns and the major league's Arizona Diamondbacks to the NHL's Phoenix Coyotes and the NFL's Arizona Cardinals. Fans can even root for their own home teams during spring-training exhibition games that bring the boys of summer to sites throughout the state every March. Longtime local favorites include the Arizona State University Sun Devils and their rivals

Elevations and Temperatures

One of the most surprising facts about Arizona is the variety of climates and landscapes. It's not all desert; it's not all lowland. In fact the terrain ranges from 70 feet above sea level at Yuma to 12,643 feet and alpine terrain atop the San Francisco peaks. Even Phoenix is at a higher elevation than you might imagine at 1,117 feet. The ride through the center of the state is a nice surprise as it climbs to 7,000 feet at Flagstaff where the great plateau of the Grand Canyon and the Navajo-Hopi Reservations begins. On a recent day in early March, high temperatures in the state ranged from a low of forty-seven degrees Fahrenheit in Flagstaff to a high of seventy-seven degrees in Yuma (with Phoenix at seventy-one degrees).

to the south, the University of Arizona Wildcats. For an even wilder sport, visitors should check out one of the many rodeos that are staged each year, demonstrating the best skills that area cowboys have to offer!

Let Arizona's hospitable residents pamper you at the day's end. Nowhere will you find your accommodations as diverse or—in many cases—luxurious. City slickers can relive their childhood fantasies at one of the many authentic guest ranches, and those in search of the ultimate in service and style can choose from dozens of top-rated resort hotels that offer activities ranging from their own water parks and European-style spas to horseback riding and championship golf. And if a day on the links is your idea of heaven, Arizona has a course for nearly every day of the year.

Even film buffs will find a fascinating array of locations that include working movie sets to scenic vistas that have served as studio "back lots" for decades. Wander among the landscapes that John Wayne galloped through, or visit the western theme park that was built for the classic film *Arizona*.

Some of the destinations in this book will have you traveling on the main road; some will take you out where the tour buses don't run. The thing about Arizona is, as film hero Buckaroo Banzai used to say, "No matter where you go, there you are."

Arizona Climate at a Glance

(Average daily high/low temperatures* by month and region)

Month	Deserts	Mountains	Month	Deserts	Mountains
January	66/37	50/21	July	100/73	89/57
February	69/39	54/24	August	98/71	85/55
March	75/42	58/27	September	96/66	82/48
April	83/49	67/34	October	87/54	72/37
May	92/56	76/40	November	75/43	59/27
June	100/65	84/47	December	67/38	51/22

* Degrees Fahrenheit

Greater Phoenix Average Temperatures

Month	Highs		Lows	
	Fahrenheit	Celsius	Fahrenheit	Celsius
January	65.2	18.4	39.4	4.1
February	69.7	20.9	42.5	5.8
March	74.5	23.6	46.7	8.2
April	83.1	28.4	53.0	11.6
May	92.4	33.5	61.5	16.4
June	102.3	39.0	70.6	21.4
July	105.0	40.5	79.5	26.4
August	102.3	39.0	77.5	25.3
September	98.2	36.7	70.9	21.6
October	87.7	30.9	59.1	15.0
November	74.3	23.5	46.9	8.3
December	66.4	19.1	40.2	4.5
Average	**85.1**	**29.5**	**57.3**	**14.0**

For Further Information about Arizona

Arizona Office of Tourism
Grand Canyon State Information Center
1110 West Washington Street, Suite 155
Phoenix, AZ 85007;
(602) 364–3700 or
(866) 275–5816 (toll-free)
www.arizonaguide.com

Greater Phoenix Convention and Visitors Bureau
One Arizona Center
400 East Van Buren Street, Suite 600
Phoenix, AZ 85004-2290;
(602) 254–6500 or (877) CALL–PHX (toll-free)
www.phoenixcvb.com

Metropolitan Tucson Convention and Visitors Bureau
100 South Church Avenue
Tucson, AZ 85701;
(520) 624–1817 or (800) 638–8350 (toll-free),
www.visittucson.org

The Four Corners:
Arizona as Part of a Southwest Itinerary

In so many ways Arizona is the heart of the Southwest. It is home to more Indian tribes than any other state in the union, and it is bordered by several major national parks, monuments, and recreation areas. Traveling from New Mexico in the east, you can develop an itinerary that might include several national monuments and national historic parks (El Morro and El Malpais between Albuquerque and Gallup, Gila Cliffs west of Truth or Consequences, White Sands near Las Cruces, or Aztec Ruins and Chaco Culture near Farmington in the northwest corner). In western Colorado you can visit Curacanti National Recreation Area between Montrose and Gunnison, then continue through the western Colorado ski country to Durango and visit Mesa Verde National Park near Four Corners. In southern Utah you'll find the beginning of the extensive chain of national parks, monuments, and recreation areas that stretches from Utah through northern Arizona to southern Nevada and includes Arches, Canyonlands, Capitol Reef, Glen Canyon/Lake Powell, the Grand Canyon, and Lake Mead/Hoover Dam; also in southern Utah are Zion and Bryce Canyon national parks. In southern Nevada adjacent to Lake Mead is the ever-popular, larger-than-life entertainment capital of Las Vegas. Finally, to the west in California is the Mohave Desert and Joshua Tree National Park.

New Mexico

Navajo and Zuni Reservations (both are partly in New Mexico and partly in Arizona)

Bisti Badlands Natural Area

El Morro National Monument

El Malpais National Monument

Gila Cliff Dwellings National Monument

Chaco Culture National Historic Park

Aztec Ruins National Monument

White Sands National Monument

Colorado

Curecanti National Recreation Area

Mesa Verde National Park

Utah

Arches National Park

Canyonlands National Park

Capitol Reef National Park

Natural Bridges National Monument

Glen Canyon National Recreation Area

Nevada

Red Rocks State Park

Valley of Fire State Park

Lake Mead National Recreation Area

California

Joshua Tree National Park

Mojave Desert National Recreation Area

Anza-Borrego Desert State Park

WEB SITES

Official site of the Arizona Office of Tourism,
with links to many cities and attractions:
www.arizonaguide.com

Grand Canyon:
www.thecanyon.com

Lake Powell Resorts and Marinas:
www.lakepowell.com

Arizona State Parks:
www.pr.state.az.us

Arizona Highways **magazine:**
www.arizonahighways.com

Arizona Game & Fish:
www.gf.state.az.us

Arizona Department of Commerce:
(including individual community profiles on every city and town
throughout the state):
www.commerce.state.az.us

Southeastern Arizona Bird Observatory:
www.sabo.org

Greater Phoenix Convention & Visitors Bureau:
www.phoenixcvb.com

State of Arizona home page:
www.azcentral.com

Metropolitan Tucson Convention and Visitors Bureau:
www.visittucson.org

Arizona Bureau of Land Management:
www.az.blm.gov

Arizona Humanities Council:
www.arizonaheritagetraveler.org

ARIZONA'S TOP TEN VISITOR ATTRACTIONS

Grand Canyon National Park
(4,672,911)

Saguaro National Park
(3,601,775)

Chase Field (formerly Bank One Ballpark)
(2,781,934)

South Mountain Park
(2,500,000)

Tempe Town Lake
(2,250,000)

London Bridge
(2,000,000)

Glen Canyon National Recreation Area
(1,861,773)

Lake Mead National Recreation Area
(1,717,975)

US Airways Center (formerly America West Arena)
(1,265,543)

The Phoenix Zoo
(1,240,000)

(according to 2004 attendance figures)

Dining and Lodging Fees

Arizona dining and lodging vary greatly throughout the state and change seasonally. Restaurants listed as *Places to Eat* are open for lunch and dinner unless otherwise noted. Pricing for rooms under *Places to Stay* is for double occupancy during high season.

Places to Eat

Up to $12	Inexpensive
$13 to $25	Moderate
$26 and up	Expensive

Places to Stay

Up to $100	Inexpensive
$101 to $200	Moderate
$201 and up	Expensive

Northern Arizona

Fredonia Area

If you'd like to visit a community that is short in the way of tourist amenities but long on history, you might want to make a stop in *Colorado City,* on Highway 389 immediately south of the Utah state line. The town, called Short Creek until 1958, has been around since the 1860s, when it was a Mormon settlement. When the Church of Jesus Christ of Latter Day Saints outlawed polygamy in 1890, church members who decided they'd rather fight than switch headed for Short Creek. This tiny agro-community became known to church officials and Arizona law enforcement officers as a haven for polygamists, and Mormons continue to be thus characterized by Hollywood and other less-informed folk.

Over the next forty to fifty years, there were several arrests for polygamy, and some questionable detective work was done by agents investigating the populace by posing as filmmakers. On July 26, 1953, the town's male population was rounded up and taken to the schoolhouse (which still stands today), where they were arrested, and the children were led away in the custody of the state. The families were eventually reunited—even in a conservative state like Arizona, the meat-hook approach to

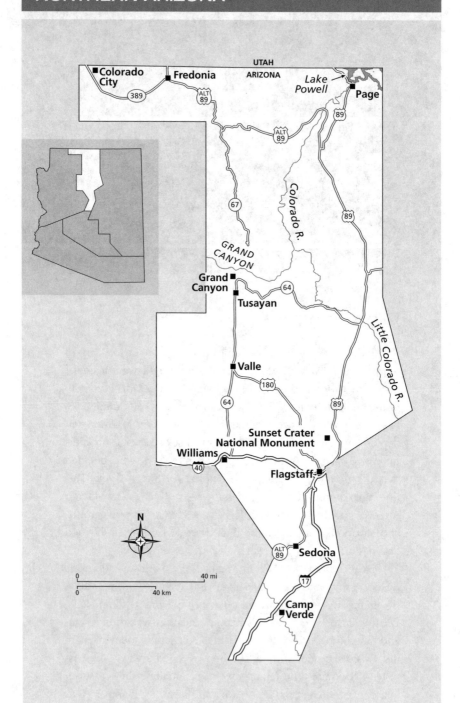

law enforcement didn't go over well. The governor responsible for the raid (conservative Republican Howard Pyle) was defeated for reelection, partly because of public disapproval of his methods in this case.

From all appearances polygamy (which court rulings have declared is legal as a religious doctrine) is still practiced in Colorado City. For decades following the raid, outsiders were not especially welcome in town, and one can hardly blame residents. Though the gingham gowns, spit curls, and many other trappings of a simpler time still abound, the community is changing enough to make a genuine effort to accommodate travelers. Visitors report that people here are friendly and more than willing to give you directions or chat about what there is to see and do in the area.

One thing you may want to do if you visit Colorado City is to stop and watch the ongoing excavation of an ancestral Puebloan (once known as the Anasazi) dwelling in the center of town. So far several rooms, storage spaces, and burial sites have been uncovered, and archaeologists believe there may be as many as two or three civilizations built on top of one another here. Locals also like to go hiking, as there are many wild areas to the north just across the Utah border. The vegetation here is typical of the high desert—junipers, sagebrush, some piñon pines—and there are distinct seasonal changes in temperature: High double- to triple-digit readings are common in the summer, and during the winter the community experiences three or four good snowfalls.

If you get hungry while visiting Colorado City, the **Vermillion Cliffs Candy Shop & Deli** (928–875–8093) at Arizona Avenue and Richard Street is open from 5:00 A.M. to 3:00 P.M. and has a full breakfast menu, along with every type of sandwich imaginable. They also make their own candy—including toffee, caramels, chocolate-covered peanuts, and date balls—and bake coffee cake, brownies, pies, and other goodies on the premises. Currently there are no motels in Colorado City; the nearest lodging is either in Hurricane, Utah, or Fredonia, Arizona.

AUTHOR'S TOP PICKS IN NORTHERN ARIZONA

Grand Canyon Railway	Museum of Northern Arizona
El Tovar Lodge	Tlaquepaque Arts & Crafts Village
Lake Powell	Pink Jeep Tours
Glen Canyon Dam	Papillon Grand Canyon Helicopters

FEBRUARY

Winterfest

Flagstaff

Sled dog races, llama games, winter sports, snow sculpture, parade, concerts, theater, art shows, historic tours, workshops, and winter star gazing.
(928) 774–4505 or (800) 842–7293

MARCH

Annual International Film Festival

Sedona

International independent cinema, documentary and animation, panel discussions featuring leading film professionals.
(928) 282–1177

Grand Canyon State Winter Games

Flagstaff

Arizona Snowbowl, slalom and giant slalom races, all ages, 5K Nordic ski race.
(928) 773–9707

MAY

Annual Rendezvous Days

Williams

Parade, black powder shoot, carnival, street dances, crafts, music.
(928) 635–4061

JUNE

Annual Wool Festival

Flagstaff

Sheep shearing, spinning and weaving demonstrations, and livestock competition at the Arizona Historical Society Pioneer Museum.
(928) 774–6272

Annual Pine Country Pro Rodeo

Flagstaff

PRCA approved, purse of $50,000 plus, chili cook-off, fashion show, parade, barn dances.
(800) 842–7293

JULY

Fair of Life Festival of Arts and Crafts Extraordinaire

Flagstaff

Wheeler Park, local and regional artisans and crafters, entertainment, classic car displays, chalk art for kids.
(928) 779–1227

Navajo Festival of Arts and Culture

Flagstaff

Museum of Northern Arizona, Navajo artists, demonstrations, storytellers, tribal dancing, music.
(928) 774–5213

Arizona Highland Celtic Festival

Flagstaff

Celtic celebration honoring the people of Brittany, Cornwall, Scotland, and Wales.
(928) 774–9541 or (800) 842–7293

Hopi Festival of Arts and Culture

Flagstaff

Museum of Northern Arizona, Hopi artists, demonstrations, tribal dances, children's activities.
(928) 774–5213

AUGUST

Flagstaff SummerFest

Flagstaff

Coconino County Fairgrounds, juried artists from across the country, fine food, live entertainment, hands-on arts and crafts for children.
(480) 968–5353 or (800) ART–FEST

Cool Country Cruise-In and Route 66 Festival

Williams

1950s-style fun with a classic car show, battle of the bands, sock hop.
(928) 635–1418

SEPTEMBER

Festival of Science

Flagstaff

Promotes science awareness and enthusiasm through field trips, exhibits, and lectures.
(800) 842–7293

Grand Canyon Music Festival

Grand Canyon

Shrine of the Ages Auditorium, musicians from around the country, jazz to classical.
(928) 638–9215 or (800) 997–8285

Jazz on the Rocks Benefit Festival

Sedona

Radisson Poco Diablo Resort, internationally known jazz festival.
(928) 282–1985

Labor Day PRCA Rodeo

Williams
(928) 635–4061

Fiesta del Tlaquepaque

Sedona

Mexican-style celebration; piñatas, mariachi bands, folklorico dance groups, flamenco/classical guitarists.
(928) 282–4838

Coconino County Fair

Flagstaff

Northern Arizona's largest county fair, featuring educational exhibits, livestock, live entertainment, a demolition derby, and carnival at the Fort Tuthill Coconino County Fairgrounds.
(928) 774–5130

OCTOBER

Celebraciónes de la Gente

Flagstaff

Museum of Northern Arizona, Diá de los Muertos (Day of the Dead) celebration, Hispanic artists, Latin music, and ballet folklorico performances.
(928) 774–5213

NOVEMBER–JANUARY

Annual Red Rock Fantasy of Lights

Sedona

Holiday lights, themed displays, holiday music.
(800) 521–3131

DECEMBER

Festival of Lights Boat Parade

Page

View from Wahweap Lodge and Marina or along the 5-mile Lakeshore Drive.
(928) 645–1004 or (928) 645–2741

One of the most spectacular nearby sights is ***Toroweap Point*** (spelled Tuweep on some maps), about 50 miles from Colorado City off Highway 389 down a lengthy stretch of graded (unpaved) road. The point, enclosed by a guardrail, juts out over the Colorado River, which lies about 3,000 feet below. Because it's closer to the river than many areas of the Grand Canyon are, you get both a spectacular view and a real sense of the power of the Colorado. A lot of visitors either don't know about Toroweap Point or decide that they'd rather see the Colorado from the South Rim of the Grand Canyon, so chances are you can spend as long as you like at Toroweap and not get elbowed aside by other visitors.

A hop and skip east is ***Pipe Spring National Monument*** (928–643–7105; www.nps.gov/pisp) on Highway 389, where an original Mormon fort (constructed of brick and wood) sits surrounded by high-desert vegetation and trees fed by underground springs. The name Pipe Spring comes from a locally famous feat of marksmanship executed by settler William Hamblin, who shot the bottom off a tobacco pipe. During the summer months there are costumed re-creations of pioneer life, but year-round you can feed the ducks in the duck pond and enjoy the serenity of this remote area. Farther east off Highway 389 is ***Steamboat Mountain,*** a natural outcropping of red stone that perfectly resembles its name. Though there are no picnic areas around the rock, weather permitting, it makes a nice 2-mile hike.

The quaint community of ***Fredonia*** (928–643–7241), also within spitting distance of the Utah border, was founded more than one hundred years ago by Mormon settlers. Some folks say the town's name is a combination of "free" and the Spanish word *doña,* meaning "lady." Accounts collected in the *Daughters*

officialarizona

State gem: Turquoise

State fossil: Petrified wood

State mammal: Ringtail

State reptile: Arizona ridge-nosed rattlesnake

State fish: Apache trout

State amphibian: Arizona tree frog

State butterfly: Two-tailed swallowtail

State song: The Arizona March Song

State colors: Blue and old gold

State tree: Paloverde

State bird: Cactus wren

State flower: Saguaro cactus blossom

State motto: Ditat Deus (God Enriches)

Official state neckwear (yes, there really is one): Bola tie

Arizona's largest newspaper: *The Arizona Republic,* Phoenix

Two newspapers in Tucson: *The Arizona Daily Star* (morning) and the *Tucson Citizen* (evening)

of the Pioneers claim that Mormons residing in Kanab would send their extra wives over the state line into the Arizona border town in an attempt to evade U.S. Marshals cracking down on polygamy.

Outside Fredonia, there are several lodges near Marble Canyon, including the **Marble Canyon Lodge** (928–355–2225 or 800–726–1789) and the **Cliff Dwellers Lodge** (928–355–2228 or 800–433–2543). The Marble Canyon Lodge is a sixty-room facility that has a restaurant that's open from 6:00 A.M. to 9:00 P.M., a convenience store, a small trading post, a gas station, a post office, and a laundromat. The rate for double occupancy ranges from $54 to $134 depending on the season. The Cliff Dweller is a twenty-two-room lodge that has a small convenience store, a gas station, a fly-fishing guide service and fly-fishing shop, and a restaurant that's open from morning through the evening hours. The rate for double occupancy is $65 to $75.

It's really the natural beauty of this area and evidence of ancient Anasazi cultures that draws visitors. Less than a two-hour drive from the city limits are Zion National Park and Bryce Canyon National Park (both in Utah), as well as Lake Powell and the North Rim of Grand Canyon.

Taking U.S. Highway 89A southeast from Fredonia leads you over the Kaibab Plateau to the **Vermillion Cliffs,** which John Wesley Powell described as "a long bank of purple cliffs plowed from the horizon high into the heavens." There are several pullouts and one scenic overlook so you can stop and take pictures of these bright-red walls of rock. At the base of the cliffs are some easy hiking trails. One difficult and unmaintained trail—known as Sandhill Crack— actually goes up the cliff. Just south of the cliffs is a marked, gravel road that leads to **House Rock Ranch,** a state-managed ranch where buffalo roam free. This road is passable most times of the year in an ordinary vehicle, although it's a bit bumpy in places and has been known to get washed out. Call the North Kaibab Ranger District at (928) 643–7395 for information on road conditions. The ranch, founded in the 1920s as part of a buffalo-raising venture that failed, is now the state-owned home of a couple who manage the remaining buffalo herd of about one hundred. There are also antelope, deer, and bighorn sheep in the House Rock Valley area, though they can all be rather elusive. The best wildlife-watching advice from locals is to drive south of the ranch on the 26-mile road until you come to the end. Then get out and walk around a bit.

Continuing east on US 89A past the Vermillion Cliffs will take you to **Marble Canyon.** In 1995 the state built a new bridge for car traffic over the Colorado River at Marble Canyon while retaining the older Navajo bridge, which is about 200 feet away from the new one, as a pedestrian crossing. This gives you the opportunity to actually walk out and stand hundreds of feet over the river that carved the Grand Canyon.

The Canyon: North Rim

Named a national park by President Woodrow Wilson in 1919, **Grand Canyon** remains the crown jewel of Arizona's tourism offerings. Drawing more than 4.6 million visitors a year, this natural wonder is a jaw-dropper no matter how many times you peer over its edge. Each time of day and each season brings a distinct palette of hues to the canyon, providing its own unique panorama. A word of caution though: The only thing separating the gazers from the gorge is a low stone wall. Unfortunately, it's not at all unusual for a hapless tourist to discover the laws of gravity a little too late. Enjoy the view, but respect the potential danger that exists—particularly for the careless.

Though many tourists choose to limit their exploration of the canyon to the views from the South Rim, there is another, very different side to this spectacular locale. The **North Rim** of the canyon is about 1,200 feet higher than the South Rim, and during the winter it gets snowed in (the only access road, Highway 67, is closed every year from mid-October to mid-May). It doesn't have as many amenities as the South Rim has, and it isn't as accessible.

The North Rim is, however, significantly more lush than the South Rim and has spectacular views. Only 10 percent of the total number of visitors to the canyon go to the North Rim, so solitude is easy to seek out. If you want to stay in the park on the North Rim, your only choice is the **Grand Canyon Lodge** (928–638–2611 or 303–29–PARKS; www.amfac.com). Fortunately, it's a nice place to stay, and the lodge building (constructed of native pine logs and limestone slabs) is built right on the edge of the North Rim not far from Bright Angel Point. The view out the windows of the dining room of this 1936 National Historic Landmark is not to be believed. In addition to the dining room (which serves traditional Western fare such as prime rib, steaks, and seafood, with some vegetarian items thrown in), the lodge also has a lobby area, gift shop, saloon, and snack shop. The National Park Service also uses the building in the evening for multimedia shows about the canyon.

For accommodations the lodge offers log cabins as well as motel rooms in a structure that was built

grandcanyonfun facts

Age: 2 billion years old

Depth: South Rim inner canyon—4,500 feet; North Rim inner canyon—5,700 feet

Width: 10 miles average

Length: 277 miles

Area: 1,904 square miles

Elevation: North Rim—8,200 feet; South Rim—7,000 feet

Visitors: more than 4.6 million per year

by the Union Pacific Railroad in the 1920s. There is also a campground on the North Rim as well as a gas station and a general store.

Now that you're here at the lightly visited North Rim, you might want to venture out on the 23-mile paved road to Cape Royal. Halfway down the road, you can stop at Point Imperial (which, at an elevation of 8,803 feet, is the highest lookout on either rim) and get a grand view of the Vermillion Cliffs to the north, the Painted Desert to the east, the Little Colorado River Canyon to the southeast, and Navajo Mountain to the northeast. Picnic tables at the Point make this a convenient place to stop for a picnic lunch. Additional lookouts along the rest of the drive offer views of such legendary landmarks as Freya Castle, Vishnu Temple, and Wotan's Throne.

Many visitors to the North Rim prefer to just wander the footpaths under the trees and gaze at the awesome marvel of the canyon. For those who prefer a farther trek, the *Phantom Ranch* overnight to the North Rim includes a room in a ranch cabin, home-cooked breakfast, lunch, and dinner, and five and a half hours of mule riding the first day, four and a half hours the second.

Lake Powell to Sunset Crater

It may be difficult to imagine Arizona as an aquatic play park (particularly because the state is more famous for its giant cacti and desert sunsets), but the truth is that this state has a plethora of lakes and rivers that are perfect for any activity from floating and meditating to shooting the rapids.

On the border with Utah sits *Lake Powell,* in the *Glen Canyon National Recreation Area.* Lake Powell began to flow into life in 1963 with the closing of the gates on *Glen Canyon Dam* on the Colorado River. Nine years later, 186 river miles had filled about one hundred canyons, creating a playground that includes 1,960 miles of shoreline and boating opportunities galore.

From the Arizona side, Lake Powell can be reached by driving on Highway 89 to Page, near the southern tip of the lake.

The Glen Canyon Dam and the *Carl Hayden Visitors Center* (928–608–6404) are located off U.S. Highway 89 about 2 miles north of Page. These attractions provide travelers with the opportunity to learn some of the area's history (even prehistory—dinosaur footprints, taken from the canyon, are on display), as well as tour the massive dam and witness its energy-producing prowess. The second-highest dam in the United States, Glen Canyon Dam has a maximum power output of 1,320 megawatts, enough power for a city of more than 1 million inhabitants. The power is sold to independent companies that utilize it in southern Arizona, Las Vegas, and as far away as Los Angeles.

Less than 5 miles northwest on US 89 is the *Wahweap Lodge and Marina*

trivia

Lake Powell, along the northern Arizona–Utah border, has more miles of shoreline than the entire Pacific coast of the United States.

(928–645–2433 or 800–528–6154; www .lakepowell.com). The marina rents houseboats and other watercraft, and the lodge provides comfortable accommodations for travelers. Its dining room features an eclectic blend of American dishes and occasionally stages live entertainment. The marina is also the location of a December Festival of Lights Parade, in which boat owners attire their craft in holiday splendor and make the trek to Glen Canyon Dam and back.

One of the most popular ways to enjoy the lake is to rent a houseboat and live on the water for a week or a weekend. These floating motel rooms range from 44 to 75 feet and can sleep as many as twelve passengers. Necessities and amenities such as refrigerators, range-ovens, toilets, showers, and gas grills are available to help you have a great vacation. Some of the more deluxe rigs even offer options like TVs and VCRs, swim slides, hot tubs, and multispeaker CD players. Prices range from $816 for three days on a 44-foot boat during the budget season (wintertime) to $8,897 for seven days in the summer season on the spiffy 75-foot Odyssey Class boat that sports a top deck with flying bridge controls.

You can rent houseboats at Wahweap and three other marinas that form an elliptical ring around Lake Powell. For reservations and information on Wahweap Lodge and Marina, Hall's Crossing Marina, Bullfrog Resort and Marina, or Hite Marina contact *Lake Powell Resorts & Marinas* (800–528–6154; www.lakepowell.com). The latter three marinas are located on the Utah side of the border.

If you'd prefer not to do your own piloting, guides from *Wilderness River Adventures* (800–528–6154) can take you from Lake Powell on a 15-mile float trip aboard a large raft. The journey starts at the base of the Glen Canyon Dam and makes a stop where you can get a close-up view of Anasazi petroglyphs; Anasazi (Ah–nah–*sah*–zee) is a Navajo word that translates as "ancient ones" and relates to a northern Arizona Indian tribe that vanished centuries ago. The float trip concludes at Lees Ferry, where Mormon pioneers used to cross the Colorado on their way back to Utah to get married. Still standing near the ferry crossing are cabins erected by settlers. There are also picnic areas and restrooms.

The beauty of the Glen Canyon area is astounding: clear mountain vistas of sand-sculpted and water-worked stones, high-desert vegetation, and sunsets of breathtaking dimensions. Over the years the region's majesty has attracted

Lake Powell's side canyons

many film companies. Notable movies filmed here include *Planet of the Apes, Maverick,* and Hong Kong director John Woo's *Broken Arrow.*

One of Glen Canyon's most famous examples of nature's creative power is **Rainbow Bridge,** which the Navajos call *Nááts'íílid Na'nízhoozhí*—meaning "rainbow extends across"—and consider sacred. At 290 feet, it's the world's tallest stone arch. Some of the lake excursion packages offered by the marinas include visits to this marvel, which can only be reached on foot or horseback.

South on US 89 you'll cross the Little Colorado River and soon arrive at the **Wupatki National Monument** (928–679–2365; www.nps.gov/wupa) near the San Francisco peaks. The monument, about 40 miles north of Flagstaff, is composed of more than 800 ruins of structures built by the ancient Sinagua Indians, who moved into the area around A.D. 1066. The ruins include a kind of handball court and a warm-air "blow hole" that releases a constant stream from deep underground. Seasonal mini-lectures are offered when visitor numbers are high. During the summer, two-hour ranger-led discovery hikes are scheduled as well. Admission is $5.00 per person, good for seven days at both Wupatki and Sunset Crater National Monuments.

Because of the elevation, the forests around here are lush with ponderosa pine (the largest spread of ponderosa pine in the world, in fact, sprouts in this area), aspen, and brilliantly colored wildflowers.

Just down the road from Wupatki is **Sunset Crater Volcano National Monument** (928–526–0502; www.nps.gov/sucr). Sunset Crater, named by Grand Canyon explorer John Wesley Powell for its orange-colored rim, erupted 900 years ago, leaving behind a 1,000-foot-high cone and a bizarre landscape of lava flow and ice caves. If Hollywood hasn't considered (or, perhaps, been permitted) to shoot a sci-fi flick here, it's an opportunity missed. The terrain resembles something you'd expect to see on an alien planet. Several easy-to-follow hiking trails take visitors around the lava flow, and picnic areas are not too far down the road.

Flagstaff Area

Fewer than twenty minutes south of US 89 is the alpine community of **Flagstaff**, set at the base of one of Arizona's most stellar mountain ranges. There are two competing theories on the origin of the town's unusual name. One says that more than 125 years ago, a flagpole made from a pine tree was placed near the site to mark the location of an underground spring so that thirsty travelers could find it. Historians generally agree that it was so named following a flag-raising ceremony marking the nation's centennial. Settlers chose a tall pine, trimmed its branches, and attached a flag to the top.

Regardless of how it got its name, the city of 64,000 is now a top getaway destination. The town is located in Coconino County, the second largest county in the United States. Over the years "Flag" (as it's known to Arizonans) has been a logging and ranching community and once was an important stop on the Atlantic & Pacific Railroad. In Arizona, Flagstaff is famous for three reasons. It is the home of **Northern Arizona University** (NAU; 928–523–9011 or 888–MORE–NAU; www.nau.edu), which is known for its forestry program; the Babbitt family, who moved into the area in the 1880s; and the Lowell Observatory, which is the site of a number of major heavenly findings.

trivia

Flagstaff garnered the honor as the world's first "International Dark-Sky City" by the International Dark-Sky Association.

Flagstaff is a city with a lot of charm. Surrounded by gorgeous scenery, including the frequently snow-capped 12,000-foot San Francisco Peaks, it has preserved many of its historic sites and much of its architecture and thus retains a small-town feel. Still, it has modern amenities that make it comfortable and convenient for residents and visitors alike. The main street, Milton Road, is lined with restaurants (both national chains and local mom-and-pop places), motels, hotels, and shopping centers; it also passes right by NAU.

Milton Road winds north through town and comes to an abrupt split where you can take a hard left and continue up Mars Hill to the observatory, veer right onto the former Santa Fe Avenue, now named Route 66 (which becomes

US 89, heading back toward Sunset Crater), then make a left onto U.S. Highway 180, which heads toward the **Arizona Historical Society/Pioneer Museum** (928–774–6272; www.arizonahistoricalsociety.org); open from 9:00 A.M. to 5:00 P.M. Monday through Saturday, $3.00 adults, $2.00 children ages 12 to 18, and the **Museum of Northern Arizona** (928–774–5213; www.musnaz .org). Daily hours from 9:00 A.M. to 5:00 P.M.; $5.00 adults, $4.00 seniors, $2.00 children ages 7 to 17. The historical society, located in the former 1908 Coconino County Hospital, has an impressive collection of photographs from Flagstaff's early days. This collection includes early twentieth-century photos and equipment from the Kolb brothers, who became famous for capturing the splendor of the Grand Canyon. Also located on the grounds are antique farming machines, an early motorized fire engine, and an original 1880s cabin.

The Museum of Northern Arizona was founded in 1928. The exhibits at the museum encompass the biology, geology, anthropology, and fine arts of both northern Arizona and the Four Corners region. The museum has displays ranging from a life-size statue of a Dilophosaurus (a carnivorous dinosaur whose remains are found only in this region), an anthropology exhibit that traces the region's history back 12,000 years, and fine arts made by Zuni, Hopi, and Navajo Indians.

US 180 also takes you up to the **Arizona Snowbowl** (928–779–1951; www.arizonasnowbowl.com), a prime skiing spot as well as a location for snowboarding and other cold-weather sports. The Snowbowl features thirty-two runs (ranging from dinky bunny hills to some that challenge very experienced skiers). Ski rentals and repairs are available, and you can sign up for beginner or intermediate lessons (also a children's ski school, beginning at age four, runs throughout the season). Lift tickets cost $44 for an all day pass (from 9:00 A.M. to 4:00 P.M.) or $36 (noon to 4:00 P.M.) on weekends and $29 for an afternoon pass on weekdays. There are two lodges—Hart Prairie Lodge and Agassiz Lodge—where you can park yourself at the end of a long day of schussing.

The **Lowell Observatory,** located at the top of Mars Hill, was built by astronomer Percival Lowell, a Mars buff who published a book about that planet's canals. It seems silly now, but Lowell erroneously believed there was life on the Angry Red Planet. He was right on the mark, however, when he predicted that a ninth planet—Planet X—would be discovered. In 1930, fourteen years after Lowell's death, astronomy assistant Clyde Tombaugh found the planet, now known as Pluto, while studying photographic plates. Visitors to the observatory can hear the full story at the visitors center (928–774–2096 or 928–774–3358; www.lowell.edu). The observatory is open daily from March to October 9:00 A.M. to 5:00 P.M., November to February from noon to 5:00 P.M.,

Famous Arizonans

Past and present residents

Rex Allen (actor)
Willcox

Charles Barkley (basketball star)
Paradise Valley

Glen Campbell (singer)
Paradise Valley

Lynda Carter (actor)
Phoenix

Alice Cooper (rock star)
Paradise Valley

Clive Cussler (best-selling author)
Paradise Valley

Ted Danson (actor)
Flagstaff

Hugh Downs (news anchor)
Carefree

Joe Garagiola (baseball Hall of
Famer/broadcaster)
Paradise Valley

Andy Granatelli (race car driver)
Paradise Valley

Paul Harvey (radio personality)
Carefree

Charles Mingus (jazz musician)
Nogales

Stevie Nicks (singer)
Phoenix

Leslie Nielsen (actor)
Paradise Valley

Nick Nolte (actor)
Phoenix

Marty Robbins (country-western singer)
Glendale

Linda Ronstadt (singer)
Tucson

David Spade (comedian)
Scottsdale

Steven Spielberg (director)
Scottsdale

Tanya Tucker (country singer)
Willcox

Dick Van Dyke (actor)
Cave Creek

Sean Young (actress)
Sedona

with evening programs starting at 7:30 or 8:00 P.M., depending on the season. Evening programs include nighttime tours and celestial viewing several nights per week. Seasonal "Night Sky" programs are offered Wednesday, Friday, and Saturday evenings. Admission is $5.00 for adults and $2.00 for children ages 5 to 17, with separate admission charges for day and evening programs.

Flagstaff hosts a popular *Winterfest,* voted by the American Bus Association as one of the Top 100 Events in North America. Winterfest activities range from wine-tasting events to jazz concerts to sled-dog races. Locations for the events vary, as do costs (some are free, others have a charge). Call the Flagstaff Visitors Center (800–842–7293; www.flagstaffarizona.org) for more information on Winterfest or other annual events.

In the summer Flagstaff's moderate temperature (the average high is eighty degrees) draws many Arizonans who want to escape the heat that builds up in the southeastern and central parts of the state. The surrounding forest area offers premier hiking and camping opportunities. The city even has an urban trails system that allows visitors and residents to access forest areas, canyons, and national monuments. The Flagstaff Visitors Center has specific maps of these trails, which include treks to the summit of Mount Humphrey (the tallest mountain in Arizona) and to many scenic aspen groves and alpine meadows in the Coconino National Forest.

Nature buffs will especially enjoy exploring the wide open spaces at the **Hart Prairie Preserve** (928–774–8892; www.nature.org). Located 14 miles north of Flagstaff, at 2601 North Fort Valley Road, this 245-acre preserve protects such endangered plants as the delicate bloomer stock and the rare Bebb's willow trees. Guided ninety-minute nature walks will introduce you to the plants and wildlife thriving in the preserve's open mountain meadows.

Special summer festivals include the **Hopi Festival of Arts and Culture** events and **Navajo Festival of Arts and Culture** at the Museum of Northern Arizona and the **Flagstaff SummerFest,** an arts and crafts festival with food and entertainment in August.

All year round Flagstaff offers the opportunity to hang out in great, funky little restaurants. The **Beaver Street Brewery and Whistle Stop Cafe** (928–779–0079) at 11 South Beaver Street, for example, is an actual microbrewery with an eclectic menu that includes everything from salads and sandwiches to wood-fired gourmet pizzas. Killer desserts include a chocolate bread pudding and a huge fruit cobbler.

Downtown, in the older section of Flagstaff (east of Mount Humphrey and north and south of the visitors center), shops, cafes, music venues, and very interesting old churches (including a Gothic cathedral that has gargoyles on its parapets—a most unusual sight in Arizona!) draw visitors year-round. The downtown shops around downtown's **Heritage Square** sell everything from outdoor gear to books to local arts and crafts. Along old Route 66 is an amazing collection of motels built during the prime years of the "Mother Road." Some look as if they could use a little attention; others are just as shiny as the day they went up.

In the midst of these nostalgic accommodations sits **The Museum Club,** aka the Zoo (928–526–9434; www.museumclub.com), at 3404 East Route 66. A historic honky-tonk owned by Shanyn and Joe Langes, the huge log-cabin building was built in 1931 by taxidermist Dean Eldredge, who used the structure to display his collection of trophy animals, antique firearms, and other bits of Americana. Five years later the museum was purchased by Doc Williams, a saddlemaker who turned the place into a nightclub. Eventually Don Scott, a former member of Bob Wills and the Texas Playboys, bought the club. For years it was the place to play for up-and-coming country talent. Stars like Willie Nelson, Waylon Jennings, and Wanda "Let's Have a Party!" Jackson shook the rafters.

Scott and his wife Thorna used to live in an upstairs apartment at the club, and some claim their spirits still haunt the honky–tonk (Don committed suicide in front of the downstairs fireplace, and Thorna died as a result of a fall down the stairs).

In 1978, Martin and Stacie Zanzucchi purchased The Museum Club, which by that time was desperately in need of repairs, and set about the time-consuming and meticulous task of restoring it to its original grandeur. They succeeded so well that the club made *Car and Driver* and *Country America* magazines' lists of the top ten roadhouses in the nation. The Zanzucchis were given the Governor's Award for Historic Preservation; The Museum Club is listed on the National Register of Historic Places. In 2005, the Langeses became the new "Zookeepers" of the club. Today, the famous roadhouse carries on its hip-shaking tradition as the "Best Place to Dance" in town.

Visitors to The Museum Club can study the display of historic photos, buy Route 66 and Museum Club memorabilia (everything from a magnet to an embroidered denim jacket), and listen to live entertainment Tuesday through Sunday nights. The club is open seven days a week. As part of Operation Safe Rides, The Museum Club offers free taxis to and from the club.

Numerous motels, ski lodges, and bed-and-breakfast inns provide accommodations in and around Flagstaff. Although just about every moderately priced national chain has a presence in Flagstaff, two properties are standouts. A venerable favorite is **Little America Hotel** (928–779–2741 or 800–865–1399; www.littleamerica.com) at 2515 East Butler Avenue. It offers all the comforts of home, a twenty-four-hour restaurant, a courtesy van, and more in a pine-shaded setting. Newer is **Embassy Suites** (928–774–4333 or 800–362–2779), 706 South Milton Road. The staff at this hotel is outstanding and the rooms, well, roomy. For a more intimate B&B style, try the **Inn at 410** (800–774–2008; www .inn410.com) at 410 North Leroux Street. Close to the visitors center, this 1907 Craftsman-style home has six guest suites and three guest rooms. Most of the suites have fireplaces and some offer Jacuzzi tubs. Locals claim that the 410 is the town's top B&B, a fact that was supported by the *Arizona Republic* in Phoenix, which lauded it as "the best bed-and-breakfast in northern Arizona." Rates range from $159 to $219 per night.

While in Flagstaff, visit the **Riordan Mansion State Historic Park** (928–779–4395) at 409 Riordan Road. Tucked away behind the Target store on Milton Road, this massive, multistory log cabin was built in 1904 for Timothy and Michael Riordan, owners of the Arizona Lumber & Timber Company. The building's architect was none other than Charles Whittlesley, designer of the El

Tovar Hotel at the South Rim of the Grand Canyon as well as Old Faithful Lodge at Yellowstone. State Park rangers give guided tours of the mansion. Tours are scheduled every hour on the hour starting at 11:00 A.M., and there are also self-guided tours of the grounds. Tour prices are $6.00 adults and $2.50 children ages 7 to 13. The last tour is at 4:00 P.M. Reservations are recommended.

Other must-sees in the Flagstaff area include **Walnut Canyon National Monument,** which comprises more than 300 rooms built into limestone cliffs as part of a prehistoric Sinaguan pueblo. The visitors center (928–526–3367; www.nps.gov/waca) has displays of pottery and artifacts recovered from the area. The monument can be reached by traveling east on Interstate 40 about 7 miles. Admission is $5.00 per person and is good for seven days.

Continue on I–40 another 26 miles to reach **Meteor Crater** (928–289–2362; www.meteorcrater.com), where 45,000 years ago a nickel-iron meteor traveling 33,000 miles per hour smashed into the Earth, creating a hole that's 570 feet deep, almost a mile wide, and more than 3 miles in circumference. Admission is $15.00 for adults, $13.00 for seniors over 60 and $6.00 for children ages 6 to 17. In the 1890s remnants of the meteor were found around the crater, and metalworkers, who failed to understand the significance of the discovery, melted down some of this material to create tools. At the beginning of the twentieth century, a mining engineer concluded that the crater was the result of a gigantic meteor, currently estimated to have been somewhere between 80 and 100 feet in diameter. For more than twenty-five years the engineer searched in vain for the main mass left from the meteor. Scientists, including Dr. Eugene Shoemaker, the Flagstaff-based astrogeologist who helped discover the Shoemaker-Levy Comet, now believe that about 80 percent of the meteor vaporized on impact. All plant and animal life within a 100-mile radius of the site was destroyed as nearly a half-billion tons of rock were gouged from the earth and showered the area.

Apollo astronauts trained in this area in preparation for the moon landings, and some skeptics actually believe that the lunar expeditions were faked on this site! In any case, you can see a spaceship landing in this crater in the John Carpenter movie *Starman.*

The crater museum complex includes the **Museum of Astrogeology** and the **Astronauts Hall of Fame,** which features a space capsule. The park grounds honor the crews of *Apollo I* and *Challenger.* There also are guided tours of the rim of the crater.

Apparently meteoric activity has not been limited to this remote location. If you fly over Arizona and study the terrain from south of Flagstaff to about the Casa Grande area and as far east as Winslow, you might notice a curious pattern of concentric rings that vary in size from 4 miles to more than 100 miles in diameter (you can see the same effect on a raised-relief map). Scientists believe these circles are the result of an ancient meteor barrage that actually scarred the earth's crust. In these circular areas are large concentrations of copper, silver, gold, and other minerals that were instrumental in the economic development of Arizona.

Many visitors to Flagstaff make Grand Canyon their next stop. An excellent way to see this natural wonder is to take I–40 west and drive about 30 miles to the town of **Williams** (800–863–0546), which is named for William Sherley "Old Bill" Williams, a famous trapper and Arizona pioneer.

This tiny Main Street locale was the last Route 66 town to be bypassed by the completion of I–40 in 1985, and with its old-fashioned street lamps and century-old brick storefronts, it offers visitors a trip back in time. If you're a fan of road memorabilia, stop by **Colors of the West** (928–635–9559) at 210 West Route 66. Across the way you'll find quality Native American arts at the **Pueblo Indian Gallery** (928–635–4966). For a dash of country charm, stop by the **Rustic Raspberry** (928–635–3024) at 309 West Route 66. These shops are open most days during daylight hours but often have shorter winter hours.

For a bite to eat, drop by **Rod's Steakhouse** (928–635–2671 or 800–562–5545), a Route 66 (known locally as Bill Williams Avenue) landmark with a steer-shaped sign on the roof. Rod's has steaks, prime rib, and seafood. For a blast to the past, travel a few more blocks west on Route 66 to **Twisters** (928–635–0266). The 1950s soda fountain serves up hamburgers and hot dogs as well as good old-fashioned sundaes, floats, and phosphates. An adjoining gift shop adds to the experience with a wide selection of Route 66 merchandise, classic Coca-Cola memorabilia, and fanciful items celebrating the careers of such celluloid characters as Betty Boop, James Dean, and Marilyn Monroe.

Williams is also the home of the **Grand Canyon Railway** (800–843–8724; www.thetrain.com). Initially built both for passengers and to serve area mines, the railway carried its first passengers to the Grand Canyon in 1901. Over time it transported U.S. presidents as well as other dignitaries and celebrities to see one of the world's most famous attractions.

Unfortunately the train couldn't compete with America's love affair with the automobile, and in 1968 it carried its last passengers. The defunct railroad was purchased in 1989 by Max Biegert, who restored not only the tracks, the engines, and the cars, but also the **Fray Marcos Hotel** (same phone number as the railway), which now serves as the railway's depot as well as a museum and gift shop.

Using historic steam engines and coach cars, the train not only takes passengers through 65 miles of glorious Arizona territory (which is especially spectacular when it's wearing a snowy winter mantle), but it also takes them back in time. While the train chugs along, passengers sit in coach cars that are decorated in original early twentieth-century style. The end car, which has an observation platform, actually uses upholstered chairs and sofas. Entertainers, including a singing brakeman dressed in period attire, perform traditional and original music about life and love on the frontier. If you take this route to the canyon, be prepared for some excitement—it's not unusual for a "train rob-bery" to take place, staged by bandits on horseback.

Beverages and snacks are served during the trip, which begins in Williams at 9:30 A.M. (be at the depot between 8:30 and 9:00 A.M.) and arrives at the Grand Canyon's South Rim at 12:15 P.M. Passengers debark at the canyon's his-toric depot and can tour the area's numerous attractions before the train pulls out at 3:15 P.M. for the trek back to Williams. You will return by 5:45 P.M. From the end of May through the first of September, there are two daily trains depart-ing at 8:30 and 10:00 A.M., returning at 5:15 and 6:45 P.M. respectively. Prices start at $60 for adults, $35 for youth (11 to 16), and $25 for children (2 to 10).

Besides being an easy and entertaining way to see the canyon, the train helps to cut down on pollution from the nearly 50,000 cars yearly that—without the railroad—would otherwise all be driven to the scenic wonder. The railway donates a portion of the ticket price to the Grand Canyon Trust, a conservation organization.

The approximately three-hour layover at the canyon gives you plenty of time to see El Tovar Hotel, Lookout Studio, Maswik Lodge and Cafeteria, Bright Angel Lodge, Hopi House, and the other attractions in the immediate area. If you wish to stay longer—especially if you want to hike or take a mule ride in the canyon—you can book a return at a different date and stay at one of the lodges within the park.

Grand Canyon: South and East Rims

When visiting the popular **South Rim,** begin at the **Canyon View Informa-tion Plaza,** where you will find some nicely presented kiosk-type information about the park. From there it's a short walk to Mather Point and your first view of the Grand Canyon. Keep in mind that this spot can be a bit more crowded than some other viewpoints.

A free shuttle system runs on four routes at the South Rim: Hermits Rest Route, Village Route, Kaibab Trail Route, and Canyon View/Mather Point Route—easing transportation along the congested rim roads. In addition, Phase I and Phase II of the 73-mile, multiuse network of trails in the Greenway sys-tem are complete and open to the public—adding easy access from Yavapai Point to Pipe Creek Vista and the Canyon View Information Plaza and the Grand Canyon Village.

The canyon is well-known for its *mule trips,* which take riders through zones of vegetation that range from pine forest to scrub desert. These can be arranged from either the North Rim or the South Rim and cover various distances. A multitude of mule trips can be arranged through the Grand Canyon National Park Lodges (303–29–PARKS or 888–29–PARKS; www.grandcanyonlodges.com), including full-day, overnight, and two-night journeys. All riders must weigh less than 200 pounds fully dressed (and, yes, they do weigh everyone!), must be at least 4 feet, 7 inches in height, and, for safety's sake, must be able to speak and understand English. These beasts do walk right along the trail's edge, so the faint of heart may want to find another activity. These treks are hugely popular, so reservations should be made as far in advance as possible.

If you're up for an adventure, legend has it that John Doyle Lee, the Mormon pioneer who is famous for Lees Ferry and infamous for his participation in the murder of more than 120 travelers at Mountain Meadows, supposedly found a gold mine somewhere on the North Rim. In the more than a century since Lee's death, numerous searchers have combed the canyon, starting at *Soap Creek* just south of Lees Ferry, and heading west as far as *Vulcan's Throne.* If Lee's contemporaries are to be believed, the gold is still out there. *Note:* Mining isn't allowed in Grand Canyon National Park, so if you do stumble across the treasure you'll have to settle for being famous but not rich!

There are so many ways to see the canyon. You can fly over by airplane or helicopter on *Air Grand Canyon* (800–AIR–GRAND; www.airgrandcanyon.com), *Air Star Airlines* (866–689–8687; www.airstar.com), or *Papillon Grand Canyon Helicopters* (800–528–2418; www.papillon.com), or you can tour by bus, using *Fred Harvey Transportation Company* (303–29–PARKS or 888–29–PARKS).

A good place to stop on the *East Rim* (though out of the range of the horseback trip) is the *Watchtower,* a Mary Colter (who also was the architect for the Hopi House and Bright Angel Lodge on the South Rim) stone reproduction of a Hopi lookout post. Visitors can climb inside, imagine how Native American sentries felt as they manned their posts 300 years ago, and get an excellent view of the canyon. The Watchtower, on the southern side of the East Rim, can easily be reached by car as part of a driving tour.

trivia

Explorer John Wesley Powell was a brave soul, venturing into such dangerous territory as the uncharted Colorado River and exploring untold canyons—yet he only had one arm.

Some visitors prefer rafting down the Colorado River to clambering around on the cliffs. About a dozen companies are licensed for canyon river trips. Some offer easygoing, half-day float trips that are perfect for any age or level of fitness. Others do the full-out, go-for-the-gusto, *The River Wild*–style three-day to three-week whitewater expeditions. In any case, you have to book your tour at least six months to one year in advance, or there's a good chance you won't get a slot. Call the park (928–638–7888) to find out about trips and companies and to call for reservations.

If you decide to visit the Grand Canyon during a month when the North Rim is closed and river or air tours aren't operating, you're still in luck—the South Rim is open year-round. Of the area's structures, *El Tovar* (303–29–PARKS or 888–29–PARKS) is the most impressive and in recent years underwent a $1-million renovation. This 1905 hotel, named for a Spanish explorer who never personally laid eyes on the canyon, has the elegant ambience of other grand hotels (like the Hotel Del Coronado, just across the bay from San Diego), yet it has an undeniable frontier simplicity and ruggedness that might make you remember the Scout lodges of your childhood. The lobby and common areas are open to sightseeing tourists, and the hotel's dining room serves Southwestern cuisine, fresh seafood, and specialty desserts and has fantastic views of the canyon. The restaurant is often booked solid, so reservations are recommended.

If you prefer a quicker meal, the *Bright Angel Fountain* is a brief stroll west of El Tovar and serves up sandwiches, salads, and very tasty, open-face frybread "tacos." It is part of the *Bright Angel Lodge* (303–29–PARKS or 888–29–PARKS), which offers roomy accommodations.

When you're ready to walk off your meal, check out *Lookout Studio,* which sells everything from fossil specimens

trivia

Only one Indian tribe occupies the bottom of the Grand Canyon—the Havasupai tribe.

(not from the park, which is protected) to books and videos about the area. At the rear of the studio, visitors can step out onto a balcony that offers a great view and a good photo opportunity.

Another popular gift shop is the Hopi House, a National Historic Landmark constructed in 1904 to look like an adobe-block Hopi village. It, too, recently underwent a $1-million renovation. **Verkamp's** (928–638–2242) just east of there, also has many gifts and souvenirs, including T-shirts and the like.

lolita's lepidopterist

During Russian author Vladimir Nabokov's first visit to Arizona in 1941, he and his party stopped at the Grand Canyon. During his visit, Nabokov—who was a serious lepidopterist as well as the author of the controversial classic novel *Lolita*—discovered an unnamed butterfly at the canyon. He called the diminutive brown butterfly *Neonympha dorothea,* after Dorothy Leuthold, the student doing the driving on the trip.

If you'd rather hike than shop, take the **Bright Angel Trail.** One of the most popular trails in the canyon, it is easily reached just west of El Tovar. You should consider yourself warned: It's a lot easier hiking down the steep switchbacks than climbing back up! This hike should only be attempted if you're wearing appropriate hiking shoes and carrying enough water and snacks. You might plan on camping out at the bottom. Before attempting the ascent you can also stay at **Phantom Ranch** (303–29–PARKS or 888–29–PARKS), a charming facility that welcomes weary hikers with a dining room and a series of cabins also designed by Mary Colter. Some cabins are basic; some are more plush. You need to make reservations well in advance. Additionally if you're intent on camping, you need a permit and a reservation. Write to Grand Canyon National Park, Backcountry Information Center, P.O. Box 129, Grand Canyon, AZ 86023 for more information. By the way, you can actually post mail from down here—it will be stamped with the postmark "Delivered by Mule from the Bottom of the Canyon."

Travelers who plan ahead may want to consider scheduling one of the excursions offered by the **Grand Canyon Field Institute** (928–638–2485 or 866–471–4435; www.grandcanyon.org/fieldinstitute). Guides from the institute take small groups of people on hiking, backpacking, and educational tours throughout the park. Among the unique jaunts and workshops are "Raptors of Grand Canyon," "Rim-to-Rim Geology Backpack," and "Backcountry Medicine." Special courses are planned for people interested in geology, human history, ecosystems, wilderness skills (including classes just for women), and photography. Fees and lengths of classes vary, as does the difficulty level of the hikes.

Reservations for all in-park Grand Canyon accommodations—also including Kachina Lodge, Thunderbird Lodge, Maswik Lodge, Yavapai Lodge, Moqui Lodge, and Trailer Village—are available by calling (303) 29–PARKS or 888–29–PARKS. A full complement of motels can also be found just outside the park entrance in the village of Tusayan.

Sedona Area and South

One of Arizona's most pleasurable drives for nearly all the senses is the route from the Grand Canyon along US 180 to the switchbacks of US 89A as it winds its way into *Oak Creek Canyon* and Sedona beyond. Especially popular in the fall, when the desert denizens travel north to view the colorful oak and sycamore leaves, the 16-mile gorge is peppered with streams and waterfalls. More than 130 species of birds call the region home, and campgrounds and hiking trails are abundant. Along the way, numerous resorts and cabins are hidden along the banks of the creek, serving up an interesting array of accommodation choices. *Garland's Oak Creek Lodge* (928–282–3343; www.garlandslodge.com; open April through mid-November) is perhaps the best known and is so popular with its regulars that many have a standing reservation each year. But others are considerably easier to book.

The Canyon Wren, Cabins for Two (928–282–6900 or 800–437–9736; www.canyonwrencabins.com), at 6425 North Highway 89A, is a cluster of four cabins located 6 miles from Sedona and is on the hilly side of the highway away from the creek. Nonsmoking inside and out, the Canyon Wren also caters to couples seeking a tranquil retreat. Continental breakfast is served daily, and each unit comes complete with a small kitchen.

Oak Creek Terrace Resort (928–282–3562 or 800–224–2229; www.oakcreekterrace.com), at 4548 North Highway 89A, is 5 miles from uptown Sedona and features two triplexes, eleven motel-style rooms, and three unique bungalows of varying layouts in a creekside setting. Nearly every unit is complete with fireplace and in-room whirlpool tub; many offer kitchenettes and outdoor barbecues. On-site Jeep Wrangler rentals are available.

Midway up the canyon is *Slide Rock State Park* (928–282–3034), a state-run facility that, as its name implies, boasts a natural water slide created by the waters of Oak Creek as they rush over naturally sculpted stone chutes. The area was once an apple orchard, and efforts are

trivia

Though it is a relatively small community, Sedona is located in both Coconino and Yavapai Counties and is completely surrounded by the Coconino National Forest.

being made to restore the original century-old buildings and continue apple production. An original apple-packing barn remains, as well as a 1926 homestead that now serves as a ranger station. For visitors, shaded picnic areas are available, and snacks and supplies can be purchased inside Slide Rock Market. Admission is $8.00 per vehicle.

On the other side of Sedona, another state park is undoubtedly more recognizable—even for folks who have never been to Arizona. **Red Rock State Park** (928–282–6907) has, for years, served as the backdrop for countless TV programs, movies, and commercials. This park is just west of Sedona off US 89A and features hiking trails that range from simple to strenuous. Maps of the 286-acre park are available from the visitors center. Admission fee is $6.00 per vehicle. Arizona's state park Web site is www.pr.state.az.us.

If you continue south on US 89A, in about 5 miles you'll reach the red-rock-ringed community of **Sedona.** Named in 1902 for Sedona Schnebly, the wife of founder T. C. Schnebly, this small town is best known as an arts community, a vacation getaway spot, and a haven for people seeking a different spiritual path. Several years ago, Sedona acquired the reputation of being a New Age center. Allegedly several electromagnetic energy sources (known as vortexes) were found in the area, and a wide variety of psychics and spiritual healers decided to tap into them by making the town their home. One New Age directory lists Sedona organizations like Center for the New Age, Sedona Psychic Wisdom, the Golden Word, and the Goddess Heart Retreat Center. The **Center for the New Age** (928–282–2085 or 888–861–6651; www.sedona newagecenter.com) at 341 Highway 179 has been providing services for more than 10 years. You can get psychic readings, healing massages, and aural photographs at the center or you can sign up for a personalized vortex tour. Four areas have been identified as possessing unusual electromagnetic forces. They are **Cathedral Rock** (off US 89A and Upper Red Rock Loop Road); **Bell Rock** (north of the Village of Oak Creek, off Highway 179); **Airport Mesa** (circling the municipal airport); and **Boynton Canyon Vortex** (Boynton Pass Road, west of Sedona off US 89A and Dry Creek Road). Some believe these outcroppings of red rock (the first two named after their respective shapes, and the latter two named for their locations) emit a palpable energy. Each area is lovely to look at, but quiet, serene Cathedral Rock west of central Sedona near Oak Creek is a personal favorite.

Hollywood filmmakers and music video, television, and television commercial producers have long been lured to Sedona, starting in the 1930s when the Zane Grey feature *Call of the Canyon* was lensed here. The pilgrimage continues today with films like De Niro's *Midnight Run* and the Johnny Depp western *Dead Man*. Glancing around at the intense, vibrant red rocks and the lush vegetation, it's easy to see why so many artists also have been drawn to this setting. Although the ***Cowboy Artists of America*** was founded here in 1965, artists of every description and from different regions, including the Southwest, have worked here. One of the most famous is painter/sculptor Max Ernst, whose surrealistic works helped to redefine art in the 1950s. Current area artists include Leslie B. De Mille, "shirt-tail cousin" to the famous film director, as well as a very talented portrait artist and sculptor in her own right, who has done a lot of work for professional golfers.

Many artists have their works on display at ***Tlaquepaque Arts and Crafts Village*** (928–282–4838; www.tlaq.com). Pronounced *T-lockey-pockey,* the center's name is a Native American word meaning "the best of everything." Designed to resemble an actual Mexican village near Guadalajara, the center's shops and galleries surround a courtyard. Each September ***Fiesta del Tlaquepaque*** is held, and strolling mariachis play while children swing at a piñata and food vendors fill the courtyard with the aroma of Southwestern cooking. Tlaquepaque is also the setting for an annual ***Festival of Lights,*** an evening event usually held on the second Saturday in December. Luminarias (more than 6,000) are placed all around the balconies, walkways, and on the fountain, bathing the village in a golden glow. The luminarias are lighted at dusk, but the festival is open from 3:00 to 8:00 P.M.

Held next door to Tlaquepaque at ***Los Abrigados*** ("the shelter") ***Resort and Spa*** (928–282–1777 or 800–521–3131), a first-class facility set on twenty acres, the annual ***Red Rock Fantasy*** (mid-November to mid-January) is a big crowd pleaser. The resort, tucked back off the main road with gorgeous views of the surrounding hills, is decorated with more than one million Christmas

Tlaquepaque Arts and Crafts Village

Sedona—Arizona's Cinematic Star

Visit Sedona for the first time and you'll likely feel as though you've been there before—and for good reason. Sedona is a star! Here are just a few of the countless productions—vintage and modern—that have used the crimson canyons as their backdrop:

Feature Films

The Karate Kid (Columbia, 1984)

Midnight Run (Universal, 1988)

The Quick and the Dead (Cates, 1987)

Riders of the Purple Sage (Fox, 1931)

Universal Soldier (Carolco, 1992)

Blood on the Moon (RKO, 1948)

Call of the Canyon (Famous Players/ Lasky, 1923)

Gun Fury (Columbia, 1953)

Television

Death Valley Days

Gambler II

Lifestyles of the Rich and Famous

Sesame Street

Commercial products

Coca-Cola, Eddie Bauer, Duracell, Frito-Lay, Kodak, Levis, and almost every foreign and domestic automaker!

lights that are lit from 5:00 to 10:00 P.M. each night. Displays ranging from salutes to the Phoenix Suns to scenes from *Babes in Toyland* are placed all around. Visitors pay a nominal admission fee (which is donated to a charity) to tour the displays. The all-suite resort has a health club with workout machines and classes, a tennis court, an outdoor pool and Jacuzzi, and three restaurants. **Steaks & Sticks** (928–204–7849) is a restaurant/nightclub that combines elements of an eatery with the essentials of a gentleman's club (cognac, cigars, and a big fireplace).

Besides the previously mentioned spots near Oak Creek, there's lots to do in the great outdoors in Sedona. Southwest of uptown Sedona on US 89A, then north on Dry Creek Road (the route you take to Boynton Canyon, site of one of the vortexes), you can enjoy an easy 2-mile hike to the 40-foot sandstone **Vultee Arch.** The naturally occurring structure is named after a pilot and aircraft designer who crashed near the arch in 1938.

If you tire of hiking, several companies can give you a lift—literally. **Northern Light Balloon Expeditions** (928–282–2274 or 800–230–6222; www .northernlightballoon.com) can take you over the Coconino National Forest for a spectacular view from the basket of a hot-air balloon. Or ramble up twisting Schnebly Road—which affords a great view of Sedona—with **Pink Jeep Tours** (928–282–5000 or 800–8–SEDONA; www.pinkjeep.com). By the way, the Schnebly Road scenic drive can be made on your own using a sturdy, high-clearance or all-terrain vehicle.

One Sedona sight you definitely shouldn't miss is the ***Chapel of the Holy Cross*** (928–282–4069) at 780 Chapel Road. This magnificent Modern Gothic cathedral was built in 1956 high in the red rocks by Margurite Brunswig Staude, a sculptor, painter, and jewelry designer who had long envisioned building a contemporary monument to God. Staude chose Lloyd Wright, son of Frank Lloyd Wright, to design the structure, but financial constraints prevented completion of his grandiose design—a 500-foot monument! Originally slated for Budapest, Hungary, the project was put on hold until Staude moved to Sedona in 1950. No services are held here. Rather, the chapel is open to anyone of any creed to come in and light a candle (for which there is a small donation), study the sculptures (some by Staude, others more than 200 years old), browse in the downstairs gift shop, and marvel at the incredible scenery. The chapel is open from 9:00 A.M. to 5:00 P.M., except Thanksgiving, Christmas, Good Friday, and Easter.

Besides the wintertime Festival of Lights and Red Rock Fantasy, annual events in Sedona include the ***Sedona Annual International Film Festival*** (March), ***Sedona Arts Festival*** and ***Sedona Art and Sculpture Walk*** (May), and ***Jazz on the Rocks Benefits Festival*** (September). Jazz on the Rocks, featuring about a half dozen top regional and national acts playing everything from swing to blues, is especially popular. It's held all day outdoors in a grassy amphitheater with Sedona's towering red rocks as a backdrop. For information about any of these events, contact the Sedona–Oak Creek Chamber of Commerce (928–282–7722 or 800–288–7336; www.visitsedona.com).

It's not hard to find a comfortable place to stay overnight in Sedona: The area is loaded with quaint bed-and-breakfast inns and has several top-notch resorts.

Despite its small size, Sedona also has a healthy assortment of eateries, from eclectic to European. A personal favorite for decent Mexican dishes and arguably the best red rock views in town is ***Oaxaca Restaurant & Cantina*** (928–282–4179) in uptown Sedona at 321 North Highway 89A. Sunday brunch at ***L'Auberge*** (928–282–1661) at 301 L'Auberge Lane is a special treat, with indoor seating in a French provincial setting or seasonally available creekside dining. There, monsieur, reservations are recommended.

When you're ready to move on from Sedona (and a word of warning: Vortex or not, the town has a very seductive character, so you may be there awhile), you can either continue south on US 89A and head to Tuzigoot National Monument, Jerome, and Prescott (all covered in another section), or you can take Highway 179 south to Interstate 17.

The interstate will steer you toward ***Montezuma Well*** and ***Montezuma Castle National Monument*** (928–567–3322; www.nps.gov/moca). Admission is $5.00 per person ages 16 and older. The well, actually a collapsed limestone cavern 1,750 feet in diameter and fed by underground springs, is a short distance from the main road. Hohokam Indian ruins dot this area. The Hohokam were an ancient Native American tribe that built elaborate communities based upon agriculture. They populated much of the state until around the late fifteenth century, when they seemingly disappeared, a phenomenon that led modern tribes to refer to these ancient ancestors by the name Hohokam, a Native American term often translated as "those who vanished." A few miles south is the "castle," a twenty-room Sinagua cliff dwelling that was built around A.D. 1100. When it was discovered during Arizona's territorial days by white settlers, it was erroneously thought to be the work of the Aztec king.

Just past the intersection of State Highway 260 and I–17 is the town of **Camp Verde** and **Fort Verde State Park** (928–567–3275). Admission is $2.00 for adults. Like a number of Arizona communities, Camp Verde is a great example of Old West architecture—and outmoded cultural interface: It sprang up as a military outpost to protect miners, ranchers, and homesteaders against Indian raids. The fort was built in 1865, and it was here in 1873 that General George Crook presided over the surrender of Apache Chief Chalipun and 300 warriors. Crook is well known in American history as a tough and savvy commander who used Apache scouts and adapted old-fashioned military tactics to work in the rugged and hostile terrain of Arizona. He also forged a trail connecting Fort Whipple (near Prescott) with Fort Apache in the Apache-Sitgreaves National Forest, a road that is still referred to as **Crook's Trail.**

Today this 138-mile trail is used primarily by hikers and horseback riders, with the most popular portion being a 25-mile section east of Camp Verde along the Mogollon Rim, a steep cliff that separates the state's northern plateau from the lower desert. The historic buildings of Fort Verde are now a museum. For museum information, call the Camp Verde Chamber of Commerce at (928) 567–9294. For information on Crook's Trail, call the Arizona State Parks at (602) 542–4174.

Arcosanti sits only a few minutes away, just off I–17 near Cordes Junction. Although Arcosanti is visible from the interstate, uninformed motorists may not know what to make of the odd-looking structures perched on the cliffside and simply zip on by unaware of what they've missed. A sort of glorious urban experiment, Arcosanti, established in 1970, is the brainchild of Italian architect Paolo Soleri. Soleri's theories of "arcology" (a meld of architecture and ecology) prompted him to construct a self-sufficient community that would produce crops and create salable products.

The buildings of Arcosanti look like nothing you've ever seen before: round and square shapes combining in asymmetrical forms amidst walls of basalt, splashed with color throughout. The effect is sort of "Frank Lloyd Wright through the Looking Glass" (not surprising, given that Soleri was a Frank Lloyd Wright Fellow). In some ways the community will remind you of the styles and decor of the early seventies—a lava lamp would look right at home here—yet it all seems timeless, like a fairy-tale kingdom.

Visitors to Arcosanti, which is open year-round, can tour the ten-acre facility, browse in the gift shop (which sells everything from Soleri's famous ceramic or bronze abstract bells to posters and T-shirts), take part in crafts and building workshops, and attend concerts at the Colly Soleri Music Center, which is named for the architect's late wife. Richie Havens, whose incomparable voice transformed the original Woodstock music festival, is a frequent guest, though the center is a venue for all types of music, including jazz and blues. Some concerts are preceded by dinner and followed by a light show projected on the canyon wall.

Arcosanti also has a bakery and a cafe. Admission to the gift shop and cafe is free, but an $8.00 donation is requested for the one-hour tour (offered every hour from 10:00 A.M. to 4:00 P.M.). For information, call (928) 632–7135 or go to www.arcosanti.org.

Places to Stay in Northern Arizona

FLAGSTAFF

Embassy Suites,
706 South Milton Road;
(928) 774–4333 or
(866) 774–4333.
Spacious rooms with mini-kitchens and separate bedrooms. Breakfast only (included). Inexpensive to moderate.

Sled Dog Inn,
10155 Mountainaire Road;
(928) 525–6212 or
(800) 754–0664.
Cozy country rooms, charming common areas, a hot tub and sauna, a decadent breakfast (included), and morning sled dog serenades. Moderate.

GRAND CANYON

BW Grand Canyon Squire Inn,
Highway 64,
P.O. Box 130,
Grand Canyon, AZ 86023;
(928) 638–2681 or
(800) 622–6966;
www.grandcanyonsquire.com
Just south of the park's entrance in Tusayan, this is the area's only resort hotel, with 250 deluxe rooms, heated pool, fitness center, restaurants, etc. Moderate to expensive.

The Grand Hotel,
P.O. Box 3319,
Grand Canyon, AZ 86023;
(928) 638–3333 or
(888) 634–7263;
www.visitgrandcanyon.com
In the Village of Tusayan near the park entrance. Similar in style and appointments to the park lodges. Offers Western weddings. Moderate.

JACOB LAKE

Jacob Lake Inn,
Junction of North Highway 89A/Highway 67;
(928) 643–7770.
A rustic lodge with cabins and rooms, restaurant, bakery, soda fountain, service station, and country store. Moderate.

LAKE POWELL

Linda's Lake Powell Condos,
P.O. Box 1258,
Page, AZ 86040;
(800) 462–7695.
Studio condos with desert or lake views. Located near Wahweap marina. Expensive.

SEDONA

Enchantment Resort,
525 Boynton Canyon Road;
(928) 282–2900 or
(800) 826–4180.
A gorgeous resort hidden in scenic Boynton Canyon. Amenities include a full-service spa, three restaurants, tennis courts, a pool, and hiking and biking trails. Expensive.

The Lodge at Sedona,
125 Kallof Place;
(928) 204–1942 or
(800) 619–4467;
www.lodgeatsedona.com
In West Sedona, this secluded bed-and-breakfast, set on 2 1/2 wooded acres, was formerly a private home and now has six rooms and

eight suites, each with a distinct theme—from Renaissance to Cherokee. Moderate to expensive.

Sedona Super 8 Motel,
2545 West Highway 89A;
(928) 282–1533 or
(800) 858–7245.
A good, reasonably priced choice on the main road with a pool. Inexpensive.

WILLIAMS

The Canyon Motel and Railroad RV Park,
1900 East Rodeo Road;
(928) 635–9371 or
(800) 482–3955.
Situated on ten acres, this remodeled 1949 motor lodge offers rooms in flagstone cottages and renovated historic cabooses and railcars. Inexpensive.

Red Garter,
137 West Railroad Avenue;
(928) 635–1484 or
(800) 328–1484;
www.redgarter.com
This bed-and-breakfast houses four rooms in a two-story 1897 brick building that

once served as a bordello and saloon. The rooms are on the upper floor and a bakery occupies the first floor. Closed December through mid-February. Inexpensive to moderate.

Places to Eat in Northern Arizona

FLAGSTAFF

Black Bart's Steakhouse and Musical Revue,
2760 East Butler Avenue;
(928) 779–3142
or (800) 574–4718.
Slightly corny, but a lot of fun, this spot features food servers who double as singers—all students at nearby Northern Arizona University. Open dinner only. Moderate to expensive.

WEB SITES FOR NORTHERN ARIZONA

Arizona Department of Tourism
www.arizonaguide.com

Flagstaff Convention and Visitors Bureau
www.flagstaffarizona.org

Grand Canyon National Park
www.nps.gov/grca

Lake Powell
www.lakepowell.com

Sedona–Oak Creek Chamber of Commerce
www.visitsedona.com

Williams–Grand Canyon Chamber of Commerce
www.williamschamber.com

**Buster's Restaurant
and Bar,**
1800 South Milton Road;
(928) 774–5155.
A steak and seafood restaurant rated the "Best Flagstaff Restaurant" by the *Arizona Daily News Sun.* Moderate.

Charly's,
23 North Leroux, Street;
(928) 779–1919.
Reasonably priced pub fare and dinners in historic downtown setting—sidewalk tables available seasonably, patio bar upstairs. Moderate.

Dara Thai,
14 South San Francisco Street;
(928) 774–0047.
Excellent oasis for Thai fare in northern Arizona. Moderate.

Pasto,
19 East Aspen Avenue;
(928) 779–1937.
Good, homemade Italian cooking with just about everything made from scratch. Moderate.

SEDONA

Blue Moon Cafe,
6101 Highway 179, Suite B;
(928) 284–1831.
Serves breakfast all day, plus burgers, sandwiches, salads, and hand-tossed pizza. Inexpensive.

Coffee Pot Restaurant,
2050 West Highway 89A;
(928) 282–6626.
Serves a huge selection of omelets and is known by locals for the "Best Breakfast in Sedona." Inexpensive.

WILLIAMS

**Miss Kitty's Steakhouse
and Saloon,**
642 East Route 66;
(928) 635–9161.
Western-style steakhouse with live music offered in the evenings. Moderate.

Pancho McGillicuddy's,
141 Railroad Avenue;
(928) 635–4150.
Dishes up large servings of Mexican food and features more than thirty tequilas at the restaurant bar. Inexpensive to moderate.

Pine Country Restaurant,
107 North Grand Canyon Boulevard;
(928) 635–9718.
Homestyle country cooking in a cozy local restaurant. Open breakfast, lunch, and dinner. Inexpensive.

Western Arizona

Lake Mead and Grand Canyon West

When it was created in the 1930s by the construction of **Hoover Dam** (702–494–2517), 110-mile-long Lake Mead was the largest artificial lake in the world. The dam itself was no small achievement either. Built to harness the awesome power of the Colorado River on the mitten tip of the Arizona–Nevada border, the dam is more than 726 feet tall and 1,282 feet long and is linked to a power plant that can generate 1.8 million horsepower. Boy, just imagine if you could tuck that baby under the hood of your car! Besides being an engineering marvel, the dam, with its art deco statues, is a work of art and is the highest in the world. Guided tours are available and depart every fifteen minutes from 9:30 A.M. to 4:45 P.M. Admission is $11 for adults, $9.00 for seniors, and $6.00 for children ages 7 to 16. Covered parking (a plus in the scorching summertime) is available. Parking fees are $7.00 per vehicle.

Just about anything you can do in a body of water, you can do on **Lake Mead.** Swimming; fishing for largemouth bass, crappie, sunfish, channel catfish, and so forth; Jet-Skiing; waterskiing; power boating; wind surfing; and scuba diving

UTAH
ARIZONA

15

Lake
Mead

GRAND CANYON

Colorado R.

NEVADA
ARIZONA

93

Peach Springs

66

Chloride

Valentine

Seligman

68

Kingman

40

40

Bullhead
City

89

Clarkdale

Oatman

Jerome

95

Chino Valley

ALT
89

Cotton-
wood

40

93

JOSHUA FOREST PKWY

Prescott

Lake
Havasu
City

89

69

Colorado R.

Parker

71

N

CALIFORNIA
ARIZONA

72

95

Quartzsite

0   40 mi

10

0   40 km

are popular activities. I've never dived here myself, but friends who have tell me it's amazingly clear for an artificial lake. If you stay in one of the neighboring towns, you can make this stop a day trip—driving up, renting a Jet Ski, and cruising around the lake for a few hours before heading back to town. If you'd like to spend more than a day at Lake Mead, consider renting a houseboat. There are more than 800 miles of shoreline, which include hidden coves and tiny backwater inlets that are perfect for lengthy exploration. There are countless areas where you can go ashore and have a picnic lunch while gazing at the surrounding mountains.

trivia

Though Arizona boasts one of the largest per capita boat ownerships in the country, all of Arizona's lakes except one—Stoneman Lake—are man-made. In fact, Lake Mead is the largest man-made lake in the United States.

The Lake Mead Visitors Center (702–293–8990; www.nps.gov/lame), as well as facilities for renting equipment or booking steamboat tours, is on the Nevada side. However, the *Temple Bar Marina* off U.S. Highway 93 in Arizona (928–767–3211 or 800–752–9669; www.7crown.com) offers camping and boat rental and launching facilities, in addition to a cafe, grocery store, motel, and cabins. RV facilities are also available.

About 40 miles south of Lake Mead on US 93, *Dolan Springs* (928–767–4473) sits at the foot of the Cerbat Mountains. Not surprisingly, given the proximity of Lake Mead, Lake Mohave, and the southwest rim of the Grand Canyon, this town is a stopping-off point for many recreation seekers.

A lot of visitors don't realize that just north of Dolan Springs off Pearce Ferry Road on the way to Meadview is the largest stand of *Joshua trees* in the world. Joshua trees are strange, spikey-topped relatives of the lily family that can reach more than 30 feet in height and outlive most humans. They were allegedly named by Mormon pioneers who believed that the upraised arms resembled Joshua leading the Israelites. Although there aren't any formal parking lots or

AUTHOR'S TOP PICKS IN WESTERN ARIZONA

Hualapai River Runners	Verde Canyon Railroad
Lake Havasu	Colorado River Indian Tribes Museum
London Bridge/English Village	Jerome

Joshua tree

picnic areas in this forest, you can easily pull off the road and get out and walk around. If you arrive between late March and early April, you may see the trees in bloom. Please note that many maps of the Dolan Springs area show a ghost town called White Hills. As a result of years of pilfering, there is virtually nothing left there, and for that reason, it isn't recommended or even accessible.

Follow Pearce Ferry Road (sometimes erroneously labeled on maps as *Pierce* Ferry Road) north from Dolan Springs to the unpaved Diamond Bar Road, turn right, and in a few minutes you'll arrive at what's commonly referred to locally as **Grand Canyon West.** The canyon's western end is 4,800 feet above the river and very different from its better-known northern, southern, and eastern boundaries. Sprinkled with high-desert vegetation, the canyon itself seems scaled down, more intimate and peaceful. Located on the **Hualapai** (pronounced *wal-a-pai*) **Indian Reservation** (888–255–9550), this wide-open rangeland has only one blip of a town, called **Peach Springs.** Hualapai Enterprises runs the **Hualapai Lodge** (928–769–2230 or 888–255–9550; www.grandcanyonresort.com), right on Route 66, which offers sixty large rooms, a gift shop, and a restaurant that's open for breakfast, lunch, and dinner daily. Some 92 miles west of Peach Springs in Grand Canyon West, the Hualapais also offer a 4-mile guided tour

Raft the River

You can take a Hualapai Indian–guided rafting trip down the Colorado River. **Hualapai River Runners** offers one- or two-day expeditions (central reservations, 928–769–2419 or 888–255–9550) starting in Peach Springs, where guides lead adventures down Diamond Creek Road to the Colorado River. This is, incidentally, the only point in the Grand Canyon where you can actually drive to the river. Two-day raft excursions include a campout on the beach. This is not an arduous trip (the guides do most of the work), so it's ideal for adults (and children age eight and older) who aren't especially experienced in backpacking and wilderness survival but want an "up-close-and-personal" view of the Colorado.

to Eagle Point and Guano Point (named after the droppings of the bats that proliferate there). A tour of the rim led by a Hualapai Indian guide includes a barbecue lunch.

Among the lesser-known, although unquestionably idyllic, settings in the area is an exotic canyon located within the tiny *Havasupai Indian Reservation.* Secluded and seemingly untouched by time and technology, the Havasu Canyon appears to be more Hawaiian than mainland, with its cascading turquoise waterfalls and flowering orchids. No doubt the biggest reason for its enduring tranquility is its remoteness—visitors must either hike or mule ride. All visitors, including campers, must make reservations with the tribe (928–448–2111 or 928–448–2201; www.havasupai tribe.com) before entering this little slice of paradise.

Minerals and the Mother Road

It doesn't take Bill Nye the Science Guy to figure out how the mining town of *Chloride* (928–565–2204), just south of Dolan Springs on US 93, got its name. Silver chloride ore, gold, and other precious minerals such as turquoise have been found in the area. Much of the area's riches were never mined, and it's not unusual to see modern-day prospectors scrambling around in the foothills of the nearby Cerbat Mountains. Before attempting this yourself, check with the chamber of commerce to get directions and to make sure you won't be stepping on someone else's claim.

If you'd rather look at rocks than dig them, check out Southwestern artist *Roy Purcell's murals.* Created in 1966 on a cliff in the Cerbats, the paintings depict images of a snake, an eagle's talon, the phases of the moon, and a princess, all sort of flowing into one another.

Several sights in Chloride, including the *Old Jail* and the *Chloride Fire Department,* are worth a look. The jail, which may remind you of the drunk tank on the *Andy Griffith Show,* is a two-cell, whitewashed building that's maintained as a museum by the historical society. The fire department houses two classic fire engines: a 1939 Ford fire engine and a 1948 Mack fire engine, both in mint condition and still in use. On the first and third Saturday of every month, a local group stages shoot-out reenactments and vaudeville entertainment at the new Western village called Cyanide Springs. For tickets and information call the Chloride Chamber of Commerce at (928) 565–2204; www .chloridearizona.com.

The Mine Shaft Market (928–565–4888) at 4940 East Tennessee Avenue sells groceries and goodies like ice cream and soft drinks. The *Tennessee Saloon,* at Tennessee and Second, is still an operating bar located in the former

JANUARY

Best in the Desert
Parker
A motorcycle race through the desert.
(928) 669–2174

Prospector's Panorama/Gold Show
Quartzsite
(928) 927–6467

Lettuce Days
Yuma
(928) 782–5712

FEBRUARY

Hobby, Crafts, and Gem Show
Quartzsite
Displays from around the country,
dealers with gems, minerals;
jewelry demos.
(928) 927–5600 or (800) 969–5464

MAY

Greater Cottonwood Antique Aeroplane and Auto Show
Cottonwood
Airport—antiques, cycles, street rods,
customs, military, kit cars, vintage and
experimental aircraft.
(928) 634–7593

Annual Paseo de Casas
Jerome
Homes and historic public buildings
from Victorians to renovated miner's
shacks; works of Jerome artists and
photographs from the Jerome Historical
Society Archives.
(928) 634–2900

Festival of Arts
Kingman
Entertainment, demonstrations,
children's art activities, food.
(928) 753–6106

George Phippen Memorial Day Western Art Show and Sale
Prescott
Courthouse Plaza—juried outdoor Western art show, "Quick Draw" and auction.
(928) 778–1385

JUNE

Old Miners Day
Chloride
Vaudeville acts, street dance, gunfights,
horseshoe-pitching contest, swap meet,
parade, live music.
(928) 565–2204

Bluegrass Festival
Prescott
Courthouse Plaza—top bands, jam
sessions, workshops.
(928) 445–2000 or (800) 266–7534

Folk Arts Fair
Prescott
Sharlot Hall Museum—traditional arts
such as quilting, woodcarving, spinning,
weaving, candlemaking; hands-on
crafts; music.
(928) 445–3122

Territorial Days
Prescott
Courthouse Plaza—arts and crafts,
games for kids, old-time photos,
entertainment.
(928) 445–2000 or (800) 266–7534

JULY

Frontier Days and World's Oldest Rodeo
Prescott
Parade, booths on the Courthouse
Plaza, fireworks, continuous entertainment, softball tournament, carnival,
melodramas, family entertainment.
(928) 445–3103

AUGUST

Arizona Cowboy Poets Gathering
Prescott
Sharlot Hall Museum—from all over the West, working cowboys who compose, recite, and sing poetry about their lives and work.
(928) 445–3122

Hualapai Mountain Arts and Crafts Festival
An arts and crafts fair at the Hualapai Mountain Resort.
(928) 757–3545

SEPTEMBER

Andy Devine Days and PRCA Rodeo
Kingman
Mohave County Fairgrounds—celebrates local history of Kingman; rodeo dance, parade, bluegrass festival, concert.
(928) 753–6106

Annual Verde River Days
Cottonwood
Dead Horse Ranch State Park—event to develop the awareness of the importance of the Verde River; fishing clinic, sand castle building, rubber duck race.
(928) 634–7593

Carrera Regatta
Lake Havasu City
Nautical Inn—poker run, boat parade, awards for the farthest miles traveled.
(909) 735–7000 or (928) 855–2141

Gold Camp Days
Oatman
Labor Day weekend parade, crazy hat contest, beard contest and a burro biscuit throwing contest.
(928) 768–6222

OCTOBER

Fort Verde Days
Camp Verde
Quilt show, BBQ, games, equestrian events, arts and crafts, reenactments.
(928) 567–9294 or (928) 567–3275

Kingman Auto and Airshow
Kingman
Kingman Airport and Industrial Park—aerobatics, parachutists, warbirds, Formula air race.
(928) 753–6106

London Bridge Days
Lake Havasu City
Free concerts, contests, country-western jamboree, costume contest, parade.
(928) 453–3444 or (800) 242–8278

Folk Music Festival
Prescott
Sharlot Hall Museum—old-time fiddlers, folk songs, bluegrass, string bands.
(928) 445–3122

NOVEMBER

Festival of Lights
Lake Havasu City
English Village and London Bridge—more than one million lights on display.
(928) 453–3444 or (800) 424–8278

Colorado River Crossing Balloon Festival
Yuma
Sunrise balloon liftoffs, sunset balloon glow, and fireworks.
(928) 343–1715

DECEMBER

Christmas Parade of Lights
Bullhead City
Lake Mohave at dusk
(928) 754–3245

Boat Parade of Lights
Lake Havasu City
Bridgewater Channel
(928) 453–3444 or (800) 424–8278

mercantile building that is thought to be about one hundred years old. Next door is the visitors center (800–578–3379) where tourists can get Arizona travel information and make reservations for rooms in several national parks, Laughlin, Nevada, and other destinations. *DJ's Cafe and Saloon* (928–565–9608) on Tennessee Avenue at Second Street serves American cuisine for dinner and spirits, too.

A great way to explore the area west of Flagstaff to the border of Nevada is to follow old *Route 66.* In case you're too young to remember, Route 66 was built more than seven decades ago as the nation's first transcontinental highway. Beginning in Chicago and ending 2,448 miles later at the Santa Monica pier, it became known as the "Main Street of America." John Steinbeck immortalized it in 1939 as the "Mother Road" in his classic novel of dustbowl-hardened Okies, *The Grapes of Wrath.* Throughout the 1930s, many an Oklahoma farmer followed the rutted tracks of the Mother Road (which hadn't been completely paved yet) out to what he hoped was a better life in the citrus fields of California.

trivia

The Beale Wagon Road, surveyed and constructed between 1857 and 1859 by Lt. Edward F. Beale, stretches through New Mexico and Arizona near the 35th parallel. The road, which was one of the major routes to California, made history as the first federally funded interstate highway.

Traveling a vastly improved Route 66 in 1946, singer/songwriter Bobby Troup wrote a song about this highway—"Get Your Kicks on Route 66"—and different versions (sung by everyone from Depeche Mode to Nat King Cole to the Rolling Stones) were hits in the 1940s, 1950s, and 1960s. The early 1960s TV show *Route 66,* about a couple of young guys cruising the Mother Road in a Corvette, introduced the *American Graffiti* generation to Route 66 and created a romanticism about the diners, drive-in theaters, and motels that lined this two-lane road.

But a death knell was in the air. In 1956 President Eisenhower had signed the Interstate Highway Act, which helped to create safer, multilane superhighways like Interstate 40. The completion in 1985 of I–40 turned much of Route 66 into a memory. Even as the last stretch of I–40 was finished, however, citizens and business owners in the old Route 66 towns of northern Arizona began banding together to save the Mother Road by marketing themselves as historic Route 66 towns to car clubs across the country and lovers of Americana around the world. Today it isn't surprising to drive along Route 66 near Kingman and see a carload of German tourists who've grown up listening to Troup's song or watching dubbed reruns of the TV show pull over to snap pictures of themselves posing in front of Route 66 highway signs.

Driving west from Williams, *Ash Fork* (928–637–0204) will be one of the first places you reach. Ash Fork, named for the area's native trees and the fact that there is a fork in the road going to Prescott, is more than one hundred years old. If you have the time, pull off Route 66 onto First Street (which becomes Double A Ranch Road), follow it across the railroad tracks to Cemetery Road, and turn east. There on a gentle slope you'll find the original *Ash Fork Cemetery,* a collection of splintering wooden crosses and weathered sandstone slabs. The locals say that the first man buried here—Tom Kane—wasn't even a resident. He was a stranger who died as a result of an accidental shooting (so much for frontier hospitality!).

Just north of the cemetery on Forest Road 124, which you can reach by following Double A Ranch Road, you'll come to another big attraction: the *flagstone quarries.* Ash Fork calls itself the "Flagstone Capital of the World," and indeed, these quarries have provided material for countless walls and floors not only all over Arizona, but nationwide via the railroad. The variety of colors and the smooth texture of Arizona flagstone have made it especially popular, and though its appeal peaked in the 1950s, it's still sought after for many types of construction.

Ash Fork also boasts the first *all-steel dam* ever built. This National Historic Engineering landmark was erected in 1898 in Johnson Canyon. The dam is one of two structures near Ash Fork (the other is a stone dam) that were built to create water reservoirs for steam trains. You can reach it (if you have a high-profile, four-wheel-drive vehicle) by taking I–40 east to the County Line Road and turning north. This dirt road bumps along until it reaches a huge cinder pit, where it joins an unmarked access road. Keep driving for about a mile. You should see a large crater that was created during the construction of the dam. You can park here and walk the short distance down to the dam. The

Ancient Messages in the Rocks

Petroglyphs, left behind by a much earlier civilization, can be seen south of Ash Fork. Head west on I–40 until you reach Crookton Road. Exit heading south, and continue on until you reach Arizona Road. This is a dirt road that shouldn't be traveled during periods of heavy rain. If there's no water on the surface, however, and you drive slowly, you should be able to negotiate it in a conventional vehicle. Continue until you reach the bridge at Partridge Creek. To the right past the bridge, you'll spot a small cliff where the drawings—many of them rectangular symbols, but some clearly representing animals—are scratched into the dark rock. The age of these drawings, along with the identity of the Native American tribe who carved them, is unknown.

mammoth steel plates, which make it look like a massive radiator, are designed to expand and contract with the temperature, and the dam shows few signs of wear after more than century of use.

Located just 5 miles northwest of Ash Fork, you can drive to **Dante's Descent,** which is also known by locals as the Devil's Hole. The natural sinkhole makes an impressive sight, plunging down more than 380 feet.

Seligman, (928–422–3939) just west of Ash Fork, is a sometime stop for Mother Road cruisers (the longest loop of Route 66 left completely intact in Arizona is the 160-mile strip from Seligman to Topock, where this road ends on the Arizona side of the Colorado River). If you're hungry, tired, or you need to refuel, Seligman has some visitors' services, including restaurants, motels, and gas stations.

As for nearby **Valentine,** it used to be that each year many thousands of Americans sent their Valentine's Day cards here to be canceled with the post office's distinctive stamp. Several years back, however, the community's postal carrier was kidnapped and murdered (a terrible crime anywhere but especially shocking here in this small, peaceful community), and the post office was closed.

In any case, the town is named for a former commissioner for Indian Affairs, not for any romantic notions. Film buffs may be interested to know that Valentine's **Hunt Ranch** (off Buck and Doe Road) is featured prominently in a scene in *Easy Rider.* Peter Fonda's character fixes a flat tire in front of the ranch, while in the background a cowboy shoes a horse.

With such a sweetheart of a name, it may not come as a surprise that Valentine is the new heart-warming home for the **Keepers of the Wild Nature Park** (928–769–1800; www.keepersofthewild.org). Located at 13441 East Route 66 (mile marker 87), this wildlife refuge is home to hundreds of exotic animals rescued from neglectful and abusive situations. The 175-acre sanctuary offers educational tours, wildlife viewing opportunities, a gift shop, and a snack shop.

Blink! You just missed it. **Hackberry,** the next stop, is that small. Hackberry, named for a regional native tree, was an 1880s mining community located just off the Santa Fe Railroad tracks. With the development of Route 66, Hackberry had a brief new life as a refueling stop for motorists. When Route 66 was diverted to a straighter path in the early 1930s, Hackberry was left stranded behind the Truxton Wash, and the town dried up faster than a sweat bead in the sun.

Farther down the road, just east of Kingman, you'll come to Hualapai Mountain Road. This 14-mile mountain drive will take you through a pine forest perfect for hiking, wildlife viewing, and picnicking at **Hualapai Mountain Park** (928–757–3859, ranger station). The nearby **Hualapai Mountain Resort** (928–757–3545), at 4525 Hualapai Mountain Road, offers three comfortable rooms and three spacious suites. This rustic retreat is light on amenities, but loaded with opportunities to get away from it all. The resort restaurant is open for lunch and dinner Wednesday through Sunday and offers a delightful breakfast on the weekends. Rooms range from $79 to $100.

Like many frontier towns, **Kingman** (928–753–6106 or 866–427–RT66; www.kingmantourism.org), about 25 miles west and south of Hackberry on Route 66, is named after one of its founders. Lewis Kingman was a surveyor whose work helped to establish the Santa Fe Railway. The town is actually much bigger than its Main Street appearance would suggest, with a population of about 25,000. Because it's within a one-hour drive of Lake Mead, Lake Havasu, Lake Mohave, and other recreational areas, it's a major stopping point for camping and boating aficionados.

Kingman is home to the **Historic Route 66 Association of Arizona** (928–753–5001; www.azrt66.com) at 120 West Route 66 in the restored Powerhouse Visitors Center, which also houses the Tourist Information Center, the Carlos Elmer Memorial Photo Gallery, a gift shop, model railroad store, and a deli/soda fountain. The Powerhouse—which was constructed as a generating station—was begun in 1907 and was fully operational in 1927. By the mid-1960s, all use of the facility ceased and it sat vacant. Demolition was too costly to be considered, and in 1986 the building was placed on the National Register of Historic Places (in all, sixty Kingman buildings enjoy the same distinction). Following a $1-million renovation, the building reopened in the fall of 1997. Organized to help preserve the vanishing way of life of mom-and-pop grocery stores and motels with names like the "Lariat Inn," the association provides some insight to visitors who want to know more about the Mother Road. They also hold a Route 66 Fun Run (where "Get Your Kicks" songwriter Bobby Troup has been featured) every May, taking riders in every type of vehicle imaginable on a trip back in time with a beauty contest, a car show, street cruising, and other activities.

For another look at the history of Mohave County, stop by the **Mohave Museum of History and Arts** (928–753–3195) at 400 West Beale Street. Here you'll discover exhibits on ranching, mining, and pioneer life. Native American artifacts and art (the Mohave, Hualapai, Chemehuevi, Havasupai, and Paiute Indians all had a presence on this corner of the state); displays of military might (there once was a gunnery school in Kingman); and movie memorabilia from actor Andy Devine (Kingman's "favorite son") are all prominently displayed in this often-overlooked, 18,000-square-foot museum. Hours are from 9:00 A.M. to 5:00 P.M. Monday through Friday and 1:00 to 5:00 P.M. Sunday. Admission is $4.00 for adults (children are free) and $3.00 for seniors. Admission fees are good for both the Mohave Museum of Art and the Historic Route 66 Museum.

If you're in the mood for more history, head over to the **Bonelli House,** (928–753–1413) at 430 East Spring Street. This two-story territorial-style mansion is named for the wealthy Swiss family that built it in 1915. Today it has been restored as a museum, and the interior has been decorated with much of the same furniture it held ninety years ago. The home is open Monday through Friday from 11:00 A.M. to 3:00 P.M. There is a donation box at the door.

You won't find any bed-and-breakfast inns right in downtown Kingman, but there are a number of motels on the Route 66 strip, ranging from the 34-room **Imperial Motel** (928–753–2176) at 1911 East Route 66 to the 148-unit **Silver Queen Motel** (928–757–4315) at 3285 East Route 66. If you're hungry, drop into **Mr. D'z Route 66 Diner** (928–718–0066) at 105 East Route 66.

Wandering into **Oatman** (928–768–6222) only a few miles from the Nevada border, a visitor might easily imagine that a time warp exists here—the town looks much the same today as it did when it was established near the turn of the twentieth century. A mining town named after a survivor of an infamous Indian attack, Oatman has braved rough economic times, but its gorgeous Mohave County scenery and Old West ambience continue to draw tourists. Oatman is a big rally point for Route 66 cruisers, including motorcycle clubs, so don't be surprised if you pull into town and glimpse a line of Corvettes or Harleys.

Clark Gable and Carole Lombard, two of the town's most famous visitors, arrived in 1939. After a ceremony in Kingman, they spent their wedding night (though some claim it was night number two) in Room 15 of the **Oatman Hotel** (928–768–4408), a two-story adobe building on Main Street. The hotel, built in 1902, is the largest adobe structure in Mohave County. The rustic hotel, which has many antique fixtures, has a full bar downstairs, a dining room, and a dance floor.

Andy Devine Country

If you're a fan of old-time Western movies, no doubt you're familiar with Kingman's most famous native son, Andy Devine. Born in 1905 in Flagstaff as Jeremiah Schwartz, he grew up in Kingman. He began his film career in the mid-1920s as a Hollywood bit player. His shambling, bearlike gait and raspy voice caused him to be cast as the comic relief in numerous Westerns, including the John Ford classic *The Man Who Shot Liberty Valance*. Devine also took roles in many vintage TV shows such as *Gunsmoke, Bonanza, The Twilight Zone, Flipper,* and *Love, American Style*. He continued working in colorful character roles until shortly before his death in 1977.

Visitors to Oatman can see staged gunfights on Main Street every weekend, hear live music in the town's four bars, and pet up to a dozen wild burros whenever they wander into town to mooch food. These descendants of pack animals have been damned by some locals as nuisances, but they've also been adopted as mascots.

Another interesting thing to do in Oatman is the **Gold Road Mine Tour** (928–768–1600; www.goldroadmine.com), which was in production from 1996 to 1998 and produced 40,000 ounces of gold a year. The price of gold seems to determine whether the mine is in full operation, but tours are offered in any case. They take you underground approximately one-eighth of a mile, and tours run all day long. Admission is $12.00 for adults, $6.00 for children younger than 12, and free for children age 3 and younger. It opens at 10:00 A.M., with the last tour at 4:30 P.M.

Oatman is the last Arizona town on Route 66. A few miles west Route 66 hooks up with Highway 95, which takes you to either the Nevada or California border.

Just east of the Nevada border on Highway 95 is **Bullhead City** (928–754–4121 or 800–987–7457; www.bullheadchamber.com). To reach it continue on Route 66 to Highway 95, then head north. Bullhead City began life more than fifty years ago as a camp for workers building the Davis Dam on the southern end of Lake Mohave. A rock formation here that resembled a bull's head led to the city's name, but it's now submerged in the lake. The dam was completed in 1953. It regulates water delivery to Mexico and generates electrical power that goes to substations in Arizona, California, and Nevada.

Bullhead City languished for years as a sparsely populated bedroom community. It began to grow in the mid-1960s when entrepreneur Don Laughlin began casino and resort development just across the Colorado River in Laughlin, Nevada, creating a need for visitor services on the Arizona side. Bullhead City was finally incorporated in 1984. Today, more than two million people a year visit Laughlin, and many of them launch their vacation from Bullhead City, where there's a $23-million airport that can accommodate planes as big as the Boeing 737. When visiting Bullhead City, stop at **The Colorado River Museum** (928–754–3399) on Highway 95, a half-mile north of the Laughlin Bridge. The museum was opened in 1990. Using photographs and models, the museum has exhibits on local Native American tribes, evidence of European exploration dating back to 1540, steamboats on the Colorado River, and wagon and camel trains that passed through this area. It is open Tuesday through Sunday from 10:00 A.M. to 4:00 P.M. A $1.00 donation is requested.

Lake Mohave can be reached by driving north on Highway 95. The lake has fishing for largemouth and striped bass, catfish, rainbow trout, and bluegill.

Fishing licenses and tackle and bait are available at the **Lake Mohave Resort and Marina** (800–752–9669; www.sevencrown.com). The marina also rents houseboats outfitted with air conditioning, a gas oven/range, freezer, microwave oven, shower and tub, stereo cassette, and other amenities. Smaller boats for skiing or fishing are also for rent. Houseboating is also quite popular on Lake Mead. The marina has several different models from which to choose.

If lounging in a casino sounds like more fun than lounging on a lake, there are eleven casinos only minutes away in Laughlin, Nevada, most of them lining the western bank of the Colorado.

There are no bed-and-breakfasts inns in Bullhead City, just hotels and motels, although some of these offer valuable options. The **River Queen Resort Motel** (928–754–3214) at 125 Long Avenue actually has an area on the property where you can fish. You can literally catch your own dinner and take it back to your room—or to one of the motel's barbecue grills—to prepare for dinner. The motel also has free shuttle service for guests to Laughlin, Nevada, and to the Bullhead City airport.

For a bite to eat, drop by **Iguana's Mexican River Cantina** (928–763–9109) at 2247 Clearwater Drive. Run for years by a guy locals know simply as "Valdo," Iguana's uses authentic Mexican recipes prepared by chefs from Sonora, Mexico.

Lake Havasu Area

South of Bullhead City and south of the Route 66 junction with Highway 95 is **Lake Havasu City** (928–453–3444 or 800–242–8278; www.golakehavasu .com). Founded in 1963, it's one of Arizona's youngest municipalities. The lake itself isn't much older, having been created in 1939 when Parker Dam was built on the California border of the Colorado River. **Lake Havasu** attracts a huge number of visitors, especially in the spring when retirees and college students flock there. In fact, in 1995, the MTV music cable channel used it as their Spring Break broadcast site. It used to clear out in the summer when Lake Havasu City often records the hottest temperature in Arizona—and sometimes in the nation. Today, though, southern Californians and Arizonans alike appear to ignore their thermometers and have turned the area into a popular summer getaway for water sports of all types.

Of course, Lake Havasu City offers more than just fun in the sun. As most of the free world knows, the city is home to the **London Bridge,** all 10,276 granite blocks of

trivia

Lake Havasu City's London Bridge is the largest "antique" ever sold to the United States.

London Bridge

which were brought over from England in 1968 by city founder Robert McCulloch of McCulloch Chainsaw fame. When the city of London put the bridge up for sale because it was too small to handle its traffic demands, McCulloch bought the bridge in a terrific publicity stunt for a mere $2,460,000. What you may not realize is that the city has gone to great lengths to complete the illusion of an English community. At the base of the bridge is the Tudor-style ***English Village.*** The shops, the streets, and even the phone booths resemble those in London. Tour guides (who are basically there to give directions) and other village dwellers dress in authentic garb. Stores in the village sell curios and gift items—some British, some not—such as glassware and candles.

The English motif continues in enterprises like the ***London Bridge Resort*** (928–855–0888 or 800–624–7939; www.londonbridgeresort.com) at 1477 Queen's Bay Road, the facade of which mimics a stone castle. The resort has boat docks, several pools, a nine-hole executive golf course, tennis courts, a workout room, and other amenities. Like many other properties around the country, the London Bridge Resort is a time share resort. When available to the public, they rent anywhere from $99 to $289 per night. Many other hotels, inns, and resorts are in Lake Havasu City, but there were no bed-and-breakfast inns at the time of this writing. For the budget-minded traveler who would like to stay close to the action, the ***Bridgeview Motel*** (928–855–5559) at 101 London Bridge Road provides the services and facilities typical of a traditional economy motel, within strolling distance of the English Village. Rates range from $50 to $135 per night.

One mile east of the English Village on McCulloch Boulevard, the city continues its re-creation of the United Kingdom with ***Shambles Village*** at 2126

McCulloch Boulevard. No, the name doesn't mean that the place is a wreck. It's a reference to old-fashioned English butcher stalls with the meat hung from the rafters. The shops include art galleries and apparel and gift shops.

For a look at a different point of view, stop by the **Lake Havasu Museum of History** (928–854–4938; www.havasumuseum.com) at 320 London Bridge Road. This new addition to Lake Havasu City features displays on the history of the region in a 3,000-square-foot building.

Another unique way to see the area is on Sea Doo watercraft. **London Bridge Watercraft Tours** (928–453–8883) at 1519 Queens Bay can take you on a guided tour from the London Bridge up the Colorado River to the **Havasu National Wildlife Refuge.** The marshland here supports a variety of birds, including white pelicans, black-crowned night herons, and kingfishers. It's also possible to see bald eagles in the winter. The Sea Doos (think of them as mini-powerboats) are large enough for two or three people, are easy to operate, and can hit speeds of 40 miles per hour—but hey, let's be careful out there!

The city has a number of major annual events, including Christmas festivities, boat regattas, and the **World Jet-Ski Racing Finals,** held every October. Call the Lake Havasu Tourism Bureau (800–242–8278) for more information about events. Additional information can be found in *Havasu Magazine* (www.havasumagazine.com).

Quartz and Camels

Due south of Lake Havasu on Highway 95 is the community of **Parker** (928–669–2174; www.parkerareachamberofcommerce.com), and a few miles farther south is **Poston,** a name that doesn't mean much to most Arizonans but that played a major role in one of the saddest chapters in American history. Beginning in the summer of 1942, and continuing until the end of World War II, nearly 18,000 Japanese-Americans were interned at the Poston camp on the **Colorado River Indian Tribes Reservation** (928–669–9211). This population made the camp the third largest city in Arizona. Though the detainees were able to create the semblance of a real community by building a pavilion and staging theatrical and musical entertainments, they were clearly prisoners within their own country.

In 1992 a monument to the camp's detainees was erected in Poston, which still contains the camp's original gym/theater. The monument is a 9-foot-tall concrete Japanese lantern with plaques that tell the story of the internment. The staff at the **Colorado River Indian Tribes Museum** in Parker can answer some questions about the Poston camp. The museum also has displays of artifacts from vanished tribes like the Anasazi and Hohokam, as well as rugs, baskets, and other crafts made by contemporary tribes like the Mohave, Navajo, and Chemehuevi.

Mention **Quartzsite** (which you can reach by driving south on Highway 95 from Parker to Interstate 10 and heading east on I–10 for a few miles) to Arizonans, and they'll probably respond "Gemboree!" The fact is that this community of about 2,000, just across the border from Blythe, California, is better known for its yearly gem shows than for anything else. It's no wonder, given that the area is laden with minerals and gems of all varieties. In January and February the Quartzsite population swells to bursting with collectors, dealers, and lookie-loos. Some of the gem selling goes on indoors, but much of the dealing is swap-meet style. Most traders will deal with the general public, but some will sell only to wholesalers. You can find some bargains here, but if you know very little about gems and minerals, caveat emptor applies. Some unscrupulous dealers, for example, will sell polished "turquoise" stones that aren't genuine. Rather, they're made by combining turquoise powder and epoxy resin. For more information on Quartzsite gem shows, contact the Quartzsite Chamber of Commerce at (928) 927–5600.

trivia

Palm Canyon, southeast of Quartzsite, is the only place in Arizona where native palm trees grow.

Quartzite Camels

Besides being a rich mining district, Quartzsite once had the distinction of being the Army's test site for integrating camels into its cavalry. The Army had employed Hadji Ali, a Syrian camel driver, to train the troops in the fine points of managing these "ships of the desert." Known as Hi Jolly to his friends, this Middle-Easterner who'd been transplanted to the American Southwest was regarded as a rather colorful character and something of a local hero. Despite Ali's best efforts, the experiment, carried out from the mid-1850s to 1864, was less than a rousing success. One explanation is that the camels couldn't get along with the Army's pack mules. In any case, the hapless animals were finally turned loose into the sun-baked surroundings, where they met an untimely death as a result of starvation or trigger-happy pioneers.

Ali died in 1902, and thirty-three years later, Governor Benjamin Moeur dedicated the **Hi Jolly Monument**, a stone pyramid topped with a metal silhouette of a camel. The monument is easily reached off the west-end bypass of I-10.

Non-Ghost Towns

To explore the west central area of the state, take Highway 89A south and west from Flagstaff. Between Clarkdale and Cottonwood lies *Tuzigoot* (an Apache name meaning "crooked water") *National Monument* (928–634–5564; www .nps.gov/tuzi). This pueblo, built by the long-vanished Sinagua Indians near the Verde River, is more than 500 years old. The Sinaguans, whose culture included farming as well as hunting and gathering, founded settlements throughout northern and central Arizona, often choosing the land near streams and hot springs as sites for building their elaborate dwellings. Besides the ruins, a nearby visitors center displays Sinaguan artifacts and sells books about the area's history. The visitors center is open daily from 8:00 A.M. to 6:00 P.M. in the summer, and from 8:00 A.M. to 5:00 P.M. in the winter. Admission is $5.00 per person age 16 and older for seven days.

Named for the tree that flourishes along area creek banks, *Cottonwood* (928–634–7593; chamber.verdevalley.com) has a handful of restored 1870s-style shops that sell everything from arts and crafts to clothing to furniture. There's also an old-time movie theater that still shows (mostly) first-run films. If you have a few minutes to spend, you may want to pull off the road and browse through some of the shops or head to a wildlife park in nearby Camp Verde. *Out of Africa Wildlife Park* (928–567–2840; www.outofafricapark.com) at 4020 North Cherry Road showcases big cats and offers a popular attraction, their daily Tiger Splash show, that involves staffers swimming with white tigers and other ferocious felines. The real attraction, however, is in *Clarkdale,* a heartbeat away.

Located north of Cottonwood on Highway 260, Clarkdale is home to the *Verde Canyon Railroad* (800–320–0718; www.verdecanyonrr.com). This 40-mile railroad was built in 1911 to take mining and other supplies and copper ore from Clarkdale northwest to the town of Drake. Over time it became popular among those who wanted easy access to the wilderness areas of Verde Canyon. The Verde Canyon Railroad's mining days ended in the 1950s, and after years of struggling financially while hauling coal, it was purchased as an excursion train in 1990. The railway uses renovated Metro New York Line coach cars, each of which can accommodate about seventy passengers. There are also open-air cars where passengers from any part of the train can stand and get a good look at the scenery as the trains ramble through the protected Verde Canyon area, a gorgeous stretch that includes a riparian cottonwood forest, desert areas, and towering red rocks.

The trip also is a wildlife lover's delight. Antelope, javelina, black hawks, and blue herons live here. Though it isn't well known to outsiders yet, more than forty bald eagles are nesting in the area. Peak viewing season is from

December through March, when the majestic birds inhabit the canyon, usually nesting within a few hundred feet of the river. During the four hour ride, singer/storytellers dressed in rustic frontier attire keep passengers entertained and help to point out the wildlife.

The railway operates year-round and even has moonlight excursions in the summer. The train operation offers cocktails, hors d'oeuvres, and deli treats. Fares start at $54.95 for adults and $34.95 for children.

Clarkdale is also the site of the *Flying Eagle Bed and Breakfast* (928–634–0663; www.flyingeaglecountry.com) at 2700 Windmill Lane. This B&B offers accommodations in a guest house or in a sunrise room attached to the main house. Flying Eagle has horseshoe and badminton courts and a spa, but the real attraction is the gorgeous view of the valley. The red rocks of Sedona are visible in the background.

Due south on Highway 89A, the former mining community of *Jerome* (928–634–2900; www.azjerome.com) is proud to call itself the "largest ghost town in Arizona." The fact is that it isn't a ghost town at all, although it nearly suffered the fate of total abandonment. Built on Cleopatra Hill in the early 1880s, the town thrived with the copper industry. At first the land beneath the town was drilled into and blasted out to form a series of tunnels (almost 90 miles in all) from which rich copper ore was extracted. Fires drove the workers out of the tunnels, however, in 1918, and surface mining became the new standard operating procedure.

The dynamiting necessitated by this strip mining caused a shake, rattle, and roll greater than anything Jerry Lee Lewis ever dreamed of, and the town discovered to its horror that it had created a massive slide zone. The *City Jail,* known as the "traveling jail," in fact, has slid 225 feet across the highway since a 1920s dynamite explosion dislodged it from its original foundation.

Unlucky Day at the First Interstate Bank

While you're in Clarkdale, stop by the *First Interstate Bank.* On a June morning in 1928, two Oklahoma desperadoes made the mistake of choosing this bank for a heist. As they began to drive away with $40,000, one of the robbers fired a round in the direction of Jim Roberts, a 70-year-old town constable who years before had been one of the most dedicated "soldiers" fighting the infamous Pleasant Valley War (a series of bloody range battles between two families of cattlemen and sheepherders) and whom Zane Grey immortalized in *To The Last Man*. Roberts calmly yanked out his nickel-plated Colt.45 SAA and shot the getaway driver in the head. The surviving holdup man bailed out as the car crashed, emptied his gun without effect at the old lawman, and decided he didn't "feel lucky."

In the early 1950s the mines closed altogether, and Jerome languished. But just as hippies discovered the Haight-Ashbury District in San Francisco in the 1960s so too did they find the Victorian buildings of Jerome to their liking, and many settled in the area permanently. Today Jerome is a thriving arts community, with renowned sculptors, painters, jewelers, and musicians plying their trades and professions here. About one-third of the community is directly involved in the arts.

Like many Arizona mining towns, Jerome is easy to navigate on foot, though some of the hills are a bit steep and walking shoes are highly recommended. You may want to explore the restaurants, B&Bs, and shops. Many of them are downtown on Main Street. A few of the fun and funky shops on Jerome's steep streets include the **Copper Rose** (928–634–0272; www.copper roseaz.com), "Northern Arizona's only natural bath and body shop"; **Nellie Bly** (928–634–0255, www.nbscopes.com), known for its impressive collection of kaleidoscopes; and **Victorian Treasures** (928–649–8099; www.victorian treasuresantiques.com), a fabulous gift shop featuring European antiques and collectibles.

Among the historic buildings to see are the **Douglas Mansion,** at the **Jerome State Historic Park** (928–634–5381) on Mine Museum Road, and the Surgeon's House. Built around World War I by James S. "Rawhide Jimmy" Douglas, owner of the Little Daisy Mine, the Douglas Mansion is a rambling adobe home that today serves as the area's museum. The mansion has a half-hour video presentation on the history of Jerome. It's open daily from 8:00 A.M. to 5:00 P.M. Admission is $4.00 for adults and $1.00 for children ages 7 to 13.

Definitely worth seeing (and staying at) is the **Surgeon's House** (928–639–1452 or 800–639–1452; www.surgeonshouse.com), the restored former residence of the Little Daisy Mine's chief surgeon, Arthur Carlson. Furnished with antiques, the Mediterranean-styled B&B recalls an earlier time when the pace of life was slower and more elegant. The owner has retained the home's charm while adding modern luxuries such as a hot tub. It can be arranged for a professional masseur to attend to your aches and pains. Spiritual consultations and walking tours of the area's highlights are also available.

For another lodging option, check into the **Ghost City Inn** (888–634–4678; www.ghostcityinn.com) on Main Street, an almost one-hundred-year-old B&B that has had many incarnations in its time, including a stint as a speakeasy. This Victorian structure, furnished in original style, has modern amenities like a Jacuzzi.

Like many small communities, Jerome tends to roll up the streets after sunset, so if you plan on arriving in town at night, make arrangements ahead of time for lodging or food. There are several quaint eateries, including the **Flat-**

iron Cafe (928–634–2733) at 416 Hull Avenue, which serves breakfast and lunch. For late-night meals, try the *Palace* (aka the *Haunted Hamburger* 928–634–0554) for ribs, burgers, and the like; or the *Red Rooster Café* (928–634–7087) for homemade soups and sandwiches. Both restaurants are within walking distance of downtown.

A Piece of the Old West

Travel southwest on Highway 89A to the other side of 7,732-foot Mingus Mountain, and you'll arrive at one of Arizona's loveliest towns, affectionately known as "everybody's hometown." But don't call it *Press-cott*. Locals prefer the pronunciation *Press-kit*. ("Just like *biscuit,*" they'll tell you). The town was named after historian William H. Prescott and began its life in the 1860s as a mining and ranching community.

In some respects, *Prescott* (928–445–2000 or 800–266–7534; www .prescott.org) looks like a cross between Flagstaff—because of its high altitude and pine trees—and Bisbee—because of its many Victorian, wood-frame homes. Residents compare it with the sorts of communities you come across in the Midwest. Of course, if you're from the Midwest, maybe that's not so exciting. We Arizonans (including Grammy-nominated jazz pianist Liz Story, who calls the town home) think it's pretty cool.

For visitors the town offers bed-and-breakfast inns, hotels, and motels. Prescott also has accommodations that are listed in the Historic Hotels of America registry. The *Hassayampa Inn* (800–322–1927; www.hassayampainn.com) at 122 East Gurley Street was built in the late 1920s as a getaway hotel for wealthy residents of Phoenix. The architecture is Pueblo Art Deco, done in red brick, and includes Arizona's first porte cochere. It has been redecorated on a regular basis without taking away the traditional character of its rooms. Near the Courthouse Square and Whiskey Row is *Hotel Vendome* (928–776–0900 or 888–468–3583; www.vendomehotel.com), which is listed on the National Register of Historic Places. It's a grandmother's cottage sort of place with quilts on the beds and a bed-and-breakfast ambience. Legend has it there's a ghost (and a ghostly cat!) in the house, which may be why the brochure says it's a unique lodging experience, not just a place to sleep.

You won't starve in Prescott: Its ninety or so restaurants range from big-name chains to mom-and-pop establishments. *Murphy's* (928–445–4044; www.murphysrestaurants.com) at 201 North Cortez Street is a former general store that is now transformed into an elegant eatery. Murphy's offers three kinds of fresh fish daily, as well as ribs, lobster tail, and other examples of American and Continental cuisine. The restaurant's lounge affords a view of

Thumb Butte, where Virgil Earp—before becoming a U.S. Marshal for Pima County—once ran a sawmill.

If you want to find out more about the area's history, the best place to go is the ***Sharlot Hall Museum*** (928–445–3122; www.sharlot.org) at 415 West Gurley Street. Hall was an early twentieth-century historian, originally from Kansas, who grew up in and around Prescott. Later in life she purchased the former governor's mansion (Prescott was twice the territorial capital) and began a museum of items relating to Arizona history. On the grounds are the Museum Center, housing the archives and research library; the Sharlot Hall Building, a rock and pine log house; the Fremont House of more sophisticated construction; a Victorian-style Bashford House; Fort Misery (which is the oldest log building associated with Arizona); the Transportation Building, exhibiting the vehicle collection; and the Governor's Mansion, built in 1864. In addition there's a ranch house, a schoolhouse, a windmill, and several gardens, including the Pioneer Herb Garden. Hours are from 10:00 A.M. to 4:00 P.M. Monday through Saturday and noon to 4:00 P.M. Sunday. Admission is $5.00 for adults.

trivia

The pine-forested central Arizona community of Prescott is known as "Arizona's Christmas City."

Prescott was named Arizona's first territorial capital in 1864, a title it relinquished to Tucson in 1867 before regaining it in 1877. The capital was moved—permanently—to Phoenix in 1889.

More than 500 Prescott buildings are listed on the National Register of Historic Places.

Another museum that attracts its share of visitors is the ***Phippen Western Art Museum*** (928–778–1385; www.phippenartmuseum.org) on Highway 89 North. Named after George Phippen, one of the founders of the Cowboy Artists of America, the museum has permanent and traveling exhibitions. Much of the work presented in the museum involves realistic depictions of cowboy life—roundups, campfires, bronc busting—but there are also impressionistic portraits of ranch hands, Native Americans, and other frontier dwellers that give startling insight into the life, work, and soul of the people of the Southwest. The museum also frequently hosts lecturers and special events related to cowboy art. The museum is open from Tuesday through Saturday from 10:00 A.M. to 4:00 P.M. and Sunday from 1:00 to 4:00 P.M. Admission is $5.00 for adults, $4.00 for seniors and students.

Historic ***Whiskey Row*** is a stretch of Montezuma Street between Gurley and Goodwin. In the "bad old days" of the West, this avenue of saloons and redlight establishments was the scene of much debauchery and gunplay, not to

Chino Valley's Claim to Fame

Although Prescott claims the privilege of being the first Arizona territorial capital, that honor rightly belongs to the little community of **Chino Valley** (928–636–2493; www.chinovalley.org), 15 miles to the north on Highway 89. In 1863 there was a mining camp in Chino Valley under the command of Lt. Amiel Whipple, and he established the capital at his fort. The most logical choice, Tucson—a much larger town with more amenities—was ruled out because of its large number of Southern sympathizers. The territorial capital was moved to Prescott the following year. There are some travelers services, including gas and lodging, in the area, but because Chino Valley is primarily a bedroom community, there are no real attractions.

mention a horrendous fire in 1900. One of the best places to visit on the Row is the **Palace** (928–541–1996; www.historicpalace.com) on Montezuma Street in the middle of the block. The original Palace burned down in the 1900 fire, but the original hand-carved mahogany bar was carried (by hand) out into the street and later incorporated into the rebuilt structure. Like many historic watering holes in Arizona, the Palace is now a restaurant and saloon that occasionally has live country-and-western music.

Prescott has been designated as Arizona's official Christmas City, and the town goes all out with decorations and merriment during the holiday season, including decorating the courthouse—smack in the center of town square—with thousands of lights.

There were many Indian wars during Arizona's frontier days, and **Skull Valley,** just west of Prescott via Montezuma Street, which becomes Iron Springs Road, is named for the grisly aftermath of an 1864 battle between Apaches and

Whiskey Row in Prescott

Maricopas. The dead warriors were not buried, and white settlers were greeted by the sight of human skulls bleaching in the sun. For years Skull Valley was a stage stop as well as the location of Fort McPherson, established here to protect settlers and overland freighters from Indian attacks. The fort was removed after only a few years of use. A number of historic buildings, however, remain. These include the Santa Fe Depot, which was built in 1898; a one-room schoolhouse built in 1917; a 1916 general store; and a 1925 gas station. Residents like Mary Kukal, who (together with her husband, now deceased) used to run the store, are helping to renovate and restore the old structures. You can see the outside of the old buildings on your own.

Places to Stay in Western Arizona

JEROME

Connor Hotel,
164 Main Street;
(928) 634–5006 or
(800) 523–3554.
Ten first-class, Victorian rooms in an 1898 hotel. Inexpensive to moderate.

Jerome Grand Hotel,
200 Hill Street
P.O. Box H,
Jerome, AZ 86331;
(928) 634–8200 or
(888) 817–6788;
www.jeromegrandhotel.net
Thirty rooms/suites in a 1926-era renovated five-story mountainside hotel.
Moderate.

KINGMAN

Days Inn West,
3023 East Route 66 Avenue;
(928) 753–7500.
A reasonably priced choice on the main drag. Inexpensive.

Historic Hotel Brunswick,
315 East Route 66;
(928) 718–1800.
A 1909 hotel located on "The Mother Road." Inexpensive.

LAKE HAVASU CITY

Howard Johnson Lodge/Suites,
335 London Bridge Road;
(800) 446–4656.
Orange roofs are the familiar sign of these lodges. Inexpensive.

Nautical Inn Resort,
1000 McCulloch Boulevard;
(800) 892–2141 or
928–855–2141;
www.nauticalinn.com
One hundred thirty-nine beachfront suites, each with a lake view and balcony or patio. Moderate to expensive.

PARKER

Blue Water Resort and Casino,
11300 Resort Drive;
(888) 243–3360;
www.bluewaterfun.com
Rooms and suites, seven dining options, casino, live entertainment, pool and water park, marina and sandy beach. Moderate.

Comfort Inn,
1290 White Spar Road;
(928) 778–5770 or
(800) 228–5150.
A reasonably priced choice on the continuation of Montezuma Street on Highway 89. Inexpensive.

PRESCOTT

Hassayampa Inn,
122 East Gurley Street;
(800) 322–1927;
www.hassayampainn.com
Sixty-eight rooms and suites. Peacock Dining Room and cocktail lounge. Charming ambience and service. Listed in the National Register of Historic Places and rumored to be haunted. Moderate to expensive.

Hotel Vendome,
230 South Cortez Street;
(888) 468–3583;
www.vendomehotel.com
Twenty-one rooms and suites within walking distance of Courthouse Plaza, museums, and shops. Wine and beer bar, cozy lobby. Listed on National Register of Historic Places. Moderate.

Places to Eat in Western Arizona

KINGMAN

The Cookery,
3300 East Andy Devine Avenue;
(928) 757–7311.
Casual American cuisine including steaks, sandwiches, and salads. Inexpensive.

Cracker Barrel Restaurant,
3520 Stockton Hill Road;
(928) 757–9000.
Family restaurant in the Western tradition. Inexpensive.

Kingman Airport Cafe,
6000 Flightline Drive;
(928) 757–4420.
Casual dining complemented by views of the runway. Inexpensive.

LAKE HAVASU CITY

Krystal's Steak and Seafood Restaurant,
460 El Camino Way;
(928) 453–2999.
Fine dining steak and seafood restaurant. Opens at 4:00 P.M. for dinner only. Moderate.

Mudshark Brewing Company,
210 Swanson Avenue;
(928) 453–2981.
Handcrafted beers, gourmet pizza, steak, seafood, and burgers. Inexpensive to moderate.

PRESCOTT

Gurley Street Grill,
230 West Gurley Street;
(928) 445–3388.
Ribs, steak, pizza, burgers, and pasta. Inexpensive.

Prescott Brewing Company,
130 West Gurley Street;
(928) 771–2795.
Handcrafted premium beer and pub-style dining in Prescott's only microbrewery. Inexpensive.

WEB SITES FOR WESTERN ARIZONA

Arizona Department of Tourism
www.arizonaguide.com

Bullhead City
www.bullheadchamber.com

Chloride
www.chloridearizona.com

Cottonwood
chamber.verdevalley.com

Havasupai Tribe
www.havasupaitribe.com

Hualapai Tourism
www.grandcanyonresort.com

Jerome Chamber of Commerce
www.azjerome.com

Kingman Area Chamber of Commerce
www.kingmantourism.org

Lake Havasu Tourism Bureau
www.golakehavasu.com

Lake Mead National Park
www.nps.gov/lame

Parker
www.parkerareachamberof commerce.com

Prescott Chamber of Commerce
www.prescott.org

Eastern Arizona

Indian Country

It's estimated that the **Navajo Nation** covers a staggering 27,000 square miles of northeastern Arizona, southeastern Utah, and northwestern New Mexico—making it larger than ten of the fifty United States. With a population of less than a quarter million, it's easy to figure out that there are many miles of wide-open territory without a human being in sight. You can see vast expanses of unbroken near-wilderness area, then, suddenly, modern homes or a collection of hogans—traditional, one-room, six-sided Navajo dwellings—pop into view. The solitude of the land is a keen reminder of what this country was like hundreds of years ago.

Therein lies one of the primary attractions of **Navajoland** (928–871–6436; www.discovernavajo.com), along with one of the biggest problems for travelers. Few people means plenty of areas with no automotive services, so if your radiator overheats, you break an axle on a rutted road, or you just get very hungry, you can be out of luck.

Here's some advice for anyone planning a trip to the reservation:

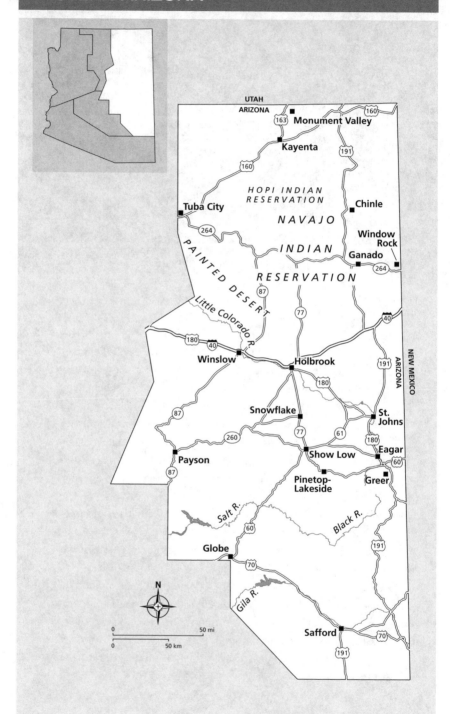

UTAH
ARIZONA

163 Monument Valley

160

Kayenta

191

160

HOPI INDIAN RESERVATION

Tuba City

NAVAJO

Chinle

264

Window Rock

INDIAN

Ganado

264

P A I N T E D   D E S E R T

R E S E R V A T I O N

87

Little Colorado R.

77

40

180

40

Winslow

Holbrook

191

ARIZONA
NEW MEXICO

180

Snowflake

St. Johns

87

260

77

61

180

Payson

Show Low

Eagar

60

87

Pinetop-Lakeside

Greer

Salt R.

Black R.

60

191

Globe

70

Gila R.

Safford

70

191

N

0   50 mi
0   50 km

1. Buy a good, detailed map of the area, showing dirt roads, and plan your route well in advance. This will save a lot of aimless driving.
2. Make sure your vehicle is in tip-top physical shape. Check fan belts, hoses, all fluid levels, tires, and so on. If anything seems suspiciously close to being worn-out or broken, have it fixed. If it's a rental vehicle, trade it in for a new one.
3. Calculate distance and gas mileage. There may not be a service station for many, many miles, so make sure you have more than enough fuel to reach your destination and get back. Whenever you come to a gas station, top off your tank.
4. If you want to go somewhere other than the Navajo Reservation visitors center (which is at Window Rock, near the New Mexico border at the junction of Interstate 40 and Indian Route 12), take a vehicle that has adequate ground clearance for rough roads. A truck or four-wheel-drive vehicle is best here. The main roads up to the reservation and to the prime attractions (for example, trading posts) are usually in good shape, but the pathways to Indian ruins and some of the more remote villages are unpaved. These are not all-weather roads, and your $40,000 sporty import—with its touchy race-tuned suspension—will be pounded into an expensive bucket of metric bolts by the time you get where you're going.
5. Travel in good weather. Again, many roads are unpaved and become all but impassable in snow or heavy rain.
6. Bring provisions in a cooler: water, trail mix, and fruit that travels well (like oranges).

And keep this very important fact in mind: When you enter the reservation, you're actually entering another nation's territory. Show respect for its laws, customs, and culture. A good practice is to stop at the visitors center first and get the rundown on what you can and can't do on the reservation. You may not be allowed to attend certain ceremonies, and at others you may be required to dress conservatively (no shorts and Hawaiian shirts). Alcohol is usually outlawed on reservation land.

AUTHOR'S TOP PICKS IN EASTERN ARIZONA

Sunrise Park Resort	Monument Valley
Tonto Natural Bridge	Petrified Forest National Park
Canyon de Chelly	Navajo National Monument

JANUARY

Hashknife Pony Express Ride
Holbrook
From Hollbrook to Scottsdale, swearing-in ceremonies, pre-dinner ride.
(928) 524–6558 or (800) 524–2459

FEBRUARY

Historic Home and Antique & Quilt Show
Globe/Miami
Transportation is provided by tour guides.
(928) 425–4495 or (800) 804–5623

MARCH

Welcome Back Buzzards
Superior
Boyce Thompson Arboretum, local flock of turkey vultures are due back to their roosts in the eucalyptus grove, bird-watching tour follows buzzard viewing.
(520) 689–2811

APRIL

Mining Country Boom Town Spree
Miami
Old-fashioned mining competitions, a wild bed race through the streets, arts and crafts.
(928) 473–4403 or (928) 473–3673

JUNE

Music Festival
Window Rock
Live entertainment, arts and crafts, book signings.
(928) 810–8540).

Strawberry Festival
Strawberry
Community Center,
seventy-plus arts and crafts booths, food.
(928) 474–4515 or (800) 672–9766

JULY

Annual Native American Festival
Pinetop-Lakeside
A juried Native American art show, artist demonstrations, and Indian music and dance performances.
(928) 367–4290 or (800) 573–4031

AUGUST

Central Navajo Fair
Chinle
All-Indian rodeo, carnival, arts and crafts market, powwow, Miss Central Navajo pageant, western concert, 4-H exhibit.
(928) 674–2052

Eagar Daze
Eagar
Concert featuring national entertainer, car show, arts and crafts, kid's zone, logging competition, and bluegrass.
(928) 333–4128

Old West Celebration and Painted Desert Classic
Hollbrook
Arts and crafts, kid's games, foot races, fun run, Native American song and dance, quilt auction.
(928) 524–6558 or (800) 524–2459

World's Oldest Continuous Rodeo
Payson
Indian dancers, floats, mountain men.
(928) 474–4515 or (800) 672–9766

Native American Art Auction
Ganado
An auction of Native American art at the historic Hubbell Trading Post.
(928) 755–3475

State Championship Old Time Fiddlers Contest
Payson
Cowboy poets, storytellers, country and bluegrass music, children's music workshop, crafts, fiddle makers, leather workers.
(928) 474–4515 or (800) 672–9766

Gila Valley Cowboy Poetry and Music Gathering
Safford/Thatcher
(928) 428–2511 or (888) 837–1841

White Mountain Apache Tribal Fair and Rodeo
Whiteriver
More than seventy years old, features all-Indian rodeos, concerts, carnival, exhibits, competition.
(928) 338–4346

Navajo Nation Fair
Window Rock
More than fifty years old, features arts and crafts, contests, exhibits, concerts, horse racing, powwow, rodeo, traditional song and dance.
(928) 871–7055

Annual Fall Festival
Pinetop-Lakeside
Arts and crafts, antique show, quilt show, 10K run, and "Run to the Pines" car show.
(928) 367–4290 or (800) 573–4031

Apache Jii Day
Globe/Miami
All-Indian celebration, crafts, paintings, baskets, quilts, dolls and clothing, entertainment by various tribes.
(928) 524–6558 or (800) 804–5623

Cowboy Christmas Arts and Crafts Show
Safford
(928) 428–2511 or (888) 837–1841

Feeling of Fall Festival
Superior
Boyce Thompson Arboretum, the sights and smells of fall, Arizona apple cider, apple pie and doughnuts, live music, special events for kids.
(520) 689–2811

Christmas Parade
Winslow
More than fifty years old, features Arizona's largest Christmas parade.
(928) 289–2434 or (928) 289–2435

Festival of Lights
Globe/Miami
Besh-Ba-Gowah Archaeological Park, luminarias, Christmas program and bonfire.
(928) 524–6558 or (800) 804–5623

Parade of Lights Festival
Holbrook
Holiday arts and crafts festival, parade of lights, and live entertainment.
(928) 524–6558 or (800) 524–2459

In general, cameras, camcorders, tape recorders, and sketch pads are forbidden in the villages. Visitors who want some record of the colorful, expressive ceremonies or powwows will have to rely on memory to preserve that experience. Occasionally Native American tribes will stage dance or drum competitions (often off the reservations) where cameras and recorders are allowed.

While you're driving, you'll notice that in many well-traveled areas of the reservation roadside vendors sell everything from katsina dolls (which are made to teach children about Hopi Katsina spirits) to rugs, baskets, pottery, and jewelry. If your interest is only in fine arts, you should be cautious when buying these arts and crafts. An experienced dealer in Native American art advises as follows: "Most good artists are going to show and sell either directly to their own clients or to galleries." Some work you see is of inferior quality, or it may actually be Mexican in origin. Unless you don't mind this, or you simply want a souvenir, stick with well-established galleries and shops. The visitors center will tell you what and where they are and can also direct you to the homes of artists and craftspeople who sell directly to the public.

Native American craftspeople can spend months or even longer working on a single piece. A lot of time and painstaking work have gone into creating the olla (*oy-yah,* a pot), bracelet, or finely woven rug you're handling. The artist has a good idea of how much it's worth. There are definite established prices, and trying to haggle over money is usually considered an insult.

Though Native American art is often cross-cultural (for example, every tribe has its share of oil painters and sculptors), as a rule of thumb the Navajos are best known for weaving and jewelry; Hopis are revered for their katsina dolls; Zunis are respected for their fetishes and jewelry; and Tohono O'odham (pronounced *Tahano Autum*) and Pima Indians are known for basketry.

In recent years, Native American artwork—everything from Pima ollas to Zuni bracelets—has become highly collectible. Blankets and rugs from the 1880s or earlier can sell for hundreds of thousands of dollars. Experts predict that prices for the works of contemporary Native American artists, who often spend as long as a year laboring on a single rug or other piece, will continue to rise. (Recently a woman who had purchased a pot some thirty years ago on a reservation for $50 had it appraised for $5,000.)

Some trading posts are worth a visit if for no other reason than to marvel at their wealth of wonderful arts and crafts as well as their sense of history. One of the best places to look or buy is the **Hubbell Trading Post** (928–755–3475; www.nps.gov/hutr), about a mile west of the tiny town of **Ganado** off Highway 264 west of Window Rock. Founded in 1878 by John Lorenzo

Native American Art

Having once made the mistake of not buying a piece of Indian pottery that by now would have doubled or tripled in value, I've decided it's high time I learned. Now living in Arizona I understand and appreciate so much of what the Indian cultures of our country are all about. For one thing, their love of the land is saving the open spaces of the West. Their reverence for the earth is also reflected in their pottery, made from the rich clay of the Arizona mesas. Utilitarian in origin, native pottery is an art form that dates back 2,000 years. Each tribe has its own way of decorating and coloring their grain and water pots—Hopi Tewa pottery is distinguished by the intricacy of their designs; Zuni use an owl motif, and the Acomas prefer figures of both animals and birds. The Navajos are known for their weaving, which is a 300-year-old craft passed from mothers to daughters, possibly with a grandmother also providing both instruction and tribal lore as part of the learning process. There are more than thirty styles of Navajo rugs, each named for the various regions of their vast reservation (nearly five million acres in total size). Geometric shapes and representations of their deities are the distinguishing features. Katsina dolls are a Hopi tradition given as gifts and teaching tools to their children. Carved from the root of a cottonwood tree, they represent dancers and spiritual beings who carry the prayers of the living to the deities who control events of everyday life. Women are particularly fond of buying native American jewelry when they visit Arizona. The Navajos and the Zunis are the tribes associated with necklaces, bracelets, rings, belts, and cluster work. Among the Navajo motifs are squash-blossom necklaces and crescent-shape pendants. Zunis are known for their combination of silver and stones. Zunis also produce fetishes, which are either polished stones that appear in the shape of a bear or carvings of wildlife (e.g., a snake) that are thought to contain a spirit.

Hubbell, this establishment has been frequented by celebrities, visiting dignitaries, and U.S. presidents. If you can't find the katsina doll, basket, or blanket you want here, it probably doesn't exist. Next door to the trading post at the visitors center, you can take a guided tour and see exhibits on Hubbell and the history of trading posts on the western frontier. Quite often Native American artisans use the area around the visitors center as a work space, and for a tip of a few dollars they'll pose for pictures.

The best place to start an exploration of the Navajo Reservation is the pueblo-style complex that houses the *Cameron Trading Post, Motel, and Restaurant* (928–279–2501 or 800–338–7385; www.camerontradingpost .com), which was established in 1916. The hotel features two-story or three-story rooms decorated in a rustic Southwestern style. The restaurant has specialties like Navajo stew and fry bread, as well as traditional burgers and sandwiches. More spectacular than the food, however, is the view from the dining room of the Little Colorado River. The trading post offers a vast assortment of katsinas, rugs, baskets, sand paintings, and pottery. Additionally, an attached gallery has high-end items, including ceremonial headdresses. Prices in the trading post and gallery are reasonable, and you can be assured of the authenticity.

Motorists unfamiliar with this vast land should understand that though many towns appear on the typical road map, services like food, water, and gasoline can be dozens of miles apart. Heading toward Kayenta and Monument Valley, the town of **Tuba City,** near the intersection of U.S. Highway 160 and state Highway 264, is a good place to stop, fill up, and stock up on supplies.

Another stop you might want to make on the way to Monument Valley is the **Kayenta Trading Post** (928–697–3541) at 1000 Main Street off U.S. Highway 163 in the town of **Kayenta.** The post, which has existed for more than forty years, offers everything from Native American jewelry, pottery, and rugs to retail groceries, videotape rentals, and even chicken feed. The store's exterior walls now sport Navajo creation-story murals, painted in 2001 by famed Navajo artist Carlos Begay.

trivia

Near Tuba City, the desert is criss-crossed by Dilophosaurus tracks, evidence that the plant-eating dinosaur the size of a horse roamed this countryside until it was annihilated by the Tyrannosaurus rex.

The capital of the Navajo Nation is **Window Rock,** located on Route 264 just a few miles west of the New Mexico border. There are several interesting attractions near Window Rock. About 3 miles west on Highway 264 you'll see the **St. Michaels Historical Museum** (928–871–4171). This stone building was a home for Franciscan friars during the 1890s. The friars came to Arizona to spread the gospel and establish schools for Native Americans. They were instrumental in helping to create a written language for the Navajos, and there are displays in the museum of some of the original Franciscan translations. There are also photographs and exhibits depicting the friars' daily lives.

Next door is the wood and brick building that houses a statue called *The Redemption of Mankind, The American Pietà*. Ludwig Schumacher, born in Germany as the son of a Nazi, rejected his father's beliefs for a life of pacifism. He immigrated to America in the mid-1980s and settled in Arizona. A craftsman by trade and a sculptor by temperament, he found a section of a juniper tree that he wanted to carve into a representation of Michelangelo's *Pietà*. Unlike the original, Schumacher's is a vertical statue, standing 16 feet tall. It depicts Jesus being taken off the cross to where Mary waits.

If you take Highway 264 east, you'll quickly arrive back at Window Rock. The **Navajo Tribal Museum and Gift Shop** (928–871–6673) and the **Navajo Arts & Crafts Enterprise** (928–871–4095) are located downtown next to the **Quality Inn Navajo Nation Capital** (928–871–4108 or 800–662–6189; www.qualityinnwindowrock.com). The museum houses intricate exhibits featuring life-size mannequins involved in tribal ceremonies and everyday activities. The arts and crafts enterprise is a Navajo organization that dates back to 1941. The purpose of this guild is to assure the quality, innovativeness, and authenticity of the crafts of its artisans. The guild also purchases arts and crafts from the Hopi, Zuni, and Santo Domingo tribes, so the selections here are very good. If you like Native American jewelry, make sure you see the Zuni pieces—especially the bracelets, which are for men as well as women.

At the one and only street light in Window Rock, take Indian Route 12 north to **Tségháhodzání** (the Navajo name for "the rock with the hole in it"). This red sandstone landmark that gave the town its name is several stories tall, with a 130-foot hole in the center. There are picnic areas nearby, as well as the hogan-shaped council chambers where the tribe's eighty-eight council members meet four times per year. The chambers are open for self-guided tours (928–871–6417). Nearby, you can visit the **Window Rock Tribal Park and Veterans' Memorial** (928–871–6647), which is open from 8:00 A.M. to 5:00 P.M. daily. The newest addition to the memorial is a tribute to the Navajo Code Talkers—a group of Navajo soldiers who created a code during WW II that was never broken.

One of the most spectacular sites on the reservation is **Canyon de Chelly** (928–674–5500; www.nps.gov/cach). Canyon de Chelly (*Shay*) is the scene of the final defeat of Navajo warriors who were holding out against troops commanded by General James Henry Carleton. In January 1864, in the final battle, twenty-three warriors died and more than 200 Navajos surrendered. You can reach Canyon de Chelly by taking Indian Route 12 north along red rock cliffs and past lush orchards. When you reach the junction for Route 7, take Route 7 (the backroad, some parts gravel) northwest to the town of **Chinle** at the entrance of Canyon de Chelly. For an alternative route on which all the roads are paved, head west on Highway 264, then north on Highway 191 to Chinle. This route is about 80 miles. Follow the highway signs to the visitors center. The center has a museum that traces the history of Native Americans in the canyon. It also has an art gallery, demonstrations of Indian arts and crafts, and an information desk. Navajo guides can also be hired here.

At the visitors center you can also get a map that will show you the route of the rim drives. You can take these roads unescorted, though you will miss the most spectacular sights. If you want to experience the Canyon more fully, you must hire a guide who will take you into the canyon (rentals include the

Exploring Canyon de Chelly

When you arrive at the entrance to Canyon de Chelly, the canyon walls are only about 30 feet high, but they eventually soar to 1,000 feet above the sandy floor. While in Canyon de Chelly, don't miss **Spider Rock Overlook.** Spider Rock is an 800-foot-tall chunk of sandstone about which there are many legends. In one Navajo version of a Bogey Man story, Navajo children are told by their parents that if they don't behave, Spider Woman—a demigod who also supposedly taught the Navajos how to weave—will take them away and leave them on top of the rock to die. Also be sure to see the **White House Ruin.** These remains of an 800-year-old Anasazi village were named for the white plaster used on one of the pueblo's walls. **Antelope House** is another set of Anasazi ruins that's worth a look. This more-than-90-room pueblo is located near a rock crevice where, in the 1920s, a mummy was recovered by archaeologists. The Anasazi sometimes wrapped their dead in ceremonial garments and placed them in hidden crevices where the weather and scavenger animals couldn't get to them. Mummies were found in the appropriately named **Mummy Cave,** also the site of a large set of ruins in the section of Canyon de Chelly known as **Canyon del Muerto** ("the canyon of the dead," so named because of burial sites uncovered here by archaeologists in the 1880s).

guide). You get the benefit of a knowledgeable Navajo guide who can tell you the history and the lore of the valley. Cameras are permitted on these trips, and usually the guides will pose for a picture provided you don't want to sell it to a photo stock agency or some such thing. Some guides will be willing to take you to villages where you can see jewelers and rug weavers at work and watch scenes of contemporary Navajo life. In some of these locations, you may be asked to leave your camera or sketch pad in the Jeep.

The steep 2.5-mile round-trip trail to **White House Ruin** is the only place where visitors can enter Canyon de Chelly without a Navajo guide. With sixty rooms in the lower section and another twenty tucked away in the cliff, this Anasazi structure housed as many as one hundred people at a time during the years between A.D. 1060 and A.D. 1275. The trailhead begins at the White House Overlook on the South Rim Drive.

West of Canyon de Chelly, off US 160, 20 miles south of Kayenta, lies the **Navajo National Monument** (www.nps.gov/nava). The 360 acres protected by the Navajo National Monument contain the ruins of three of the most intact Anasazi cliff dwellings. Stop at the visitors center (928–672–2700) 9 miles north of US 160 on Highway 564. Like most visitors centers on the reservation, there is an exhibit hall, an arts and crafts shop, and presentations on Navajo history. Best of all, the center is next to a moderately strenuous 5-mile round-trip hiking trail that takes you to a view of the ***Betatakin Ruins.*** Betatakin, situated about 700 feet below the rim of the canyon, has about 135 rooms that were built sometime between A.D. 1250 and A.D. 1300. You'll need binoculars or a spotting scope to see much detail, but even from a distance they are impressive.

If you're feeling adventurous and want a truly off-the-beaten-path experience on the Navajo reservation, sign up for a hike to ***Keet Seel*** (928–672–2366), a 160-room, well-preserved Anasazi settlement. After trekking the 8.5 miles to the remote cliff dwelling you can climb up ladders with a ranger to walk the streets of this ancient civilization. People began settling in Keet Seel in A.D. 950, nearly 300 years before construction began in Betatakin. In A.D. 1250, a new group of settlers arrived and a steady influx kept the village growing until it contained more than 150 rooms—making it the largest of its kind in the state. The diversity of Keet Seel residents is reflected in the building styles used to construct the four distinctly different kivas, three common streets, and a retaining wall stretching 180 feet along the eastern half of the village.

Betatakin and Keet Seel tours are conducted daily from Memorial Day weekend through Labor Day weekend. Free tickets for the Betatakin hike are handed out at 8:30 A.M. and 11:00 A.M. daily on a first-come, first-serve basis with a limit of twenty-five hikers for each tour. Free permits are available for the Keet Seel tour with a limit of twenty people a day. Reservations can be made up to two months in advance for Keet Seel. The Navajo Nation is on daylight saving time and is one hour ahead of other Arizona locations during the summer months.

Exploring Canyon Mysteries

The sandstone walls of the extensive *Tsegi Canyon* system cradle the remains of an ancient civilization that inhabited lands that are now part of the vast Navajo Nation. The Anasazi, a word meaning the "ancient ones" or "ancestors of the aliens" in the Navajo tongue, inhabited the vivid landscape found in southeastern Arizona for nearly a thousand years before finally mysteriously abandoning their far-flung dwellings.

Deep within the sandstone canyons, three cliff dwellings are protected by Navajo National Monument—Inscription House, Betatakin, and Keet Seel. Visitors can take a 5-mile round-trip hike led daily by Navajo guides to the base of a looming cave measuring 450 feet high and 370 feet wide. Nestled inside are the crumbling ruins of Betatakin. An 18-mile round-trip hike into a tributary canyon of the system leads to Keet Seel, one of the largest and best preserved cliff dwellings in the state. However, the location of Inscription House is kept secret in hopes of preserving the crumbling vestige of the small dwelling.

While on the hikes, beware of rockfall hazards, watch for flash floods and stay on trails to avoid quicksand. Livestock pollute the stream so all water must be carried in. Take a minimum of two liters of water per person for the Betatakin hike and four quarts for the Keet Seel hike. The trails run primarily through Navajoland, and all hikers must stay on designated paths.

Don't leave the Navajo reservation until you've seen *Monument Valley* (435–727–5870; www.navajonationparks.org), where numerous Westerns, including John Ford classics like *Stagecoach,* were filmed. You can reach Monument Valley Navajo National Tribal Park by driving north on US 163. Though it straddles the Utah–Arizona border, most of the park is actually within Arizona. The nearly 30,000-acre valley spills across the landscape like a watercolor set of purples, reds, and golds. Jutting up at irregular intervals are tremendous mountains of sand-sculpted rock. The valley is unquestionably one of Arizona's most widely photographed sites, with its soaring sandstone monoliths and cliff formations that bear curious names like the Three Sisters and the Mittens. Many of the accommodations, such as *Gouldings Trading Post, Lodge and Museum* (801–727–3231 or 435–727–3235; www.gouldings.com), are located north of the Arizona border. The *Monument Valley National Navajo Tribal Park Headquarters and Visitor Center* is also in Utah, about 5 miles past the state line off US 163. Watch for the crossroads on US 163, and take the one that goes to the right. The visitors center offers dramatic views of Monument Valley. You can purchase a permit at the visitors center to take your vehicle on a 17-mile loop

Monuments of Time

Pulitzer-prize winner N. Scott Momaday described Monument Valley: "You see the monoliths that stand away in space, and you imagine that you have come upon eternity. They do not appear to exist in time. You think: I see that time comes to an end on this side of the rock, and on the other side there is nothing forever."

This desert highland, situated at 5,564 feet, began to form twenty-five million years ago as a vast inland sea. When the waters receded, all that remained were expansive beds of red sandstone, which the wind used to sculpt the massive monuments— grain by grain, year by year.

Hogans nestle along the road and farther out into the valley, where the Navajo people live and play as they have since they first came to this region in the late fifteenth century. Since that time, the Navajo were only parted from its stark beauty after their forced removal to New Mexico between 1864 and 1868. Ninety years later, the Navajo Tribal Council designated the 29,816-acre Monument Valley National Navajo Tribal Park to preserve the lifestyle of the Navajos residing within its boundaries.

Hogan at Monument Valley

drive through the valley, but the road is poorly maintained and bumpy. You'll have a much better time if you hire a guide at the visitors center to take you by Jeep or horseback on a tour of the full canyon.

One place that nearly everyone visits on the Navajo Reservation is **Four Corners National Monument** (928–871–6647), the only place in the nation where four states (Arizona, Utah, Colorado, and New Mexico) converge. There's a marker at this point, and few Arizona vacations are complete without a photo of the travelers straddling this landmark. Four Corners is easily reached by taking US 160 northeast.

There isn't an endless array of motels and eateries on the reservation, but of the few, most are well known and time-tested. In Kayenta the **Best Western Wetherill Inn** (928–697–3231) has fifty-four rooms, no restaurant, but a small gift shop and an indoor pool. About 10 miles away is the **Anasazi Inn at Tsegi Canyon** (928–697–3793; www.anasaziinn.com), which is only a few minutes away from the Navajo National Monument and has great views. There's a twenty-four-hour restaurant and a gift shop but no pool. In Chinle the **Thunderbird Lodge Motel** (928–674–5841 or 800–679–2473; www.tbirdlodge.com) has a cafeteria that's open until 9:00 P.M. and a gift shop. Canyon tours are also available through the motel.

For restaurants try **Amigo Cafe** (928–697–8448), off US 163 just north of US 160; it serves Mexican, American, and Navajo cuisine.

Tucked entirely within the Navajo Reservation is the comparatively tiny 1.5-million-acre **Hopi Reservation** (928–734–3283; www.hopi.nsn.us), home to about 8,000 people. This rocky terrain has been inhabited by the Hopi and their ancestors for hundreds of years. In fact the village of **Oraibi** on the third mesa (plateau) is the oldest continuously inhabited town in the United States, having been settled around A.D. 1100.

Inscription Rock

One place you're sure to want to visit on the Hopi Reservation is *Inscription Rock.* Take Route 264 east until it ends at the Keams Canyon Trading Post. After a 2-mile hike along Keams Canyon, you'll come to a dam. Nearby is a sandstone wall that bears the 1864 signature of Kit Carson. Carson, a buffalo hunter and sometime army scout, was the man General James Carleton ordered to deliver an ultimatum to the Navajos—that they must relocate to the Bosque Redondo reservation by the Pecos River or be destroyed.

The reservation's villages are grouped on three separate mesas, with the *Hopi Cultural Center* (928–734–2401 or 928–734–6650; www.psv.com/hopi .html) accessible from the second mesa off Highway 264. The center has a museum, a motel, a gift shop, and a restaurant with authentic cuisine. The motel's front desk staff is an excellent source for information about any tribal dances and ceremonies that the public may view. Though friendly, the Hopi closely guard their privacy and religious rituals. Some areas of the Hopi Reservation are open to tourists, whereas others are not. And although the Hopi do invite visitors to observe many of their colorful ceremonies, the use of cameras, video or audio recorders, and sketch pads is strictly forbidden. Hopi dances traditionally begin in December, with ceremonies stopping in July, but call ahead if you'd like to plan your visit to coincide with these events.

Wild West Country

Just south of the Navajo reservation, near the junction of Route 77 and I–40, is the town of *Holbrook* (928–524–6558 or 800–524–2459). About 100 years ago, Holbrook was known as "the town too tough for women and children." Cowboys shot it out in saloons like the Bucket of Blood, and some of the killings associated with the Pleasant Valley War took place here. To get a look at what the town used to be like, drop by the 1898 *Navajo County Courthouse* (928–524–6558 or 800–524–2459) at 100 East Arizona Street. You can tour the sheriff's office and the jail and see exhibits depicting everything from the area's geologic history to an old-time barber shop. It's open from 8:00 A.M. to 5:00 P.M., Monday through Friday.

Once a year (usually in January) the town offers visitors a chance to obtain a very unusual souvenir: a letter delivered by the *Pony Express.* In commemoration of the area's history and as a kickoff to other festivities, a team of riders known as the *Hashknife Pony Express Riders* sets off from the Holbrook

Post Office on a three-day trek to Scottsdale through the White Mountains. They carry thousands of letters with them, and each is canceled with a special mark that designates it as a Pony Express delivery. The riders' arrival in Scottsdale heralds the official kickoff of the city's annual Parada del Sol celebration. For more details about having a letter sent in this manner, contact Holbrook Postmaster, Pony Express Ride, Holbrook, AZ 86025.

For restaurants in Holbrook try the **Wayside Cafe** (928–524–3167) at 1150 West Hopi Drive (Route 66). It serves Mexican and American food Monday through Friday. **Romo's Cafe** (928–524–2153) at 121 West Hopi Drive has been serving up Mexican favorites since the 1960s. Holbrook does not have any bed-and-breakfast inns but it does have more than 1,000 motel rooms, ranging from simple mom-and-pop–style lodging to more elaborate chain accommodations. **The Best Western Arizonian** (no, we don't normally spell it that way) **Inn** (928– 524–2611) at 2508 East Navajo Boulevard has a pool and restaurant. A favorite place to stay for families is the route 66 icon **Wigwam Motel** (928–524–3048) at 811 West Hopi Boulevard.

The **Petrified Forest National Park** and Painted Desert (928–524–6228; www.nps.gov/pefo/) are a short drive north from town on I–40. The **Painted Desert,** north of the freeway, provides vistas of green desert vegetation with mountains of red and purplish hues. If you're wearing polarized sunglasses, the effect can be quite striking. Conversely, if you're not wearing sunglasses, or if they're of the nonpolarized variety that don't block stray light, the scenery will look washed out and you'll wonder why you bothered to stop. If you plan to take pictures here, the same rule applies. If you can, use a polarizing filter on your lens or wait until the sun is at an angle, just after sunrise or just before sunset.

trivia

Arizona has its own "Triassic Park," actually the Petrified Forest National Park, where the remains of Triassic reptiles have been unearthed and ancient trees turned to stone 225 million years ago.

Across the road, the **Petrified Forest** is a marvel of the unique properties of nature. Littered across the landscape are giant chunks of what were once logs, part of a conifer forest that thrived millions of years ago. Long before humans walked the earth, the forest was covered by water, and sediments settled on the trees. Gradually, as the trees decayed, all that was left was hardened stone in the shape of the original tree. Because these fossils haven't been polished, you often have to look really hard to see the array of colors lurking in the stone.

Before heading off to see the sights, stop at the visitors center and grab a descriptive brochure. You'll probably want to see **Agate Bridge,** where a petrified log fell over a canyon. One story has it that more than 100 years ago, on a $10 bet, a cowboy rode his horse over that bridge—not a feat I'd care to duplicate! Another place to stop is **Newspaper Rock,** where ancient Indian tribes chiseled in all the news that was fit to chip.

By the way, it's illegal to remove any pieces of wood from the park, and, really, the stuff is so nice in the gift shops you'd be foolish to risk the fine. Stop by the **Gray's Petrified Wood Co.** (928–524–1842) gift shop on Highway 180 at Highway 77, and you'll see many crafts made from petrified wood, as well as polished chunks of the material. Admission to the museum is free, and it's open from 8:00 A.M. to 6:45 P.M. every day with extended summer hours.

The Winslow area has long been inhabited. Hopi archaeological remains in the nearby **Homolovi State Park** (928–289–4106) date back many hundreds of years. The park, located off I–40 via Route 87, sprawls over 4,000 acres at 4,900 feet and has campgrounds and hiking trails, some of which will take visitors to petroglyphs and an old Mormon cemetery. Two of the Hopi-Anasazi sites are open to the public. Several other sites are still being excavated. In the past, the park has held "dig days" when visitors were allowed to help with certain aspects of the research. Write to the park officials at HC63–Box 5, Winslow, AZ 86047 to see about such special events. Also worth a look are the exhibits in the **Hubbell Building,** another old-fashioned trading post that sells Native American arts and crafts.

Winslow (928–289–2434; www.winslowarizona.org) itself, founded in 1881, has quite a history. Named for Gen. Edward F. Winslow, president of the St. Louis & San Francisco Railroad, the community was raised on the three Rs: ranching, railroading, and Route 66. The **Old Trails Museum** (928–289– 5861) at 212 North Kinsley Avenue has displays of all three stages of the area's history, as well as artifacts from its Native American history.

For a peek at more history and a beer or two, drive over to **Minnetonka Trading Post** (928–289–2561), which once was part of a shack owned by the legendary Hashknife Ranch. The Hashknife Ranch was part of the Aztec Land and Cattle Company, in the 1880s one of the largest ranching enterprises in the Southwest. The front wall of the building is made of petrified wood. Today it's a popular honky-tonk for cowboys.

Not all the sites being excavated are as old as the Anasazi ruins at Homolovi. The remnants of **Brigham City,** a rock fort founded in 1876 by Mormon settlers near the banks of the Little Colorado River, are currently being unearthed and prepared for public display. You can view the work taking place from North Road, an access strip just east of the golf course. Access can be limited at times.

Aircraft aficionados may want to make the drive along Second Street to Highway 87 and out Airport Road to the **Winslow-Lindbergh Regional Airport** (928– 289–2429), which is named after the famous pilot, Charles Lindbergh. This airport is unique because it has the longest runways in North America. In addition, it was designed by Charles Lindbergh (on his honeymoon, no less!) and built by Howard Hughes. The airport saw extensive military use during World War II, and today you still may be able to see old planes there because it's a slurry base for converted bombers used in fighting forest fires.

No visit to Winslow is complete without a stroll over to the park to see *"The Corner."* The Glenn Frey/Jackson Browne song "Take It Easy"— recorded first by the Eagles on their debut album and later by Browne— recounts an incident that occurred on the corner of Second (actually Route 66) and Kinsley. Every year the town holds a "Miss Flatbed Ford" contest in honor of the famous song's lyrics. Winslow has even built a "Take It Easy" park on this corner, using the space created by a fire that leveled the old Winslow Drugstore. The park is designed to resemble a 1944 photograph of the corner, depicting a long, lean cowpuncher lounging against a lamppost and speaking to a shorter cattle driver. T-shirts of this scene are available for sale.

trivia

In its heyday, Winslow's La Posada Hotel housed such celebrity guests as Clark Gable and Carole Lombard, Douglas Fairbanks and Mary Pickford, Charles and Anne Morrow Lindbergh, Gary Cooper, Jimmy Durante, John Wayne, Howard Hughes, Will Rogers, Harry Truman, and Franklin Roosevelt, as well as Japanese royalty.

Winslow has attracted filmmakers as well as musicians. Oliver Stone came to town to film part of *Natural Born Killers*. The kickoff scenes were shot in the **Red Sands Bar,** which has been closed for years but was refurbished as a roadside diner just for the film.

One of the most exciting projects in Winslow in years was the renovation and reopening of **La Posada** (928–289–4366; www.laposada.org), a Fred Harvey hotel located by the Santa Fe Railroad tracks at 303 East Second Street. The hotel, a National Historic Landmark, is a 60,000-square-foot Spanish Mission–style palace designed by famed architect Mary Jane Colter and built in 1930 at a cost of more than $1 million dollars; it was frequented by many celebrities. During World War II, as many as 3,000 troops were fed in the dining hall each day. It closed in 1958 as the result of declining rail travel. It has fifty rooms.

Winslow has many chain restaurants as well as cafes, such as the **Brown Mug** (928–289–9973) at 308 East Second Street. It is open every day but Sunday. The **Casa Blanca Cafe** (928–289–4191) at 512 East 3rd Street is open daily.

You won't find any bed-and-breakfast inns in Winslow, but the dozen-and-a-half motels range from simple to sophisticated. The ***Best Western Adobe Inn*** (928–289–4638 or 800–528–1234) at 1701 North Park Drive has an indoor pool and hot tub, as well as a restaurant that's open for breakfast, lunch, and dinner.

Apache and Mormon Country

The ***Apache Sitgreaves National Forest*** (928–333–4301; www.fs.fed.us/r3/asnf) is an impressive stand of vegetation (about two million acres) that ranges from about 3,500 feet in elevation to more than 11,000 feet above sea level. Flora and fauna from many diverse environments can be seen here. Three dozen campgrounds, several hundred thousand acres of wilderness or primitive area blocked to vehicles, and nearly 900 miles of trails are here for those who love hiking and camping.

Many small towns, including Heber, Show Low, Pinetop-Lakeside, and Alpine, lie within the forest boundaries, and quite a few others are within an hour's drive or less. Widely used by vacationers during ski season, this area is also a cool (well, mostly) summer retreat. Bluegrass festivals and other activities help to draw visitors from all over the country.

Incidentally, it's within this stand of forest that Travis Walton, who lived in the Heber area, claimed to have been abducted by a UFO on November 5, 1975 (an intriguing refutation of his story is presented in Philip J. Klass's *UFO Abductions: A Dangerous Game*). Walton's story was told in the *National Enquirer* and in the 1993 film *Fire in the Sky,* which was filmed around the area.

Settled in 1878, ***Snowflake*** (928–536–4331) was one of the first Mormon communities founded in Arizona. Believe it or not, it wasn't named after an ice crystal—rather, it was built by Erastus Snow and William J. Flake. Flake was responsible for the actual acquisition of the land. He bought the land from rancher James Stinson, only to discover it also had been given to the Santa Fe Railway, and then to the Hashknife Ranch. Like many Mormon settlers in Arizona, Flake met with hostility regarding his religious beliefs and, in 1884, he was arrested for polygamy and spent some months in the gruesome Yuma Territorial Prison.

The town follows Brigham Young's City of Zion design—wide boulevards and neatly squared-off city blocks. Today in the downtown area, many of the original homes—ranging in style from Greek Revival to Victorian to bungalow—look exactly as they did one hundred years ago. You can take a self-guided tour of the exterior of the historic homes year-round. You can also arrange for an interior tour of several of the homes. To schedule a tour, call the Snowflake/Taylor Chamber of Commerce at (928) 536–4331. Every July the

Mogollon Rim Overlook

If you visit the forest, be sure to take the *Mogollon Rim Overlook* trail, which is accessible from Highway 260. This easy, 1-mile hike through pine forest affords magnificent canyon views where you'll be tempted to sit, listen to the wind, and observe the squirrels. The squirrels seem to like watching people, too—just don't move too fast.

community celebrates its heritage with Pioneer Days, during which there are guided house tours by costumed Snowflake residents, parades, theatrical productions, and other events.

Situated along Route 191, *St. Johns* (928–337–2000), the Apache County seat, prides itself on having a major *Equestrian Center* (928–337–4517) located next to the airport. The center has facilities for cross-country competition, dressage, and other events; however, no riding rentals for visitors are offered here. Call to find out if any horse shows are scheduled during your visit to the White Mountains. The *Apache County Museum* (928–337–4737) is also located here at 180 West Cleveland Avenue. Artifacts of the area's history and prehistory—including a 24,000-year-old set of woolly mammoth tusks— are on display. The museum is open from 9:00 A.M. to 5:00 P.M., Monday through Friday. Guided tours are available upon request.

You can certainly be forgiven if you think the communities in the White Mountain region blend together. It's easy to forget which town is on what side of which lake. In simple terms, *Show Low* (928–537–2326 or 888–SHOW–LOW; www.showlowchamberofcommerce.com) was named after an 1875 card game that supposedly established the town's ownership. It is west on Highway 60 and just south of *Fool Hollow Lake Recreation Area* (928–537–3680). The town of Pinetop-Lakeside is south of Show Low along Highway 260. Sunrise Park Resort lies to the southeast along Highway 273.

The entire *White Mountains Apache Reservation* (928–338–1230; www .wmat.nsn.us) area is loaded with recreational opportunities: lakes, streams, nature trails, golf courses, and even *Hon-Dah* (Apache for "welcome") *Resort Casino* (928–369–0299 or 800–929–8744; www.hon-dah.com) on Highway 260 just south of Pinetop-Lakeside. Many of these enterprises are owned by the White Mountain Apache tribe, which has done a phenomenal job with developing visitor services while maintaining the natural look of the terrain.

One of their finest accomplishments is the *Sunrise Park Resort* (928–735–7669 or 800–772–SNOW; www.sunriseskipark.com), Arizona's largest ski resort. Three mountains—Sunrise Peak (10,700 feet), Apache Peak (11,000 feet), and Cyclone Circle (10,700 feet)—comprise the skiable terrain, which is laced with sixty-five trails and served by modern, high-speed quad, triple, and double chairlifts.

trivia

Eastern Arizona is home to much of what is considered to be the world's largest stand of virgin ponderosa pine.

Day lodges on each of the peaks provide food and full rental facilities for skis and snowboards. Additionally the one-hundred-room **Sunrise Resort Hotel** (800–554–6835) provides accommodations, whirlpool spas, and saunas just 3 miles from the base of the mountain. The season starts in early December and, weather permitting, runs through late March or longer. Because the resort has extensive snowmaking equipment, it isn't totally dependent on Mother Nature; on a sunny, warm day in Phoenix, you can hop in your car and in four hours or so be in the snow.

About 30 miles south of Hon-Dah on Highway 73 is **Fort Apache Historic Park** (928–338–1230). This historic piece of frontier and military history operated from 1870 to 1922. Its primary mission was to keep the peace between white settlers and northern tribes of Apaches. General Crook used the fort as a base of operations during his expeditions against Geronimo and Cochise. Today the fort is a museum, with many of its buildings intact, including officers' quarters, horse barns, and a cemetery. Among the exhibits on display in the **White Mountain Apache Cultural Center** (928–338–4625; www.wmat.us/wmaculture .shtml) are some on the history of the Apache tribe in Arizona.

You'll find many little cafes and family restaurants in the White Mountains. For lunch try **Johnny Angel's Diner** (928–367–1956) at 436 East White Mountain Boulevard in Pinetop.

There's little evidence of it now, but more than one hundred years ago **Springerville** (928–333–2656; www.springerville.com) was one of the toughest towns in the Arizona territory. Because the dense foliage of what is now the Apache-Sitgreaves National Forest provided so many excellent hiding places and made tracking difficult, a countless number of stolen horses and cattle ended up here. Even the tattered remnants of the Clanton gang, after an infamous shoot-out in Tombstone, decided to avail themselves of this area's greater tolerance of lawless activity.

The town's name is actually the result of the hard-luck nature of its early days. Henry Springer, a merchant, went broke attempting to help out some ranchers, and as an ironic twist the town founders decided to name it after him.

Springerville's history as a pioneer outpost is honored by being one of twelve sites in the nation to have a **Madonna of the Trail Statue.** These statues, made of algonite stone that incorporates Missouri granite to achieve a glowing hue, were placed on points along the National Old Trails Road by the Daughters of the American Revolution in the late 1920s. The statue depicts a sturdy, stoic pioneer woman in homespun clothes, cradling one child in her left arm and holding a rifle in her right, while another child clings to her skirts. To find the statue, drive down Main Street to the post office; the Madonna is directly across the street.

About 2 miles north of town is *Casa Malpais* ("house of the badlands") *Pueblo Archeological Park* (928–333–5375). This Hopi and Zuni ruin and National Historic Park was first reported by an archaeologist in 1883. Stone walls, pottery, and other features of the site indicate that it was occupied for several hundred years before being abandoned in the fifteenth century. Some areas related to the site remain off-limits to the public, but there's still plenty to see, including a museum on Main Street in Springerville and a field laboratory. Lectures and tours are conducted on a frequent basis. For more information write to Casa Malapais Pueblo, 318 East Main Street, Springerville, AZ 85938.

The tiny towns of *Greer* and *Alpine* (fewer than 1,000 residents total) have some visitors services, including quaint lodges and cabins, but most shops and restaurants in the area are in Springerville. For a quick meal, try *Booga Reds* (928–333–2640) at 512 East Main Street, which offers homemade Mexican and American food from 6:00 A.M. to 9:00 P.M. every day. (The name, by the way, is a nickname given to the owner by an old cowboy.)

Motels, guest ranches, and cabins are spread throughout the White Mountains area, including *Oakwood Inn B&B* (928–537–3030 or 800–959–8098) at 6558 Wagonwheel in Lakeside, and the *Tal Wi-Wi* ("where the sun rises first") *Lodge* (928–339–4319 or 800–476–2695; www.talwiwilodge.com) in Alpine. The Tal Wi-Wi Lodge, incidentally, features some suites that have fireplaces and hot tubs.

Round Valley Ensphere

There's another unusual, albeit modern, structure you may want to take a look at: the $11 million *Round Valley Ensphere.* Located 2 miles south of Springerville in the nearby town of *Eagar* (928–333–4128; www.eagar.com), this dome looks a bit like something out of *The Jetsons* and boasts the distinction of being the first domed high school stadium in the country. Built in 1992, the dome is 440 feet in diameter and covers a total floor area of 189,000 square feet. Besides a football field, the dome can accommodate up to seven removable basketball courts. It also has tennis courts and 5,000 seats.

Henry and Tonto

If you take Highway 260 west from Show Low, you'll travel a scenic route through the Apache-Sitgreaves National Forest, across the Mogollon Rim and down into the Tonto National Forest. There are many small towns along the way in which you can stop for gas and travel supplies. The area also features scads of National Forest campgrounds and developed hiking trails. Within a few hours you'll reach **Payson** (928–474–4515 or 800–672–9766; www.rim countrychamber.com), only about 90 miles from the major metropolitan area of Phoenix, yet close to immense stands of ponderosa pine and numerous lakes and streams. As you might expect, this small community of about 15,000 is a recreational stop for people on their way to the White Mountains, as well as a vacation spot for world-weary warriors from the Phoenix area.

Nature trails, campgrounds, and various frequent festivals keep this area active. In August Payson is the location of **The World's Oldest Rodeo.** In September, the **Fiddlers' Contest** brings the region's finest pickers and fiddlers to the pine country. In October a regional **fine arts festival** is held here, and in December, Payson kicks off the holiday countdown by lighting **Christmas trees at the Swiss Village.** The **Swiss Village Shopping Plaza** is at the southern tip of town. It is a small collection of gift shops, restaurants, and a hotel, the **Best Western Payson Inn** (928–474–3241 or 800–247–9477; www.bestwesternpaysoninn.com). Though rather touristy, the shops have some interesting handmade items (check out the Payson candle factory; 928–474–2152), and the Alpine-style village is an unusual sight in the midst of an Arizona forest. Those seeking a more off-beat shopping experience can stop at one of the quirky antique shops, such as **Granny's Attic Antique Market** (928–474–3962) at 800 East Highway 260.

Just north of here up Highway 87 is the **Tonto Natural Bridge State Park** (928–476–4202; www.pr.state.az.us/Parks/parkhtml/tonto.html), a limestone formation that's believed to be the largest such formation (400 feet long) in the world. A bit farther north are the tiny mountain towns of **Pine** and **Strawberry** (928–474–4515 or 800–672–9766; www.rimcountrychamber.com). The **Strawberry Schoolhouse,** built in 1884, is the oldest standing one-room schoolhouse in the state. It held its last classes in 1907, and today it's a historic state monument that's open for tours on the weekends.

Globe (928–425–4495 or 800–804–5623; www.globemiamichamber.com), a town of about 7,500, is a mining community with strong links to Arizona's past. You can reach Globe by driving south on Highway 87 to Highway 188, which soon becomes Highway 88 beyond the Tonto National Monument. Continue south on this scenic route through the pines of Tonto National Forest, and you'll soon enter Globe. From the Phoenix area, it's an easy jaunt east on US 60. In the downtown area, more than two dozen historic buildings date from just before the turn of the twentieth century until the late 1920s. They range in style from territorial adobe to Queen Anne Victorian. You can drop by the ***Gila County Historical Museum*** (928–425–7385)—the former Globe-Miami Mine Rescue Station, built in 1920—at 1330 North Broad Street, on US 60 next to the chamber of commerce to look at exhibits of how the community grew and changed. The museum is open Monday through Friday from 10:00 A.M. to 4:00 P.M. and from 11:00 A.M. to 3:00 P.M. Saturday. Also worth a look is the town's ***Cobre*** ("copper") ***Valley Center for the Arts*** (928–425–0884), in the building that used to be the Gila County Courthouse. It has been lovingly restored as a venue for the Copper Cities Community Players and also houses visual arts studios. You can take a self-guided tour and browse in the gift shop, which sells everything from handpainted furniture to stationery. The center is open Monday through Friday from 10:00 A.M. to 5:00 P.M., Saturday from 10:00 A.M. to 4:00 P.M., and Sunday from noon to 4:00 P.M. Donations are gratefully accepted.

Follow Broad Street through Globe for about 1.5 miles, and you'll see a clearly marked road leading to ***Besh-Ba-Gowah*** ("metal house") ***Archaeological Park*** (928–425–0320 or 800–804–5623). This Salado pueblo settlement was built around A.D. 1225 on top of what was once a Hohokam pit house. The site has been restored to allow visitors a self-guided tour. You can climb around in the ancient settlement using ladders to follow the same paths original occupants took to get to the roof or down to the first floor. An on-site museum houses artifacts retrieved from the excavation, including the world's largest single-site collection of Salado pottery. Admission is $3.00 for adults and $2.00 for seniors. Children under 12 are free. It's open from 9:00 A.M to 5:00 P.M.

Besh-Ba-Gowah

After you've worked up an appetite crawling in and out of the pueblo, try a homestyle meal at *Judy's Cook House* (928–425–5366) at 2280 East Highway 60 in Globe. Refreshed, you can prowl Globe's half-dozen or so antiques or gift shops, such as *Past Time Antiques* (928–425–2220) at 150 West Mesquite.

As for accommodations, several bed-and-breakfast inns in Globe provide rest for the weary. *Cedar Hill B&B* (928–425–7530) at 175 East Cedar is an early twentieth-century wooden home built by one of the area's most influential families. Antiques (including a queen-size brass bed) have been used in furnishing the rooms, and amenities like cable TV in the living room help you feel comfortably at home. Call for current rates. A relatively new—but very old—find is the *Noftsger Hill Inn* (928–425–2260 or 877–780–2479; www.noftsger hillinn.com), a bed-and-breakfast that has guests sleeping in the actual classrooms and janitor's closet of the old Noftsger Hill School at 425 North Street. Owners Rosalie and Dom Ayala purchased the property from the previous owners in 2001 and have six rooms currently available—all furnished in "comfortable antiques." Rates are $75 to $100 per night.

Arguably the best reason to visit the *Safford* area is to drive up Swift Trail to the summit of *Mount Graham* (928–428–4150), a 10,713-foot peak in the Pinaleño Mountains known as a "sky island," as its lofty green peak appears to be a lush island hovering in the clouds. This mountain has had an interesting history over the years. More than one hundred years ago when there was a fort nearby, injured soldiers were taken up Mount Graham to recuperate in the pine-scented air. For a number of decades there have been cabins, Christmas tree farms, and campgrounds on the mountain.

More recently the University of Arizona and the Vatican have each built telescopes on the peak. The University of Arizona has an international reputation for its astronomical research, which has been based at several locations in southeastern Arizona. The Vatican's involvement in celestial research dates back to the time of Galileo. Together the university and the Catholic church were able to create telescopes on Mount Graham whose data augment each other's. The Mount Graham telescopes have thrilled astronomers because the scopes are on the cutting edge of technology, but they have angered some environmentalists, who feel the vehicular traffic created by the telescope projects threatens the already endangered Mount Graham red squirrel. University of Arizona biologists are monitoring the squirrels for potential negative impact. To date, there are no signs that the observatory construction has negatively affected the squirrels.

The telescopes aren't visible from the ground, and indeed they are all but invisible in the forest (on a visit to the site, I couldn't detect them until I was only a few hundred yards away). They also are off-limits to anyone without an official U.S. Forest Service permit, which keeps unwanted traffic off the final dirt road to the top where the squirrels live.

Although you can't drive up Swift Trail to where the scopes are, there are many beautiful areas on the mountain where you can pull off and have a picnic. There are also several scenic overlooks where you can see gorgeous, sweeping vistas of the valley all the way down to Safford. If hiking is on your agenda, there are nine major trails on Mount Graham. One of the best is the moderately difficult 14-mile Round the Top Mountain Trail, which meanders through shady pine forest and also offers some good views of the countryside. Visit or write the Safford-Graham, County Chamber of Commerce (1111 Thatcher Boulevard, Safford, AZ 85546, 928–428–2511 or 888–837–1841; www.visitgraham county.com) for detailed hiking maps. Whenever you visit Mount Graham, bring a jacket, because it's chilly even in the summer.

As an aside, on your way up Swift Trail you'll pass a *Federal Penitentiary* on your left where Watergate conspirator John Ehrlichman was imprisoned for a while. Other favorite activities in Graham County include hunting for fire agates at the *Black Hills Rockhound Area* (928–348–4400); taking a cotton gin tour (928–428–0714) during the ginning season from October through December; and searching for views of the more than 300 species of birds that inhabit the region (928–428–2511 or 888–837–1841).

About a half-hour drive to the south, along State Route 266 off Route 191, is the town of *Bonita* (no chamber of commerce). Like a lot of Arizona towns, this one can claim a rather wild and woolly heritage. Bonita's old, two-story general store is no longer open; it was formerly known as George Atkins' Saloon. Right out front on August 17, 1877, Francis P. Cahill, a strapping Irish laborer, picked a fight with a youngster known as Henry Antrim. He called Antrim a pimp. Skinny, buck-toothed Antrim—a known horse thief and ne'er-do-well—was no match for Cahill. When the big man rushed him, the eighteen-year-old kid pulled a pistol and gut-shot his tormentor. Cahill died the following day, and the boy who went on to be called William H. "Billy the Kid" Bonney chalked up his first kill. Some stories dispute this and insist that Billy began killing in another state at the age of twelve, but it seems likely that those tales are the sort of tabloid fabrications that were rampant in Victorian times (some things don't change).

From Bonita it's a quick drive north to *Fort Grant,* the site of an even more infamous frontier tragedy. In March 1871, about a half-mile outside what was then Camp Grant, lived a settlement of several hundred Apaches—mostly women and children—who were under the care of the camp's commander, Lt. Royal Whitman. Though the camp seemed peaceful and Whitman had reason to be optimistic about future relations between the Apaches and the U.S. government, a group of men from Tucson, including some civic leaders, held the opposite view. On April 28 they rode out from Tucson with a force of about one hundred Papagos and Mexicans to attack the Apache camp in retribution for previous Indian raids, which actually had nothing to do with the Camp Grant Apaches.

On the morning of April 30, the raiders leveled the peaceful Indian camp, slaughtering all the inhabitants. In the aftermath Whitman and his troops buried the dead and tried to assure other Apaches in the area that the U.S. Army had not played a part in the massacre. President Grant ordered the Arizona territorial governor to find the men responsible for the carnage. The leaders of the raid were brought to trial in Tucson, but all were acquitted. Today Fort Grant is a penitentiary, and there are no visitor services.

For more information on the original Camp Grant story, check the *Graham County Historical Society* (928–348–0470) archives located in the old high school in Thatcher, which has exhibits detailing the frontier history of Graham County.

WEB SITES FOR EASTERN ARIZONA

Arizona Department of Tourism
www.arizonaguide.com

Eagar Chamber of Commerce
www.eagar.com

Globe-Miami Chamber of Commerce
www.globemiamichamber.com

Graham County Chamber of Commerce
www.visitgrahamcounty.com

Hopi Office of Public Information
www.hopi.nsn.us

Navajo Nation Tourism Office
www.discovernavajo.com

Payson Chamber of Commerce
www.ci.payson.az.us

Pinetop-Lakeside Chamber of Commerce
www.pinetoplakesidechamber.com

Rim Country Regional Chamber of Commerce
www.rimcountrychamber.com

Show Low Chamber of Commerce
www.showlowchamberof
commerce.com

Springerville Chamber of Commerce
www.springerville.com

St. Johns Chamber of Commerce
www.stjohnschamber.com

White Mountain Apache Reservation
www.wmat.nsn.us

Winslow Chamber of Commerce
www.winslowarizona.org

Places to Stay in Eastern Arizona

GREER

Greer Lodge and Cabins,
44 North Main Street;
(928) 735–7216;
www.greerlodgeaz.com
Lodge rooms and cabin
rentals, full-service spa,
restaurant and bar, gift shop,
and three private lakes.
Moderate to Expensive.

Hidden Meadow Ranch,
620 County Road 1325;
(928) 333–1000
or (866) 333–4080;
www.hiddenmeadow.com
Ten guest cabins, dining
room (three meals a day
included), private pond,
guest horses, mercantile.
Moderate to expensive.

HOLBROOK

Motel 6,
2514 East Navajo Boulevard;
(928) 524–6101.
Moderately priced motel-
style lodgings with a swimming pool and a laundry.
Moderate.

KAYENTA

Holiday Inn,
Junction US 160 and 164;
(928) 697–3221.
Modern facility, conveniently
located near Monument Valley. Remember: Navajoland
is alcohol-free! Moderate.

PAYSON

Days Inn & Suites,
301-A South Beeline
Highway;
(928) 474–9800
or (800) 329–7466
Motel with fireplace, pool
with spa pool, pets OK.
Moderate.

**Mountain Meadows
Cabins,**
25 miles east of Payson off
Highway 260 in Christopher
Creek;
(928) 478–4415;
www.mountainmeadows
cabins.com
Six cabins with kitchens and
fireplaces. Inexpensive to
moderate.

PINETOP-LAKESIDE

Rainbow's End Resort,
Route 2,
Box 1330,
Pinetop-Lakeside, AZ 85929;
(928) 368–9004;
www.rainbowsendresort.com
Charming accommodations
on Rainbow Lake. Inexpen-
sive to moderate.

Woodland Inn and Suites,
458 East White Mountain
Boulevard;
(928) 367–3636.
Motel-type accommodations
with continental breakfast
and in-room coffee. Pets OK
with a $10 fee. Inexpensive.

SAFFORD

**Olney House Bed and
Breakfast,**
1104 Central Avenue;
(928) 428–5118 or
(800) 814–5118;
www.olneyhouse.com
A historic house with two
cottages and a full breakfast
(included). Moderate.

SHOW LOW

Days Inn,
480 West Deuce of Clubs;
(928) 537–4356 or
(800) 329–7466.
Full-service, 122-room inn
with in-room refrigerators
and microwaves. Free buffet
breakfast. Moderate.

THATCHER

**Black Rock Ranch Wilder-
ness Retreat,**
Black Rock Road,
P.O. Box 543,
Thatcher, AZ 85552;
(928) 428–6481;
www.blackrockranch.com
Five cabins, dining room,
wildlife watching, and Western adventures at a working
cattle ranch. Moderate.

TUBA CITY

Quality Inn,
Main Street and
Moenave Avenue,
P.O. Box 247,
Tuba City, AZ 86034;
(928) 283–4545.
On the Navajo Reservation.
Inexpensive.

WINSLOW

Days Inn,
2035 West Highway 66;
(928) 289–1010.
Near the interstate with
restaurants and gas
stations nearby.
Moderate.

Places to Eat in Eastern Arizona

HOLBROOK

Jerry's,
2600 Navajo Boulevard;
(928) 524-2364.
A family-style diner serving American food. Inexpensive.

PAYSON

Cucina Paradiso,
512 North Beeline Highway;
(928) 468-6500.
Casual Italian dining in a relaxing atmosphere. Inexpensive to moderate.

El Rancho Mexican Restaurant,
200 South Beeline Highway;
(928) 474-3111.
Tacos, enchiladas, burritos, and other Mexican favorites. Inexpensive.

Macky's Grill
1111 South Beeline Highway;
(928) 474-7411.
This casual Payson restaurant serves American food for lunch and dinner and offers a full children's menu. Inexpensive to moderate.

PINETOP–LAKESIDE

Chalet Restaurant and Bar,
348 West White Mountain Boulevard;
(928) 367-1514.
Seafood, ribs, and the only sushi bar in Navajo County. Open Tuesday through Saturday at 5:00 P.M. Moderate.

Charlie Clark's Steak House,
Highway 260,
P.O. Box 1283,
Pinetop-Lakeside, AZ 85929;
(928) 367-4900.
Consistently good food and service for true carnivores. Look for the horse on the roof! Inexpensive to moderate.

Christmas Tree Restaurant,
Woodland Road,
P.O. Box 1617,
Pinetop-Lakeside, AZ 85929;
(928) 367-3107.
Posh dining among the pines. This curiously named eatery was a longtime favorite of the late humorist Erma Bombeck. Closed Monday and Tuesday. Moderate.

SAFFORD

El Coronado,
409 Main Street;
(928) 428-7755.
Mexican specialties and American mainstays. Inexpensive.

Manor House Restaurant and Rock'n Horse Saloon,
415 East Highway 70;
(928) 428-7148.
Seafood, steaks, pasta, Mexican entrees, and pizza. Inexpensive to moderate.

WINSLOW

Casa Blanca Cafe,
512 East Third Street;
(928) 289-4191.
A family-owned restaurant serving up hearty Mexican specialties. Inexpensive to moderate

Turquoise Room at La Posada,
303 East Second Street;
(928) 289-4366.
Serves up a stylish Southwestern-inspired menu of dishes such as pork carnitas, Churro lamb cassoulet, and elk medallions. Open for breakfast, lunch, and dinner. Moderate to expensive.

Central Arizona

The Valley of the Sun and Phoenix

The **Valley of the Sun** cuts a diagonal swath from Wickenburg in the northwest to Florence in the southeast with Arizona's primary gateway, **Sky Harbor International Airport**, located almost exactly in the center and encircled by the major interstate highways that provide access in every direction, to every region of the state. Covering approximately 2,000 square miles of the **Sonoran Desert**, the Phoenix metro-plex is made up of twenty-two separate cities and towns, the best-known of which are Phoenix (the core city), Scottsdale (best known for its resorts and art galleries), and Tempe (home of Arizona State University and excellent coffee shops). Gaining in popularity and in recognition are Mesa and Apache Junction in the east valley, Florence and Casa Grande to the south, and Glendale (known for its antiques shops and as the new home for the NFL Arizona Cardinals and the NHL Phoenix Coyotes) and Wickenburg (which bills itself as the dude ranch capital of the world) in the west valley.

For information about the Valley of the Sun, your best starting point is the **Greater Phoenix Convention and Visi-**

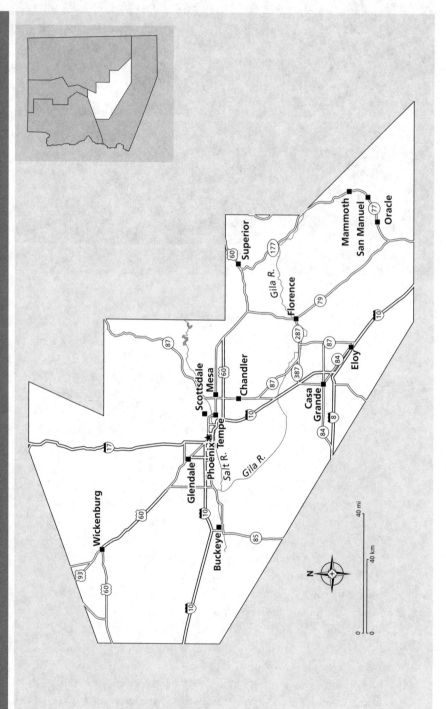

CENTRAL ARIZONA

tors Bureau (602–254–6500 or toll free/877–225–5749, www.phoenixcvb .com) in Phoenix. When you get to town, the CVB has a downtown walk-in information center (602–452–6282) that is open Monday through Friday from 8:00 A.M. to 5:00 P.M. at 50 North Second Street. There is a second walk-in information center (602–452–6281) at the *Biltmore Fashion Park* at 2404 East Camelback Road. The center is located between Macy's and Pavilion Christofle. Hours are from 10:00 A.M. to 7:00 P.M., Monday through Wednesday, from 10:00 A.M. to 8:00 P.M., Thursday and Friday, from 10:00 A.M. to 6:00 P.M., Saturday, and from noon to 6:00 P.M. Sunday.

If you were born to be wild and you're looking for a unique way to see the Valley (or even the rest of Arizona), you may want to contact *Blue Sky Street Eagle* (480–557–9400 or 866–766–2626; www.streeteagle.com) at 1755 West University Drive, Suite 120, Tempe. The company offers experienced riders the opportunity to climb aboard a Harley-Davidson or BMW bike and take off on an adventure. Employees can either offer you advice on where to ride or arrange a guided tour for groups of five or more riders.

Phoenix is the fifth largest city in the nation, with more than 1.5 million residents within city limits and about 3.2 million total in the greater Phoenix area. Towns spread out along Interstate 10 and Interstate 17 like strands of a giant spider web, covering the Valley of the Sun with attractions that are sure to ensnare travelers. The Valley is made up of a myriad of pseudo-, micro-, and full-scale communities, and it can be quite daunting to find your way around if you don't have a detailed map. To the west of Phoenix are the suburban communities of Sun City West, Surprise, El Mirage, Youngtown, Sun City, Peoria, Glendale, Buckeye, Wickenburg, Litchfield Park, Goodyear, and Avondale. To the east are Paradise Valley, Scottsdale, Tempe, Mesa, and Apache Junction. Farther south are Guadalupe, Ahwatukee, Chandler, Gilbert, Sun Lakes, Higley, Queen Creek, and Casa Grande. And that's just a partial list!

AUTHOR'S TOP PICKS IN CENTRAL ARIZONA

The Arizona Center	The Phoenix Zoo
Arizona Science Center	Desert Botanical Garden
Heard Museum	Grady Gammage Memorial Auditorium/ASU
Rawhide Wild West Town	
Chase Field	Orpheum Theatre

TOP ANNUAL EVENTS IN CENTRAL ARIZONA

JANUARY

West Valley Native American Invitational Arts Festival
Litchfield Park
150+ Native American artisans.
(623) 935–6384

Phoenix Arizona Stock Show and Arizona Working Ranch Horse Competition
State Fairgrounds
(602) 258–8569

Annual FBR Open
Various locations
One of the PGA Tour's top events, with the finest golfers in the world.
(602) 870–4431

FEBRUARY

Gold Rush Days
Wickenburg
Senior rodeo (50+ years old), gold-panning, carnival, western dances, arts and crafts, BBQ, gem show, mucking, and drilling.
(928) 684–5479

Arizona's Renaissance Festival
Apache Junction
Sixteenth-century European village.
(520) 463–2700
(February and March)

Lost Dutchman Days
Apache Junction
Includes professional rodeos, gold panning.
(480) 982–3141

O'Odham Tash
Casa Grande
Largest all–Native American rodeo, arts and crafts.
(520) 836–4723 or (800) 916–1515

Native American World Championship Hoop Dance Championship
Phoenix
Heard Museum—top Native American dancers from the United States and Canada.
(602) 252–8848

Arizona Scottish Highland Games
Mesa
(602) 431–0095

Gliding over the desert in a hot-air balloon is an interesting way to travel off the beaten path; so is doing it yourself with a parasail or sailplane (aka glider). Flying adventures are available in several corners of the Valley. For glider flights *Arizona Soaring/Estrella Sailport* (520–568–2318; www.azsoaring.com) is located south of the city, in Maricopa, a short drive off I–10. They offer rides and instruction seven days a week from 11:00 A.M. weekdays, and from 9:00 A.M. weekends. Northwest of the city is *Turf Soaring School* (602–439–3621; www.turfsoaring.com) at the Pleasant Valley Airport in Peoria. They are open every day from 9:00 A.M. to 5:00 P.M. Hot-air balloon rides are available from *Unicorn Balloon Company* (480–991–3666 or 800–755–0935; www.unicornballoon.com), which launches near Scottsdale Airport, and *Hot*

All-Arabian Horse Show
Scottsdale
Two thousand of the world's most beautiful Arabians, Half-Arabians, and National Show Horses.
(480) 515–1500

MARCH

Annual Jaycees Rodeo of Rodeos
Phoenix
Nearly seventy years old—traditional rodeo and concert.
(602) 254–6500

Heard Museum Guild Annual Indian Fair and Market
Phoenix
Features more than 300 of the nation's top Native American artists.
(602) 252–8848

Civil War Battle Reenactment
Picacho Peak
(520) 466–3183

Arts Festival
Scottsdale
Rated among the top in the country.
(800) 877–1117

Old Town Tempe Spring Festival of the Arts
Tempe
Second largest arts and entertainment festival in the Southwest.
(800) 283–6734

APRIL

Gaslight Antique Walk
Glendale
Seventy-five stores, specialty shops, and restaurants stay open from 6:00 to 9:00 P.M. third Thursday of the month.
(623) 930–2960

Culinary Festival
Scottsdale
Great Arizona Picnic, Le Tour Culinaire.
(800) 877–1117

MAY

Sweet Onion Festival
Glendale
Onion seeds, fresh veggies and onion, onion recipe books, onion recipe contest.
(602) 470–8086

(Continued on page 92)

Air Expeditions Inc. (480–502–6999 or 800–831–7610), which launches from a site in North Phoenix. Early morning is the traditional time to balloon, and Hot Air Expeditions (HAE) makes it an occasion available year-round with a champagne breakfast catered by Vincent Guerithault, chef of a well-known Phoenix restaurant, Vincent's on Camelback. HAE also does a sunset trip during the winter months with champagne and hors d'oeuvres catered by Chef Vincent (who does a mean chocolate truffle, by the way). Also offering balloon flights—plus Jeep safaris, parasailing, horseback rides, and raft expeditions—is *Adventures Out West* (480–991–3666 or 800–755–0935; www.adventuresout west.com). They also offer combination Jeep-balloon trips (one with a western breakfast option) and may give a discount on the other activities they offer. As

TOP ANNUAL EVENTS IN CENTRAL ARIZONA

JUNE

Grand Canyon State Summer Games
Phoenix
Olympic-style competition in twenty-two different sports. Athletes of all ages and abilities, with one category available for elite athletes.
(480) 517–9700

JULY

Summer Spectacular Art Walk
Scottsdale
(800) 877–1117

Downtown Cooldown
Tempe
Featuring twenty tons of snow.
(480) 921–2300

AUGUST

Bring in the Clowns
Scottsdale
The largest clown gathering in the Southwest.
(800) 877–1117

SEPTEMBER

Fiesta Septiembre
Wickenburg
Desert Caballeros Western Museum—arts and crafts, folklorico dancers, mariachi bands, mercado, salsa contest.
(928) 684–5479 or 684–0977

OCTOBER

Cowboy Artists of America Sale and Exhibition
Phoenix
(602) 257–8382

NOVEMBER

Fountain Festival of Arts and Crafts
Fountain Hills
(480) 837–1654

Celebration of Art
Glendale
Outdoor street festival.
(623) 930–2960

a guideline to prices, flights with Adventures Out West range from $165 to $215 per person.

Jeep tours are another great way to see the desert. Two companies operating in the Valley of the Sun are *Arizona Desert Mountain Jeep Tours* (480–860–1777), which offers a choice of five four-hour itineraries and operates twice a day, seven days a week; and *Desert Storm Hummer Tours* (480–922–0020 or 866–374–8637; www.dshummer.com), which gives you three to four hours in one of those double-wides that are billed as the most powerful four-by-four vehicles on earth.

Phoenix emerged from the ashes of Hohokam settlements, prospector claims, and military camps around 1850. It was long an agricultural center,

Arizona Temple Christmas Lighting
Mesa
Five hundred thousand plus lights in the
garden and a lighted reflection pool.
(480) 964-7164

Thunderbird Balloon Classic
Scottsdale
Continuous entertainment, 130 balloons.
(800) 877-1117

Fantasy of Lights
Tempe
Downtown illuminated, city tree lighting,
fireworks, multiple live entertainment
stages.
(480) 894-8158

**Bluegrass Festival and
Fiddle Championship**
Wickenburg
(928) 684-5479

DECEMBER

Pueblo Grande Indian Market
Phoenix
Native American artisans,
traditional foods.
(602) 495-0901

Las Noches de las Luminarias
Phoenix
Desert Botanical Gardens—7,000+ lit
luminarias line the garden pathways,
musical groups perform.
(480) 941-1225

Zoo Lights
Phoenix
Phoenix Zoo—600,000+ lights, lighted
animal exhibits.
(602) 273-1341

Fiesta Bowl Block Party
Tempe
Thirty-plus musical groups on five
different stages, pep rally.
(800) 635-5748

**Cowboy Christmas, Cowboy
Poets Gathering**
Wickenburg
Desert Caballeros Western
Museum—poetry, ballads, stories,
singin', and storytellin'.
(928) 684-5479

diverting water from the Salt River to irrigate many acres of farmland. In true colorful Western fashion, the man most credited with envisioning the irrigation potential of the Valley was Jack Swilling, a drug-addicted Confederate deserter who led the Battle of Picacho Pass (more on this later in this chapter). Probably the biggest contrast between the Valley of the Sun and other areas in central and southern Arizona is that Phoenix and its environs are much greener, with sizable lawns, countless public parks, and many nonnative trees.

All this greenery provides some much-needed summer shade. Many areas of the Southwest are hot during the summer, but Phoenix has the reputation as a true hot spot, with 100-plus-degree temperatures the norm throughout the summer. As miserable as that may sound, particularly to those from the north, the area's nearly nonexistent humidity—coupled with the zillions of swimming pools that dot the landscape—makes it relatively bearable even in the dead of summer. Even locals will talk about soaring highs of 115 and 120, but thankfully, those days are as rare as snow in the desert.

Sports fans may want to begin their exploration of the Valley at the home of the National Basketball Association's Phoenix Suns, as well as the Women's National Basketball Association's Phoenix Mercury, and the American Football League's Arizona Rattlers. US Airways Center is also one of the best places in the Valley to see musical performers, ice shows, rodeos, and whatever. *US Airways Center* (602–379–7800; www.usairwayscenter.com) can be found at 201 East Jefferson Street. The exit is well marked from I–17 North, and once you find Jefferson Street, just keep your eyes peeled for the giant basketball mural. The arena is the modern, gray brick building on the opposite side of the street. Several businesses within the arena cater to fans and tourists. On the first level, the *Teamshop* (602–514–8321) sells posters, key chains, wearables, and other items related to the Suns and other Phoenix-area teams. *The Lexus Club* restaurant (602–379–7719) on the second level is open during events. For lunch during the weekdays or dinner Monday through Saturday, dine on classic Italian fare at *il Palazzetto* (602–514–8500), which, at 211 East Jefferson Street, is adjacent to the US Airways Center. *Chase Field* opened in 1998 as the home-field for the world-champion Arizona Diamondbacks. Even when the Arizona Diamondbacks aren't playing, this massive, $350-million, retractable-roofed stadium is worth seeing—perhaps over lunch at *Friday's Front Row* (602–462–3503), a casual eatery built right into the stands that's open daily. Here, too, you can shop for sports memorabilia at *Teamshop* (602–462–6700). As an aside, Chase Field is the first ballpark ever to be built with its own swimming pool off right field. Only in Phoenix!

Just north of US Airways Center is *Majerle's* (Mar-leez) *Sports Grill* (602–253–0118; www.majerles.com) at 24 North Second Street. This is the place that Suns' former star "Thunder Dan" Majerle built with his phenomenal three-point shooting ability. Besides being a great pub and restaurant (with menu

It's a Cool 100° Outside

According to the National Climatic Data Center's summer heat stress index comparison, Phoenix's low humidity results in more comfortable summer weather than most would imagine. Although the outdoor temperatures average 100.5 degrees Fahrenheit, it feels like it's only 96. Compare that with Dallas, where the average high may be only 93, yet high humidity makes it feel more like 109.

Chase Field Fun Facts

The park's retractable roof has six operable telescoping panels that, when open, provide 5.25 acres of open sky.

The roof is driven by two 200-horsepower electric motors that consume between $1.20 and $2.00 worth of electricity to open or close the roof.

The park has 650 television sets, 81 concession stands, and 580 bathroom stalls.

Using as much cooling power as 2,285 average homes, the 8,000-ton air-conditioning system takes about four hours to lower the temperature inside the stadium from 110 to 72 degrees.

About 17,000 tons of structural steel were used to build the park.

items named after the players and probably the best french fries available anywhere), the grill is packed tighter than an overstuffed gym bag during Suns' games, when you can watch the action on a projection TV. Hours here are from 11:00 A.M. to 1:00 A.M. daily. Another popular spot that has sprung up within walking distance of the sports and entertainment venues is *Sliders American Grill* (602–462–3800) at 201 South 4th Street.

Alice Cooper'stown Phoenix (602–253–7337; www.alicecooperstown .com) at 101 East Jefferson Street was opened by the legendary hometown boy and rock star known as Alice Cooper. Basically a sports and music bar, Cooper'stown is located near the US Airways Center and Chase Field. Since it opened in 1998 it has been a hot spot for celebrity sightings and is known as a place to see and be seen. The menu features barbeque and waitstaff sport the Alice Cooper trademark teardrop. Also near the sports venues with an equally sports-oriented format is the 24,000-square-foot *Jackson's on 3rd* (602–254–5303; www.jacksonsonthird.com) at 245 East Jackson Street near Third Street.

A themed eatery at 3 South Second Street, where the trademark Fender guitar shape heralds your arrival, is the *Hard Rock Cafe* (602–261–7625; www .hardrock.com). The restaurant displays mucho memorabilia, including instruments and costumes donated by musicians. Outdoor seating is available, illuminated by an unusual flame-spouting fountain.

Your best bet to sample the variety of nightlife Phoenix offers is the classy downtown complex called *The Arizona Center* (602–271–4000; www.arizona center.com). Located between Third and Fifth Streets north of Van Buren Street, it's a complete dining, shopping, and entertainment complex. There's the *AMC Arizona Center 24 Theatres,* a twenty-four-plex movie theater

(602–956–4AMC) that shows first-run features in their full digital sound splendor and offers reduced ticket prices for the early shows. You'll find familiar formats at **Uno's Chicago Grill** (602–253–3355) and **Hooters** (602–495–1234). You'll also find local favorites: **Mi Amigo Mexican Grill** (602–256–7355), **Sam's Cafe** (602–252–3545), and **Lombardi's** (602–257–8323) for wood-fired pizza and Italian seafood specialties. For something quicker and cheaper, stop by one of the smaller eateries where you can get everything from gourmet coffee at **Starbucks** (602–258–2472) to ice cream concoctions at **Cold Stone Creamery** (602–252–5572).

For concert lovers, **Cricket Pavilion** (602–254–7200; www.cricket-pavilion .com) at 2121 North 83rd Avenue offers about three dozen events per year, including most of the top pop/rock and country acts that tour Arizona. The Pavilion, which seats about 20,000 under the stars, has provisions for video screens and adjacent areas for booths that sell everything from bottled water to concert tees to margaritas. During major events such as Jimmy Buffett's annual visit, the Pavilion turns into Party Town, with a forest of colorfully decorated Parrotheads—which is what Buffett fans call themselves—bopping to the tunes.

The Valley is a great place to hear up-and-coming musical acts, and as you might expect, there are a lot of hip clubs. Your best bet for finding the hot new spots in town is to look for one of three local freebie publications distributed from street stands and in local restaurants and shops. *The Rep* and *Get Out* are published by the local newspapers; another source is *New Times,* a fairly hefty read that does a good job covering the Valley's nightlife.

They may have built this city on sports and rock and roll, but art and architecture also offer significant appeal. Several key buildings were designed, built, or influenced by master architect Frank Lloyd Wright; some of them are private residences, but four are public buildings that can be toured. The most impressive is **Taliesin** (Welsh for "shining brow") **West** (480–860–2700; www.frank lloydwright.org) at 12621 Frank Lloyd Wright Boulevard, Scottsdale. Built against the foothills of the McDowell Mountains just outside of Scottsdale, this winter retreat was begun in 1937 by Wright, who made many changes to it over time (the original structure used canvas flaps instead of glass windows). Today, it's the headquarters of the Frank Lloyd Wright Foundation, which operates a school of architecture and maintains an archive of the master's designs. Taliesin West has a gift shop and offers tours that range from a one-hour overview to an in-depth, behind-the-scenes study. Special events at the site include desert walks and nighttime city-light gazing.

Wright also had an influence on one of Phoenix's best-known resorts, the **Arizona Biltmore Resort and Spa** (602–955–6600 or 800–950–2575; www.arizonabiltmore.com) at 2400 East Missouri Avenue, which at one time

A Musical Spawning Ground

Phoenix is well known as a stepping stone to the recording mecca of Los Angeles. Over the years this city has given the world the Tubes, jazz/pop vocalist Rickie Lee Jones, and Francine Reed (a gospel/blues vocalist who recorded with Lyle Lovett). The Valley's most memorable contribution to the music industry is probably glam/heavy-metal/shock-rock god Alice Cooper. Alice (aka Vincent Furnier) attended Cortez High School (8828 North 31st Avenue), if any of you rock fans want to see where this self-styled bad boy got his start. Together with his band, the Earwigs, he first recorded in the Valley on the Santa Cruz label. Away from the stage, he lives a quiet life north of Phoenix in beautiful Paradise Valley. He plays golf and has, on occasion, dispensed advice to local bands. At one time he owned a Native American art gallery in Scottsdale.

was run by the Wrigley chewing gum family. Though most believe that the resort was designed by Wright, it was actually at the hand of his former apprentice, Albert Chase McArthur. The story goes that McArthur invited the famous architect to oversee construction of the hotel, which he did quietly for a few months before completely removing himself from the project. Nevertheless, Wright's touch can be seen in the block structure of the resort as well as in its distinctive spire. You have to be a guest to get a guided tour, but you're welcome to look around the lobby and other public areas.

If you're still looking for the "Wright stuff," drop by **Grady Gammage Memorial Auditorium** (480–965–3434; www.asugammage.com) on Apache Boulevard and Gammage Parkway in Tempe. This structure, on the grounds of Arizona State University, was actually begun after Wright's death and was completed in 1964. The circular building has been extensively praised for its physical beauty as well as its acoustics. Tours are conducted during the academic year from September through May, and the center regularly hosts touring Broadway groups that perform such hits as *Cats, Phantom of the Opera,* and *Movin' Out* to sold-out crowds.

Last on a tour of Wright structures would be **The First Christian Church** (602–246–9206) at 6750 North Seventh Avenue, Phoenix, which could perhaps win an award as the Frank Lloyd Wright building completed most posthumously. Though this slant-roofed structure with its repeated triangular motif was drafted in 1950, construction didn't take place until 1970. In any case, the design is breathtaking. Tours are available by special arrangement.

Architecturally, **Downtown Phoenix** has a lot to admire. The copper-domed 1900 historic **State Capitol** building (602–542–4675; www.dlapr.lib.az.us/museum) at 1700 West Washington Street is now a historical museum. (The

DASH around Downtown Phoenix— It's Free!

Whether your reason is tired feet or summer heat, the **DASH (Downtown Area Shuttle)** (602–253–5000; www.valleymetro.com) is the easy way to see downtown Phoenix. These orange and purple minibuses run every six to twelve minutes from 6:30 A.M. to 11:00 P.M., Monday through Friday. They take you past—or near—all the major downtown hotels, restaurants, theaters, and sights, including Heritage Square, the Arizona Science Center and Phoenix Museum of History, Chase Field, and the Arizona Center. Plus, in the middle of the day (from 11:00 A.M. to 2:00 P.M.) the route is extended to include the State Capitol, the Mining and Mineral Museum, and the Hall of Fame. Best of all, DASH is free. Look for a stop where you see the signs with a dashing jackrabbit.

actual government offices now occupy the modern, nine-story tower that rises behind the historic dome.) You can wander about at your own pace, or take one of the guided tours to peer into exhibits on the state's political past. The State Capitol building is open from 8:00 A.M. to 5:00 P.M., Monday through Friday with guided tours at 9:30 A.M., 11:00 A.M., and 1:00 P.M. Also worth a look in the downtown area are Heritage Square, St. Mary's Basilica, and the Old County/City Hall complex.

The **Heritage Square** complex (602–262–5029; www.rossonhouse museum.org) at Seventh and Monroe Streets is a group of historic houses from the original Phoenix townsite. Now the buildings house museums, boutiques, a bistro, and a gift shop/tearoom surrounding a cool, green courtyard. The **Arizona Doll and Toy Museum** (602–253–9337) is located here, as are the Phoenix Museum of History, the Arizona Science Center, and the **Victorian Rosson** and **Silva Houses.** For a bite to eat you can drop by the **Teeter House** (602–252–4682; www.theteeterhouse.com) or for dinner, **Pizzeria Bianco** (602–258–8300). Hours vary on the various attractions, and some are closed during the summer, so call ahead to avoid disappointment.

The **Arizona Science Center** (602–716–2000; www.azscience.org) at 600 East Washington is the kind of place where Carl Sagan would have felt right at home. Now located in a $47-million building just east of the Phoenix Convention Center, the facility is a hands-on (and in some cases, whole-body-on) learning complex that encompasses Arizona's largest planetarium, a wide-screen theater, and 350 interactive exhibits that beg to be touched and explored.

Next door is **The Phoenix Museum of History** (602–253–2734; www.pm oh.org) at 105 North Fifth Street, between Washington and Monroe Streets where interactive exhibits highlight territorial and early statehood days in Arizona and emphasize the multicultural heritage of the state.

St. Mary's Basilica (602–354–2100) at 231 North Third Street is a soaring edifice that seems out of place, yet is oddly natural amid all the modern downtown structures. Built in 1881, it is the oldest Catholic church in the city and a popular place for weddings and other major events. If there aren't any services taking place when you visit, you can walk around inside and marvel at the various forms of architecture that were used in constructing this Phoenix landmark (call for hours). It also, interestingly enough, has its own gift shop selling religious articles and mementos.

The *Herberger Theater Center* (602–254–7399; www.herbergertheater .org) at 222 East Monroe Street is an understated earth-tone structure that provides space for eight performing arts groups—including the very popular (and deservedly so) Arizona Theatre Company, which uses professional actors from stage and screen to perform original and time-tested works in Phoenix and Tucson. The company's season usually runs October through May.

Along Washington Street en route to the State Capitol you'll find a small off-the-beaten-path museum worth considering. The *Arizona Mining & Mineral Museum* (602–255–3795 or 800–446–4259; www.admmr.state.az.us) at 1502 West Washington and 15th Avenue, which honors the industry that built Arizona and made it the number-one mining state in the country for nonfuel production. You'll see turquoise, smithsonite, wulfenite, malachite, azurite, and pyrite; you'll also see some gold.

The Old County Courthouse

No tour of the downtown area is complete without a look at the *Old County Courthouse* on Washington Street between First and Third Avenues. The county structure, thought to be the largest terra-cotta–surfaced structure in the state, is a grand old courthouse built in the late 1920s. On the second floor is the courtroom where the famous Miranda trial took place. The 1963 case, involving Ernesto Miranda, who was arrested for a rape that occurred near Bethany Home Road and 17th Street in Phoenix, threw a harsh spotlight on police interrogation tactics and resulted in the Miranda Rights ruling ("You have the right to remain silent. If you give up the right to remain silent . . . ").

Ironically, the building also played a key role in one of Clint Eastwood's cop films. In *The Gauntlet,* Eastwood plays a Phoenix policeman who has to provide protection for a witness. In the film's climax, Eastwood drives a bus through downtown Phoenix and runs it up the steps of the Old County Courthouse. The structures in the County/ City complex are public buildings; as such they are open to visitors, but no tours are offered.

If you're hungry after a downtown tour, a great place to eat is ***Tom's Tavern*** (602–257–1688), centrally located on the corner of Washington and First Avenue. Seating is indoors and out (with misters in the summertime), and the politically driven menu offers sandwiches named after local office holders, past and present. Hours are from 7:00 A.M. to 8:00 P.M., Monday through Friday. For breakfast, lunch, and dinner, check out ***Kricket's*** (602–258–3411) at 401 North First Street in the downtown Ramada Inn. Kricket's is decorated with photographs and other memorabilia that reflect the city's past, and it offers American and Southwestern cuisine.

Another choice in the neighborhood is at ***Seamus McCaffrey's Irish Pub & Restaurant*** (602–253–6081) at 18 West Monroe Street.

While you're downtown, be sure to get a look at the Spanish Colonial–style ***Orpheum Theatre*** (602–262–7272 for tickets) at 203 West Adams Street. Built in 1929, the theater was used for films and vaudeville performances. Mae West and W. C. Fields both graced this stage. Following an exhaustive, meticulous $14-million restoration project, the Orpheum reopened in early 1997. Broadway road shows play here.

Before leaving central Phoenix, the ***Heard Museum*** (602–252–8848 or 602–252–8344; www.heard.org) is an Arizona "must-see" located at 2301 North Central Avenue near Monte Vista Road. Long known for its vast collection of Native American art, both the exhibit space and the parking area have been recently expanded to allow more visitors more ways to appreciate the craftsmanship and design abilities of the Native Peoples of the Southwest. Barry Goldwater's collection of hand-carved katsina dolls is there; so is the doll collection of the Fred Harvey Corporation. Also fascinating to see and study are baskets,

America's Heroes: Phoenix's Firefighting Museum

Among the many unusual places to visit in Phoenix is the largest firefighter museum in the world. **The Hall of Flame** (602–275–3473; www.hallofflame.org) at 6101 East Van Buren Street has almost one hundred antique and classic fire engines as well as firefighting artifacts of all types. The fire engines date as far back as 1725 and are as new as 1961. One of the carriages was used to fight the 1871 Chicago Fire. Photos, artwork, badge and arm patch displays, and even a fire safety exhibit for kids round out the items of interest here. Admission is $6.00 for adults, $5.00 for seniors, $4.00 for children ages 6 to 17, and $1.50 for ages 3 to 5. It's open from 9:00 A.M. to 5:00 P.M., Monday through Saturday, and from noon to 4:00 P.M., Sunday.

Finding an Address in Phoenix

The Greater Phoenix area is built in the Western tradition of squares. It's exactly 1 mile from one main road to the next, often with a semi-main thoroughfare at the halfway point. The only things that stand in the way of this perfect patterning are the buttes and mountains that pop up here and there in the Valley of the Sun. Finding an address east to west is fairly simple. The numbering begins at Central Avenue and moves logically and predictably either west through the avenues or east through the streets, so you know that 2400 East Camelback is at 24th Street or 4300 West Indian School is at 43rd Avenue. North-South addresses are not as simple—numbering begins at Washington Street downtown, but you have to know that Camelback Road is 5000 North. Similarly, when you get into other towns in the Phoenix metro area, you'll find they too have a First Street or a Fifth Avenue and in some cases—Scottsdale or Tempe for example—it's the roads running north–south that are named and some of the east-west streets that are numbered. Go figure! And be sure you know which city you're in, because numbering starts again—and goes town by town—when you get into what's called the East Valley (see below). Here's a bit of help with some of the more well-traveled thoroughfares in the Greater Phoenix area:

Street or Road Name	Numbers Begin At
Washington	0 North/South (1000 North in Tempe)
Van Buren	300 North
Roosevelt	1000 North
McDowell	1600 North
Thomas	2900 North
Osborn	3400 North
Indian School	4100 North
Camelback	5000 North
Lincoln	6600 North
Glendale	7000 North
Northern	8000 North
Shea	10600 North
Thunderbird	13800 North
Bell/Frank Lloyd Wright	17000 North
Pinnacle Peak	23400 North
Southern	6000 South (3300 South in Tempe; 1200 South in Mesa)
Elliot	10800 South (7600 South in Tempe; 3000 South in Chandler)
Ray	14000 South (1000 South in Chandler; 1600 in Gilbert)

trivia

Arizona is known as the Copper State. It produces more than 65 percent of the nation's domestic supply.

jewelry, pottery, and textiles. The artist-in-residence program gives you a chance to meet and hear artists discuss their work; plus, you can see replicas of traditional Indian dwellings including a Navajo hogan, an Apache wickiup, and a Hopi corn grinding room. The museum is open from 9:30 A.M. to 5:00 P.M. daily. Admission is $10 for adults, $9.00 for seniors, $5.00 for students, and $3.00 for children ages 6 to 12. There are free guided tours offered at noon, 1:30 P.M., and 3:00 P.M. daily.

There's a two-fer waiting to be discovered at Phoenix's Papago Park, and they're side-by-side on Galvin Parkway east of downtown. *The Phoenix Zoo* (602–273–1341; www.phoenixzoo.org) at 455 North Galvin Parkway is the only zoo in the country that is 100 percent privately funded; it's spacious, neat, and amusing, which is why it's also regarded as one of America's finest. Designed as a series of habitats, it includes an African veldt, a South American rain forest, and a traditional Arizona farm. Docents and teen volunteers make the exhibits come alive, and a Disney-style tram covers the entire complex. Two worthwhile special events during the year are "Boo at the Zoo," when children visit wearing Halloween costumes; during the holidays, "Zoo Lights" is a must-do. It's a month-long celebration (late November to early January) when the trees and the cacti are lit every evening until 10:00 P.M., and mimes, magicians, and carolers appear in the central courtyard or on the pathways. The zoo is open 364 days of the year (closed only December 25); hours are from 9:00 A.M. to 5:00 P.M., except in summer to early fall (June 1 through September 30) when hours are 7:00 A.M. to 4:00 P.M. weekends and holidays, and 7:00 A.M. to 2:00 P.M. on weekdays. Next along the road is *Desert Botanical Garden* (480–941–1225; www.dbg.org) at 1201 North Galvin Parkway, home to one of the world's largest and most diverse collections of desert plants as well as fine examples of Native American housing styles. It's a great place to learn more about cacti and their nasty habits before you set off on a desert hike; it's also an eye-opener to the beauty and delicacy of desert wildflowers, bushes, and small trees. Events here during the year include spring and fall plant sales, Music in the Garden, Jazz in the Garden, and, like its neighbor the zoo, there's a winter holiday celebration of lights called "Las Noches de las Luminarias" each year. The Botanical Garden is open every day except July 4, Thanksgiving, and December 25; hours are from 7:00 A.M. to 8:00 P.M. May through September, and from 8:00 A.M. to 8:00 P.M. October through April.

North on Central Avenue from downtown is the *Phoenix Art Museum* (602–257–1222; www.phxart.org) at 1625 North Central Avenue at McDowell

Road, which houses a wide-ranging collection of art works, including American, European, Spanish Colonial, Latin American, and Asian paintings and sculptures. Of particular interest to visitors may be the museum's collection of Western American works featuring the works of Southwestern artists. Children will enjoy both the ArtWorks Gallery—a hands-on, "brains-on" activity room for children—and the Thorne Miniature Rooms, which show how people lived during historic periods in the United States and Europe. Admission is $9.00 for adults, $7.00 for seniors and students, and $3.00 for ages 6 to 17. The museum offers free admission on Thursday. Guided tours are held daily at 1:00, 2:00, and 6:00 P.M., with additional tours offered at 11:00 A.M. and 2:00 P.M. on Saturday

The *Phoenix Public Library* (602–262–4636) at 1221 North Central Avenue is an exceptional research and reading resource. The building also is of architectural interest. You can also see exhibits there relating to city life in Phoenix. One not-to-be-missed example of cooperation among residents is the library's centennial quilt, which hangs in the central area of the first floor near the children's book section.

One of the Valley's most unusual attractions is the *Mystery Castle* (602–268–1581) at 800 East Mineral Road near South Mountain Park in Phoenix. This eighteen-room stone structure, which also incorporates wire rims from a Stutz Bearcat, was put together completely by hand. The mystery comes from the fact that the builder never told his family about the work. He had always promised his daughter that he would build her a castle, and one day he left their home in Seattle and came to Phoenix to undertake the project. She only found out about the castle when his will was read, and she lives there to this day. The castle has thirteen fireplaces, lots of antiques, and the general sense of being smack dab in the midst of somebody's dream. You can tour this unique home Thursday through Sunday from 11:00 A.M. to 4:00 P.M., October through May only. The cost is $5.00 for adults and $3.00 for children ages 5 to 15.

The *Pioneer Arizona Living History Museum* (623–465–1052; www .pioneer-arizona.com) at 3901 West Pioneer Road on I–17, 1 mile north of Carefree Highway, is a group of more than two dozen buildings, some authentic, and some reproductions that are used by reenactors to re-create the image of the frontier West. Visitors can see metalworking, dressmaking, carpentry, and other activities going on just as they were more than one hundred years ago. Open Wednesday through Sunday, from 9:00 A.M. to 5:00 P.M., October to May and from 8:00 A.M. to 2:00 P.M., Friday through Sunday from June to September.

The *Pueblo Grande Museum* (602–495–0901 or 877–706–4408; www .pueblogrande.com) at 4619 East Washington Street is an actual Hohokam village that was abandoned around A.D. 1450. The museum's exhibit rooms have permanent displays of artifacts and also serve as a venue for workshops such as

Mystery Castle

pottery making and archaeology. Hikes to nearby ancient petroglyph sites are also a featured event. Guided tours are held on Saturday at 11:00 A.M. and 1:00 P.M. and Sunday at 1:30 P.M. For almost twenty years the museum also has held an annual Indian market (usually in December), where more than 500 artists sell their works. The market also features traditional music and dancing, food, and beverages.

If you're in the mood to shop during your trip to Phoenix, you're in luck—the Valley is flush with shopping centers. One of the first, and still one of the best, is the west side *Metrocenter* (602–997–8991 or 602–997–2642; www .metrocentermall.com) at 9617 Metro Parkway (at I–17 off Peoria Avenue). A sprawling complex of more than 200 shops and restaurants, it also boasts a multiplex theater, an indoor arcade, and an outdoor amusement park. The whole complex is surrounded by hotels and eateries.

Another cool place to shop is the *Biltmore Fashion Park* (602–955–8401; www.shopbiltmore.com) at Camelback and 24th Streets. The shops here aren't joined by enclosed corridors, but the inner court is shaded, so it's pretty comfortable year-round. There are boutique-style shops, nationally known retailers such as Macy's and Saks Fifth Avenue, plus Williams Sonoma, Ann Taylor, Escada, Ralph Lauren, and Border's Books and Music, among others.

Scottsdale and Its Neighbors

Scottsdale, as a community, began in 1888 when Army chaplain Winfield Scott purchased land to grow citrus and other crops. Over the years the town has emerged as a world-renowned resort destination, offering great shopping, public parks, nationally recognized museums, frontier-type attractions, and galleries galore.

Cosanti and Cause Bells

In addition to the architectural work of Frank Lloyd Wright that is so much a part of the Phoenix-Scottsdale landscape, you'll also want to try to see the more fantastical and futuristic work of Italian architect Paolo Soleri. **Cosanti** (480–948–6145 or 800–752–3187; www.cosanti.com) at 6433 East Doubletree Ranch Road, Scottsdale, is an example of his concept of blending desert landscaping with earth-formed concrete structures. Everywhere you walk among the courtyards, terraces, and gardens, there are bronze and ceramic windbells tinkling. Designed by Soleri and his artisans, these Cause Bells, as they are known, represent national and global issues. You can watch them being made; you also can buy them to provide funding for the various organizations that work on solving world problems. Cosanti is open from 9:00 A.M. to 5:00 P.M., Monday through Saturday and from 11:00 A.M. to 5:00 P.M., Sunday. The foundry is open to the public in the morning—it's best to call first. Donations accepted.

In fact Scottsdale is *loaded* with galleries. In at least three separate areas—Main Street Arts and Antique District, Marshall Way, and Fifth Avenue Shopping Area (in which there are more than 200 specialty shops)—you can stroll for hours and get a close-up look at everything from traditional Native American arts and crafts to nineteenth-century fine art. You can easily walk or take Scottsdale's local transportation—a trolley—to these various areas, but you may want to take your car, because you'll no doubt buy something!

Faust Gallery (480–946–6345; www.Faustgallery.com) at 7103 East Main Street represents emerging and established Native American artists, with katsinas, pottery, paintings, and other works. *American Fine Art Editions, Inc.* (480–990–1200 or 800–466–8276; www.americanfineartgallery.com) at 3908 North Scottsdale Road, represents the contemporary art scene very well with an eclectic collection of original work by internationally acclaimed twentieth-century artists (Neiman, Wyeth, Picasso). *Borgata* at 6166 North Scottsdale Road is a Mediterranean-style complex of about forty shops and eateries, with cobblestone paths, fountains, towers, and all the ingredients of a fairy-tale setting (albeit one that takes plastic!). If all the shopping makes you hungry, wander into *Cafe Terra Cotta* (480–948–8100), a nouvelle-style, informal yet sumptuous place created by restaurateur Donna Nordin (who was named by PBS as one of the great chefs of the Southwest) and her husband Don Luria. The cuisine, well

trivia

The Phoenix/Scottsdale area is home to more Mobil Five-Star and AAA Five-Diamond resorts than any other destination in the United States.

flavored and tailored to Arizona tastes, is very moderately priced, and menu selections include everything from vegetarian items to seafood to fare that leans toward more traditional continental offerings.

If you're staying at a hotel or resort way north in Scottsdale, you'll be glad to know there are art museums within reach. Or if your wandering takes you north to Carefree, you will also find an extension of the *Heard Museum* of Native American art and crafts located in el Pedregal Festival Marketplace on Scottsdale Road and Carefree Highway (for information on Heard Museum North, call 480–488–9817).

A Carefree Life

About twenty minutes north of Fountain Hills are the twin communities of Cave Creek and Carefree. *Cave Creek* was a mining community one hundred years ago, and over time it has become a diverse town of a little more than 3,000 residents. Nearby *Carefree* is a bedroom community that began development in the 1950s and today serves as home to famous faces such as news anchor Hugh Downs and actress P. J. Soles (*Halloween, Carrie, Rock and Roll High School*). Carefree also is the location of the largest, most accurate sundial in the Western Hemisphere. This impressive timepiece, which sweeps out of the earth like a giant scimitar, can be found off Cave Creek Road and Sunshine Way. One stop you should definitely make in Carefree is *el Pedregal* ("the place with many stones") at 34505 North Scottsdale Road (480–488–1072; www.elpedregal.com). This Morrocan-influenced marketplace has clothing stores (including several Western boutiques featuring the ultrahot retro-forties ranch-wear look), gift shops, and several eateries. The inner courtyard is used for music and dance performances, as well as visual arts events. The center is also home to the Heard Museum North (480–488–9817), a satellite facility of the acclaimed downtown Phoenix museum.

el Pedregal

About 12 miles east of Scottsdale is the community of *Fountain Hills* (480–837–1654; www.fountainhillschamber.com). Fountain Hills can be reached by taking Shea Boulevard east through the desert foothills until it runs into Fountain Hills. Besides being home to the *Tallest Fountain in the World* (560 feet, as verified in the *Guinness Book of World Records*), this picturesque town has a number of local sights that are worth a look. If you want to try for your own record, hit the jackpot at *Fort McDowell Casino* (800–THE–FORT; www.fmcasino.com), where visitors challenge Lady Luck twenty-four hours a day, seven days a week; there's a free shuttle, if you need it. *Saguaro Lake,* an artificial reservoir on the Salt River, offers a number of boating, waterskiing, and swimming opportunities, as well as a steamboat paddle wheeler (480–984–5311 or 480–984–2425; www.saguarolake.net) that does regular tours and dinner cruises. You can reach Saguaro Lake by taking Highway 87 north until you reach Bush Highway. Head south on Bush Highway, and it will take you to the lake.

While you're in Fountain Hills, drop by for a bite at *Que Bueno* (480–837–2418) at 13207 North LaMontana Drive. This Mexican restaurant has won plaudits for its homemade salsa and features savory desserts like chocolate chimichangas.

The West Valley

On the western side of the Valley—accessible by heading west out of downtown Phoenix on I–10—is the tri-city area of Avondale, Goodyear, and *Litchfield Park* (623–932–2260; www.southwestvalleychamber.org). Litchfield Park sprang to life as a company town in 1916 when Goodyear Tire and Rubber executive Paul Litchfield purchased the land to use as a cotton farm back in the days when cotton cords were utilized in automotive tires. Today the town is best known as the location of *The Wigwam Resort* (800–327–0396 or 623–935–3811; www.wigwamresort.com) at 300 Wigwam Boulevard. This four-star resort is composed of charming adobe casitas that were initially built for Goodyear officials. The Wigwam is especially favored by golfers because it features three eighteen-hole golf courses. Two of these, the Gold Course and the Blue Course, were designed by well-known golf-course architect Robert Trent Jones Sr. The Gold Course, which was selected by *Golf Digest Magazine* as one of the top seventy-five courses in America, is a whopping 7,100 yards long. Because of the Wigwam's off-the-beaten-path loca-

trivia

There are more than 200 golf courses in Greater Phoenix—making it one of the top five golf destinations in the world!

tion, it also offers guests amenities such as horseback riding and trap and skeet shooting.

Not surprisingly for an area that was raised by the rubber giant, nearby **Avondale** is home to **Phoenix International Raceway** (602–252–2227; www.phoenixintlraceway.com), the location of the world's fastest paved 1-mile oval track. The raceway attracts huge crowds; famous drivers such as Mario Andretti, Emerson Fittipaldi, and Al Unser Jr.; and brings hundreds of millions of dollars into the tri-city coffers.

Wickenburg and Northwest of Metropolitan Phoenix

At the junction of Routes 93 and 60, **Wickenburg** (928–684–5479; www .wickenburgchamber.com) is a frontier town that's been a popular getaway destination for decades. Within a half-dozen or so miles there are five guest ranches that offer dudes and dudettes a close-up glimpse of the cowboy way of life. Because of this concentration of lodges serving the "City Slicker" set, Wickenburg has earned the title of "The Dude Ranch Capital of the World."

Prospector/farmer Henry Wickenburg, a native of Prussia, founded the town some 130 years ago after discovering the largest gold-producing strike in the history of the state. He called his mine the **Vulture Mine** (602–859–2743). If you're interested in viewing the remains of Wickenburg's mining camp, it's about a dozen miles from town. Drive about 2.5 miles west of Wickenburg on U.S. Highway 60, turn left onto Vulture Mine Road, and continue for 12 miles. The pavement will end, and you'll be on a dirt road that can be a bit bumpy (don't attempt this drive during or immediately after a rainstorm). When you pull off the road, you'll see Vulture Peak, a tall hill with a crease in the middle of its summit. Vulture Mine is just to the southwest of the peak.

The remains of the wood and adobe buildings that once made up the Vul-

The Code of the West

If you're fascinated by the "Code of the West" (as is nearly anybody who grew up watching *The Rifleman* and *Wanted: Dead or Alive*), head for the Circle K store in Wickenburg near Tegner and Wickenburg Way. Behind the store is a 200-year-old **mesquite tree**, known as the "jail tree," which was used from 1863 to 1890 as a place to chain miscreants before the town had a jail.

ture camp can still be explored. Though the mine mostly dried up around the turn of the twentieth century, some limited excavation is still being carried on in the area. Be careful to confine your explorations to buildings and hillsides that aren't marked as private property.

Mining is no longer a major portion of Wickenburg's economy. The lovely scenery—which ranges from creosote bush and cacti to oak and pine trees— draws visitors. Ranching and agriculture have helped to keep the city's coffers well stocked.

If you drive in from the west off US 60, you can continue on the roadway that becomes Wickenburg Way, center of many of the area's hotels and restaurants. U.S. Highway 89/93 also leads into the town; once in the town limits, it's called Tegner Street. Either way, it's easy to get around, and most of Wickenburg's attractions are in the downtown center grid.

There's a lot of history in this town, including many buildings that date from the turn of the twentieth century or earlier. One of the most interesting is the **Hassayampa Building** near Apache and Frontier Streets. Originally built as a hotel for railroad passengers, it had nine separate fireplaces and a huge kitchen. Today it's office and shop space. Other locations worth stopping by to have a look at include **Hyder's Livery Stable** across the street from the Hassayampa Building. The stable, with its distinctive rock wall, is much classier than the simple barn-like buildings you generally see in Western towns. When it ceased being a stable in the 1920s, it was turned into a garage and auto dealership. The **Upton House** on Washington Street, west of Apache Street, was built from locally produced bricks. It was once occupied by one of the wealthiest families in the area.

trivia

"Hassayampa" is actually an Apache word that means "river that runs upside down." Oddly, the preserve is one of the few locations where the river does not run underground.

Nearby on Frontier Street and Wickenburg Way is the **Desert Caballeros Western Museum and Park** (928–684–2272; www.westernmuseum.org) at 21 North Frontier Street. The museum displays modern artwork from members of the Cowboy Artists of America in addition to pieces by American masters like Frederic Remington. There are also period rooms depicting Wickenburg's early years. The small park adjacent to the museum features a life-size statue by Joe Beeler of a cowboy kneeling beside his horse. The museum and museum store are open year-round, Monday through Saturday, from 10:00 A.M. to 5:00 P.M. and Sunday from noon to 4:00 P.M. Closed major holidays. Admission is $6.00 adults, $4.50 seniors, and $1.00 children ages 6 to 16.

Wickenburg is better known for its current hospitality than for its earlier law enforcement policies. Its guest ranches range from a cozy, historic hacienda to an elaborate resort that has its own golf course. Among these is *Rancho Casitas* (928–684–2628), which is closed during the summer and has separate cottage-style houses with kitchens and fireplaces. It also has a pool and horseback riding facilities. *Kay El Bar Ranch* (928–684–7593 or 800–684–7583; www.kayelbar.com) is a traditional adobe guest ranch with a pool and horseback riding; it is open mid-October to May 1. *Flying E Ranch* (928–684–2690 or 888–684–2650; www.flyingeranch.com) is an actual working cattle ranch that also has a tennis court, pool, spa, and sauna; its season is November to May. *Williams Family Ranch* (928–308–0589; www.williamsfamilyranch.com) is another working cattle ranch offering cowboy adventures September through May. *Rancho de los Caballeros* (928–684–5484 or 800–684–5030; www.sunc .com) caters not only to horse lovers but also to tennis buffs and golfers; it is open from October to May.

In keeping with Wickenburg's frontier history, area restaurants include steakhouses and several establishments serving Mexican fare, but you also can find Chinese cuisine, fish and chips, and several cafes that have home-cooked specialties. *The Horseshoe Cafe* (928–684–7377) at 207 East Wickenburg Way has American cuisine and is open daily year-round from 5:00 A.M. to 1:00 P.M. *March Hare* (928–684–0223) at 170 West Wickenburg Way features homemade baked goods, salads, stews, and sandwiches. It is open year-round, Tuesday through Saturday from 11:00 A.M. to 2:00 P.M. Another cool hangout is *Screamers* (928–684–9056) at 1141 West Wickenburg Way, a 1950s-style diner named after the owner's daughters—I swear I'm not making this up! Screamers features a variety of dishes, including chicken, fish, hamburgers (even a Hawaiian Burger), hotdogs, and more. They're open Monday through Saturday, from 6:00 A.M. to 8:00 P.M. and Sunday from 10:30 A.M. to 8:00 P.M.

A must-see attraction is the *Hassayampa River Preserve* (928–684–2772; www.nature.org), about 4 miles southeast of town on US 60. The 660-acre preserve, managed by the Nature Conservancy, is a refuge area for birds like the zone-tailed hawk and the yellow-tailed cuckoo. It's not unusual to see the white posteriors of mule deer as they frolic through the brush. You may also see tracks made by raccoons, bobcats, and mountain lions. The preserve's office is in a restored home that once belonged to a group of settlers who fell victim to the Indian wars in the 1880s. Admission is $5.00 for adults. The preserve is closed Monday and Tuesday.

Ghost towns are scattered throughout this rugged area, including Stanton, where prospectors are said to have picked up gold nuggets the size of potatoes, and Congress, home of a legendary tunnel that led from the general store to the town's hotel. Hidden Castle Hot Springs, east of Wickenburg, was at one time an exclusive spa where soothing natural hot spring water provided therapeutic relief for an impressive guest list that included President John F. Kennedy.

The city of **Glendale** (623–930–4500 or 877–800–2601; www.visitglen dale.com) has some delightful off-the-beaten-path surprises to offer. Best known locally as Arizona's antiques capital, a recent expansion of the **Old Town Glendale** antiques shopping area has turned some of the former Craftsman bungalow-style homes of nearby **Catlin Court Historic District** into shops and restaurants (streets and alleys are gaslit in the evenings every third Thursday of the month); there's a walking tour leaflet you can use to see the entire neighborhood. A free trolley connects these downtown areas, or it's a short walk through lovely Murphy Park. Kitty-corner from the park is **The Bead Museum** (623–931–2737; www.thebeadmuseum.com), a fascinating collection of beads from around the world, historic to contemporary. Beads come in all shapes and sizes and traditionally have been decorated with various techniques or simply left unadorned. Over the centuries they have been used for trade and currency, as amulets, and, of course, for jewelry and personal adornment. The

somethingold

West of Phoenix, the city of Glendale was named by *USA Today* as one of the ten best places in the country to shop for antiques.

museum is open Monday, Tuesday, Wednesday, Friday, and Saturday from 10:00 A.M. to 5:00 P.M., Thursday 10:00 A.M. to 8:00 P.M., and Sunday from 11:00 A.M. to 4:00 P.M. Also along the trolley route or a fairly easy walk from Old Town is **Cerreta Candy Company** (623–930–1000; www.cerreta.com) at 5345 West Glendale Avenue, a family-operated chocolate factory where you can watch candy being made, buy gift assortments, and enjoy a sample or two.

In recent years, Glendale has made a play for major league sports venues—acquiring both the NHL Phoenix Coyotes and the NFL Arizona Cardinals. During the 2003–2004 season, the Phoenix Coyotes Hockey Club started playing in the **Glendale Arena** at the Westgate City Center (623–850–PUCK; www.phoenixcoyotes.com). In 2003, the city broke ground for the **NFL Arizona Cardinals Stadium,** (480–603–1062; www.arizonacardinalsstadium .com) located south of the Phoenix Coyotes Arena at the Loop 101 and Bethany Home Road. The stadium, designed by architect Peter Eisenman, is built in the shape of a barrel cactus and seats 63,000. It opened for the 2006 season and will host the Super Bowl XLII Championship game in 2008.

On the opposite side of the Valley, **Tempe,** one of the oldest communities in the area, is known as the home of **Arizona State University** (ASU; 480–965–9011; www.asu.edu). The previously mentioned Grady Gammage Memorial Auditorium is definitely worth your time.

For a different kind of art work, wander into the ASU campus and head for the *J. Russell and Bonita Nelson Fine Arts Center* (480–965–2787). The 49,700-square-foot center, designed by Antoine Predock, is itself a work of art. The lavender-hued structures that make up the center are boldly geometric yet reflect the shapes you find in the Sonoran Desert. Inside, along with performing arts spaces, are 8,000 works of art in the ASU Art Museum, including an extensive collection of contemporary ceramics and Latin American folk and fine art.

ASU, incidentally, is where Jerry Lewis's character worked in his best-loved film, *The Nutty Professor;* you may recognize some of the buildings on campus from the film. *Sun Devil Stadium* was also the site of Super Bowl XXX. Tempe, however, doesn't need special events to draw a crowd. The whole downtown area is packed with college hangouts—pizza, Chinese food, coffeehouses, microbreweries—if you can't find something here that tempts your palate, you aren't really hungry.

The East Valley and Points South

Just east of Tempe is *Mesa* (800–283–6372 or 480–969–1307; www.mesachamber .org), another surprise in the Valley of the Sun. Graced with a face-lift in recent years, the downtown area is the site of *almost* everything you might want to see or do. The expanded *Mesa Southwest Museum* (480–644–2230; www.ci .mesa.az.us/swmuseum) at 53 North Macdonald Street has the largest exhibition of animated, full-scale, "roaring" dinosaurs west of the Mississippi, plus an exhibit of sea life from the Jurassic and Paleozoic periods. A 50-foot waterfall, caves, and re-creations of Hohokam Indian dwellings are also part of the museum's exhibits. The museum is open Tuesday through Saturday from 10:00 A.M. to 5:00 P.M., and Sunday from 1:00 to 5:00 P.M. Closed on holidays. Set among gardens, *The Arizona Temple Visitors Center* (480–964–7164) at 525 East Main Street is a well-known landmark in this city that was founded by the Mormons in 1878. Known for both its Easter Pageant (largest annual in the world) and its displays of twinkling lights during the holidays, the main attraction is its 10-foot Christus sculpture by Bertel Thorvaldsen.

Not far away is a museum that will be of special interest to aviation buffs or anyone with an interest in seeing preserved military aircraft of World War II. *The Arizona Wing of the Confederate Air Force* (480–924–1940) is located adjacent to Falcon Field Airport near the crossroads of McKellips and Greenfield Roads. The Arizona Wing displays several of the greats of World War II, restored and maintained not just for display in Arizona but in flying condition and ready for takeoff to events around the country each year. Among their aircraft are the American B-17 *Sentimental Journey,* which is considered the most authentically restored of all the B-17s flying today; plus there is an example of a German Heinkel, and two restored B-25 bombers of the type Jimmy Doolittle flew.

The Lower Salt River Recreation Area, which can be reached easily from Mesa, is a popular summer spot for "tubing" and river rafting trips. Weather permitting, the Salt is crammed with people on inner tubes, drifting lazily while their portable stereos compete for audio dominance. Others take guided tours of the river. Three companies not far from Mesa that provide equipment and transportation are *Salt River Recreation, Inc.* (480–984–3305; www.saltrivertubing.com), *Cimarron River Rafting Co.* (480–994–1199; www.cimarronadventures.com), and *Desert Voyagers Guided Raft Trips* (480–998–7238; www.desertvoyagers.com).

A little farther south in Chandler, you can visit a piece of the Old West at *Rawhide Wild West Town* (480–502–5600; www.rawhide.com) at 5700 North Loop Road, Chandler. It's a re-created 1880s frontier town, complete with shoot-outs and melodrama; stagecoach, camel, and burro rides; and a number of Old West restaurants and shops.

At the eastern end of the Valley of the Sun sits *Apache Junction,* located at the intersection of Highway 88 and US 60. This town boasts several well-attended annual events. Ironically, given the town's name and very Southwestern heritage, one of the major yearly amusements is a *Renaissance Festival* (520–463–2700; www.royalfaires.com). Held weekends and holidays from mid-February through late March, this 30-acre re-creation of life in sixteenth-century England features performances by jugglers, musicians, dancers, and other entertainers. This merriment is intertwined with jousting matches and falconry demonstrations. There also are more than 200 vendors of food and crafts, and you can even see trained fleas perform. Incidentally, the "sister city" for this event is Sherwood Forest, England. Apache Junction celebrates its mining heritage in February with *Lost Dutchman Days.* Legend has it that sometime in the late 1880s Dutch miner Jacob Walz discovered a gold mine in the Superstition Mountains just outside of Apache Junction. The Superstitions, a 160,285-acre volcanic mountain range, is rocky and rugged throughout. When Walz died in 1891 without revealing the location of his mine, many treasure seekers flocked to the area to hunt for the Dutchman's riches. To this day no one has uncovered the location. Lost Dutchman Days events include a rodeo, a parade, and a carnival.

You can delve into the region's mining history any time of year by following the *Apache Trail,* a circular route into the *Tonto National Forest* that takes you to the *Goldfield Ghost Town* (www.goldfieldghosttown.com) a re-created 1890s mining town that features tours of a former mine, a scenic railroad, and includes the *Superstition Mountain Lost Dutchman Museum.* At the museum you can learn how prehistoric Indians lived in the area, see a model of the entire Superstition Mountain wilderness area, and study exhibits that tell you about natural history—rocks, ores, animals, and reptiles. One exhibit contains photos, furniture, and equipment from a family home; another displays equipment and clothing from the mounted troops that are part of Arizona history; and, perhaps most fun, there are twenty-three maps that show possible locations of the Lost Dutchman Mine. For tours contact **Goldfield Ghost Town and Mine Tours** (480–983–0333) at 4650 North Mammoth Mine Road. The route continues to Canyon Lake where you can ride the **Dolly Steamboat** through the inner waterways of the "Junior Grand Canyon" and learn more about plants and animals that live near the lake. Next stop, **Tortilla Flat, Arizona** (480–984–1776; www.tortillaflataz.com), population six, where the combination restaurant, motel, saloon, gift shop, grocery store, and U.S. Post Office is a convenient place to stop for a burger, chili, or an ice-cream cone.

I recommend that you contact a tour company if you'd like to get a close-up look at the Superstitions. Many hikers and prospectors have died because they didn't know the terrain well enough.

Traveling south from Apache Junction on US 60 takes you to **Superior** (520–689–5752; www.superior-arizona.com). Known by several names since the 1880s, the town was a mining center for about one hundred years. Lately Superior has earned a bit of a reputation as a movie set, serving as the setting for *The Prophecy,* a horror flick, and Oliver Stone's *U-Turn*. Word has it that Stone selected the town because it retained a 1950s ambience, and set designers left behind many of the facades they created on the town's main street. Today visitors make the trek to Superior to tour the nearby **Boyce Thompson Arboretum** (520–689–2811 or 520–689–2723). The arboretum contains more than 1,500 species of plants, as well as many birds and animals. Its specialties are desert and arid-land plants, including cacti and wildflowers of many colorful varieties. Created in 1924, it's the oldest and largest botanical garden in Arizona. There are more than six hiking trails throughout the grounds. Ranging from easy half-mile strolls to moderately rugged 3-mile hikes, these trails are especially popular in the fall and winter when the mild weather in this area encourages people to enjoy the great outdoors. In the vicinity is **Picket Post Mountain,** where in 1927 Colonel Boyce Thompson built a home into the stony face of a cliff. The house is now a museum, maintained just as Thompson, a copper magnate, left it. It's open from 8:00 A.M. to 5:00 P.M. daily. Dogs are permitted if leashed, and picnic tables are available. Admission is $7.50 for adults and $3.00 for children ages 5 to 12.

Also nearby are the **Apache Tears Caves.** The caves contain many fine examples of black obsidian, known in the Southwest as "Apache tears." This dense, glassy volcanic rock is popular in many Southwestern jewelry designs. Visitors can chisel off an Apache tear for a small fee. The name Apache Tear comes from a heartbreaking story. Just south of Superior is **Apache Leap** in Queen Creek Canyon. (You can reach this location by taking Highway 177 south from Superior and watching for the turnoff to Apache Leap.) According to legend, it was on this site some 120 years ago that a cavalry detachment from Camp Pinal cornered seventy-five Apache warriors. Rather than submit to capture, they threw themselves off the cliff. Upon hearing of the warriors' fate, the women of the tribe cried tears that turned to stone. Despite the tragic history of this spot, today it's a good place to drive to for a get-away-from-it-all picnic lunch.

If your next destination is the Tucson area, take Highway 177 south and you'll soon enter the tri-city area known as **SMOR** (San Manuel, Mammoth, Oracle Region). This area has a long history as a mining and ranching community, though today SMOR is better known for recreational offerings such as hiking, horseback riding, and bird-watching. North of Oracle on U.S. Highway 79 is the **Tom Mix Monument,** a stone pillar topped by a metal silhouette of a riderless horse. This vaguely macabre statue commemorates the approximate spot where silent movie Western hero Tom Mix was killed when he drove his 1937 Cord automobile off the road. The horse (Tony, Mix's favorite mount) has been stolen from the monument several times over the years, so don't be too surprised if it seems to have moseyed off!

Also near the SMOR is the famous (or, depending upon your perspective, infamous) **Biosphere II** (520–838–6200; www.bio2.edu) on State Route 77. The Biosphere II was originally designed by a team of researchers put together by Texas billionaire Edward Bass to create a totally self-contained environment in the form of a giant, pyramid-shaped greenhouse that could be used to study how ecosystems work and also provide a prototype for civilizations of the future (i.e., on other planets). Plagued by personnel problems and dogged by allegations of cultism, the project, which planned to seal a group of researchers inside the facility for two years, became the butt of many jokes. Even the TV series *Cheers* made fun of the concept by putting character Lilith inside such a facility.

In 1993 things came to a head when members of Biosphere II's scientific advisory board resigned, citing concerns over imprecise experiments. The following year, Bass, who reportedly had paid $150 million to build Biosphere II, stepped in and removed key members of the management team. Since then, the new management team, a subsidiary of Columbia University, has turned away from the concept of sealing crew members inside the five-story, 7.2-million-cubic-foot greenhouse. Instead they've concentrated on specific experiments dealing with assessing methods of irrigation, creating air-purification products that can be used in homes and commercial buildings, and pursuing other proj-

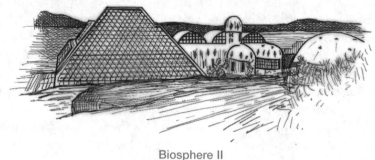

Biosphere II

ects that produce tangible results. Today visitors can tour portions of the facility and see environments ranging from a tropical rainforest to a coral reef. You can drop in at a Biosphere II laboratory and see actual experiments or shop in the gift shop and eat lunch or dinner in the restaurant. There also is a twenty-seven-suite hotel—the Inn at the Biosphere—in the neighborhood. Admission to the Biosphere is currently $19.95 for adults and $12.95 for children ages 6 to 12 for a guided tour. It's open from 9:00 A.M. to 4:00 P.M. daily.

Nearby **Oracle** has a long history as a mining community. In fact in 1902 Buffalo Bill Cody staked out a gold claim in this area and for a while lived in a cabin above one of his mines. He squandered a large portion of his fortune on what was essentially a hoax (there was virtually no gold, and the tungsten ore he found was not enough for him to recoup his investment).

Like many Arizona towns Oracle has a dedicated group of artists of various disciplines and abilities. The artists range from potters to landscape painters to bronze sculptors. They host an annual weekend **Oracle Festival of Fine Art** (520–896–9200), usually in March. During the festival there are tours of the artists' studios, art discussions, and performing arts events. Oracle has a number of galleries and shops that display local artists' work year-round. For information on the SMOR area, contact San Manuel/Mammoth/Oracle Chamber of Commerce (520–385–9322), P.O. Box 416, San Manuel, AZ 85631.

Another off-the-beaten-path route to Tucson is through **Florence,** home to **Pinal County Historical Museum** (520–868–4382) and the McFarland Historical State Park. Florence is also a stone's throw away from such attractions as a group of petroglyphs and coke ovens off Kelvin Road, which is off a four-wheel-drive trail over private property. Check with Greater Florence Chamber of Commerce (520–868–9433 or 800–437–9433, P.O. Box 929, Florence, AZ 85232). In town the visitors center is at 291 Bailey Street, in the historic district.

The **McFarland Historical State Park** (520–868–5216), on the corner of Main and Ruggles in Florence, was named after Ernest W. McFarland, the only

American known to have served his state as an elected official in all three branches of government. It's the site of the *first Pinal County Courthouse,* an adobe block building constructed in 1878 that housed prisoners and provided offices for lawmen until 1891, when a larger facility was constructed. It was quite a hellhole in the early days. Before improvements to the building in 1882, the jail was a windowless adobe cubicle with one entrance that was covered by burlap. Prisoners were chained to a boulder buried in the center of the jail. Visitors can see the improved 1882 jail, the sheriff's office, and the court recorder's office. A nearby archive houses exhibits related to the governmental career of Ernest McFarland. McFarland Historical State Park is open for self-guided tours Thursday through Monday from 8:00 A.M. to 5:00 P.M.

The *second Pinal County Courthouse,* built in 1891, still exists as well. Located on Pinal between 11th and 13th Streets, it is a large, rather ornate red brick building with a clock tower. Incidentally, this is the courthouse where Pearl Hart, the last known stagecoach robber in the United States, was tried in 1899 and sentenced to five years in the Territorial Prison at Yuma. Guided walking tours of Florence's historic downtown district can be arranged by calling (520) 868–5216.

trivia

If any of the terrain around Florence looks to you like Martians could land and feel right at home, you're not alone in your opinion. The 1953 George Pal–produced film *War of the Worlds* was partially shot here.

If you'd like to hang around Florence for a while, check into the *Inn at Rancho Sonora* (520–868–8000 or 800–205–6817; www.ranchosonora.com) at 9198 North Highway 79, a 1930s adobe guest ranch. The rooms have been renovated and redecorated in Western fashion, but with the modern comfort conveniences of dual-paned windows and air conditioning. The inn also has a pool and a hot tub. Rates start at $59.

From Florence you can take Highway 287 west and Highway 87 south to the *Casa Grande National Monument* (520–723–3172; www.nps.gov/cagr). Casa Grande was a Hohokam settlement built around A.D. 1150. Theories abound, including everything from family dwelling to astronomical observatory, regarding the purpose for the large adobe structure that still stands here in the midst of the desert. It's one of the best-preserved sites of its kind in the state. Stop by the visitors center to get a brochure and take the self-guided tour. If you have the time, stay for one of the informative talks given by a park ranger on the history of the Casa Grande ruins. The visitors center is open daily from 8:00 A.M. to 5:00 P.M. Admission is $5.00 for adults.

The major annual event for this area is the **O'Odham Tash,** a celebration of Native American culture usually held in February. Festivities are open to the general public. You'll hear traditional music of several varieties, including Waila, a kind of rock-and-roll polka. Watch colorful ceremonial dancers compete for awards and browse through arts and crafts, including baskets, rugs, paintings, and jewelry. You can also sample O'Odham cuisine. An all-Indian rodeo rounds out the events. Contact the Casa Grande Chamber of Commerce (800–916–1515; www.casagrandechamber.org) for more information.

Continuing on Highway 87 south takes you past farming communities that sprout forth like an emerald beard across the stubbly face of the desert. Highway 87 merges into I–10 a few miles south of the tiny town of Picacho. Just east of the town is **Picacho Peak** (520–466–3183), a craggy, saguaro-dotted mountain that in the spring is covered with wildflowers. This is the site of the Battle of Picacho Pass, Arizona's only Civil War battle (military purists insist it was only a skirmish).

In any case, the military engagement took place on April 15, 1862, when Union troops commanded by Lt. James Barrett fired upon Confederates led by Lt. Jack Swilling. This is the same Jack Swilling who later was instrumental in digging Phoenix's irrigation canals. On the day of the Battle of Picacho Pass, however, he was intent only on pursuing victory for the Southern cause. In the ensuing action, Barrett and two Union privates were killed. Fearing that more Union troops were on the way, Swilling's forces retreated. That was a wise move because within a few days the Union Army marched through Picacho Pass on the way to Tucson. Each spring (usually March), reenactors stage this battle as well as scenes of frontier life. Picacho Peak is a state park, with facilities including restrooms, picnic areas, campgrounds, and an easy to moderately difficult nature trail.

Places to Stay in Central Arizona

GLENDALE

Best Western Phoenix/Glendale,
7116 North 59th Avenue;
(623) 939–9431 or
(800) 333–7172;
www.bestwestern.com
Near Old Town Glendale and
Catlin Court. Inexpensive.

MESA

Marriott Phoenix Mesa Hotel and Convention Center,
200 North Centennial Way;
(480) 898–8300 or
(800) 228–9290.
Not far from downtown with
273 spacious rooms. Inexpensive to moderate.

PHOENIX

Hyatt Regency Phoenix,
122 North Second Street;
(602) 252–1234 or
(800) 233–1234;
www.hyattphoenix.com
Right downtown across from
the Civic Plaza with 712
rooms and suites. Rooftop
revolving restaurant for great
view of the entire Valley of
the Sun. Moderate.

WEB SITES FOR CENTRAL ARIZONA

**Apache Junction Area
Chamber of Commerce**
www.apachejunctioncoc.com

Arizona Department of Tourism
www.arizonaguide.com

**Carefree/Cave Creek
Chamber of Commerce**
www.carefree-cavecreek.com

Chandler Chamber of Commerce
www.chandlerchamber.com

Fountain Hills Chamber of Commerce
www.fountainhillschamber.com

Glendale Chamber of Commerce
www.visitglendale.com

**Greater Casa Grande
Chamber of Commerce**
www.casagrandechamber.org

**Greater Phoenix Convention
and Visitors Bureau**
www.phoenixcvb.com

Mesa Chamber of Commerce
www.mesachamber.org

**Northwest Valley Chamber
of Commerce**
www.northwestvalley.com

Peoria Chamber of Commerce
www.peoriachamber.com

**Scottsdale Area Chamber
of Commerce**
www.scottsdalecvb.com

**Southwest Valley Chamber
of Commerce**
www.southwestvalleychamber.org

**Tempe Convention and
Visitors Bureau**
www.tempecvb.com

Wickenburg Chamber of Commerce
www.wickenburgchamber.com

Pointe South Mountain Resort,
7777 South Pointe Parkway;
(602) 438–9000 or
(877) 800–4888;
www.pointesouthmtn.com
This luxury resort at South Mountain has championship golf, an athletic club and spa, six restaurants and The Oasis—"Arizona's Ultimate Water Adventure."
Moderate to expensive.

SCOTTSDALE

Caleo Resort and Spa,
4925 North Scottsdale Road;
(480) 945–7666 or
(800) 528–7867;
www.caleoresort.com
This lovely resort is located in downtown Scottsdale near the art galleries and shops in the Old Town District. Expensive.

The Phoenician,
6000 East Camelback Road;
(480) 941–8200 or
(800) 888–8234;
www.thephoenician.com
Located at the base of Camelback Mountain, this renowned resort offers a golf course, a spa, a tennis garden, nine pools and eleven restaurants. Expensive.

TEMPE

Tempe Ramada,
1701 West Baseline Road;
(480) 413–1188 or
(800) 633–8300;
www.ramada.com
Right off I–10, near Peterson House Museum and not too far from downtown Tempe. Inexpensive.

Places to Eat in Central Arizona

GLENDALE

Haus Murphy's,
5819 West Glendale Avenue;
(623) 939–2480.
German food on the main street of Old Town Glendale. Inexpensive to moderate.

MESA

Mango's Mexican Cafe,
44 West Main Street;
(480) 464–5700.
Another Mexican possibility in the heart of downtown shopping not far from Mesa Southwest Museum. Inexpensive to moderate.

PHOENIX

Fry Bread House,
4140 North Seventh Avenue;
(602) 351–2345.
This small downtown restaurant has some of the best Indian fry bread in town. Inexpensive.

Red Devil Italian Restaurant,
3102 East McDowell Road;
(602) 267–1036.
This Italian restaurant is often voted the best pizzeria in town. Inexpensive to moderate.

SCOTTSDALE

5 & Diner,
9069 East Indian Bend Road;
(480) 949–1957.
In Scottsdale Pavilions Mall off Pima Road. Fifties diner with jukeboxes playing the oldies. Breakfasts, burgers, and blue-plate specials. Inexpensive.

Southern Arizona

The Southwestern Corner

Yuma (928–783–0071 or 800–293–0071; www.visityuma.com), on Interstate 8, exists among several worlds: It's only a few minute's drive from either the California state line or the Mexican border. It's also in the midst of a desert area, yet it's bordered by the Colorado River and has more than 150,000 acres dedicated to agriculture.

Despite its dichotomies, **Yuma** has a long, colorful history as a distinctive part of Arizona. It was originally named Colorado City (after the river) and then Arizona City, finally taking the name of the Native American tribe that had long called the area home. Puns were inevitable, and a few years back the suggestion was made that the town adopt the slogan "You'll Love Our Sense of Yuma."

In the nineteenth century the town was a crossing point for the famous Mormon Battalion as well as Kit Carson and California gold seekers. In the 1850s the invention of the shallow-draft steamboat made Yuma a major stop on the Colorado River for boats taking supplies to army posts or mining camps. Its territorial prison, built in 1875, housed some of the

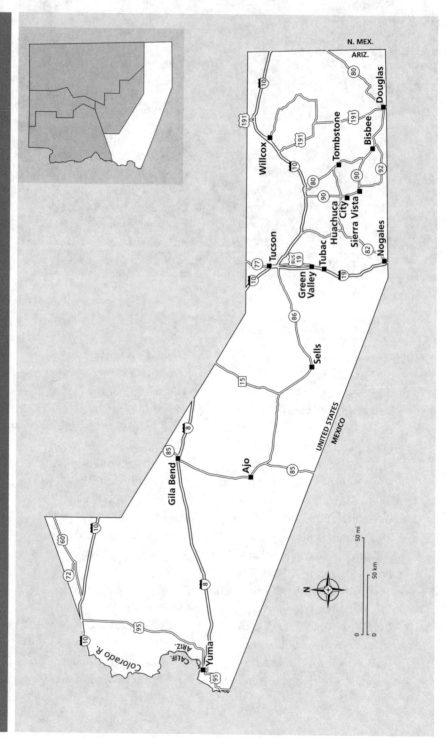

SOUTHERN ARIZONA

West's most notorious desperados, and in modern times the town has become not only an important agricultural center (labor organizer Cesar Chavez grew up here) but also the site for a Marine Corps Air Station and an Army Proving Ground.

For history buffs, Yuma has a number of interesting museums. The **Yuma Crossing State Historic Park** (928–329–0471) at Fourth Avenue, located beyond the railroad tracks along the river behind City Hall, was a vital distribution point for military equipment from 1864 to 1883. Several original buildings, including the quartermaster's office and the commanding officer's quarters, have been restored. The depot is operated as a living history museum, complete with authentically costumed guides. It's open daily from 9:00 A.M. to 5:00 P.M. Admission is $3.00 for adults.

The Yuma Territorial Prison State Park (928–783–4771) at One Prison Hill Road at the east end of First Avenue is another popular attraction. No film about the Old West is complete without at least one reference to this infamous Iron Bar Hotel. Historians argue over whether the prison, built in 1876, was actually a "hellhole," as it's often depicted. Certainly inmates would have found it cramped, dark, and hot. Yet it had one of the first libraries in the state, electric fans, and many brief prison sentences. There are video presentations on the history of the prison every 35 minutes beginning at 8:00 A.M. Visit the prison on Sunday October through April, and you can watch Old West shoot-outs staged by the Yuma Vigilantes. It's open from 8:00 A.M. to 5:00 P.M. Admission is $4.00 for adults.

One of the strangest bits of history in the area is the **McPhaul Bridge,** 18 miles north of Yuma on Highway 95. The bridge, sometimes referred to locally as the "swinging bridge to nowhere," was built in 1929 as a route across the Gila River. When the Gila was rerouted for agricultural projects, the bridge was

AUTHOR'S TOP PICKS IN SOUTHERN ARIZONA

Arizona-Sonora Desert Museum	Ramsey Canyon Preserve
Kitt Peak National Observatory	Bisbee shops and galleries
Tanque Verde Guest Ranch	Chiricahua Mountains
Mission San Xavier del Bac	Club Congress
Tubac	Sabino Canyon
Kartchner Caverns State Park	

JANUARY

Tucson Gem, Mineral and Fossil Showcase

Tucson
The world's largest marketplace gem and mineral show.
(800) 638–8350

Wings over Willcox

Willcox
Sandhill Crane Celebration, guided tours, includes a "hawk stalk," seminars, workshops, field trips, bird-watching.
Third weekend in January.
(520) 384–2272 or (800) 200–2272

FEBRUARY

Territorial Days

Benson
Crafts, auto show, music, dances, games, reenactments, auction, exhibits, contests, balloon festival.
(520) 586–2842

Cochise Cowboy Poetry and Music Gathering

Sierra Vista
Storytellers, reciters, singers and musicians, nationally recognized artists.
Second weekend in February.
(520) 459–3868 or (800) 288–3861

Festival of the Arts

Tubac
Juried artists, entertainment, and demonstrations.
(520) 398–2704

Arizona State Museum's Southwest Indian Art Fair

Tucson
More than 200 Indian artists displaying their work.
(520) 626–8381

La Fiesta de los Vaqueros

Tucson
More than eighty years old, this PRCA rodeo is America's largest outdoor, midwinter rodeo.
(520) 741–2233 or (800) 964–5662

Jaycees Silver Spur Rodeo Parade

Yuma
For more than fifty years, the largest in Yuma.
(928) 344–5451

MARCH

O'odham Day Celebration

Ajo
Tohono O'odham basketweaving demonstration and storytelling.
The third Saturday in March.
(520) 387–6849

Territorial Days

Tombstone
Arizona fire cart championship races, all-pet parade, and gunfight reenactments.
(520) 457–9317 or 888–457–3929

APRIL

La Vuelta de Bisbee

Bisbee
Top amateur men and women cyclists from throughout the United States and abroad wind up and down the roads of historic Old Bisbee.
(520) 432–5421 or (877) 424–7234

Pima County Fair

Tucson
(520) 762–9100

MAY

Wyatt Earp Days
Tombstone
Gunfights, public hanging, saloon girls, fashion show, parade, dancing, live country/western band.
(520) 457–9317 or (888) 457–3929

Waila Festival
Tucson
Dance performances and craft demonstrations by the Tohono O'odham.
(520) 628–5774

Cinco de Mayo
Tucson
A celebration of the Mexican holiday commemorating the Puebla battle of May 5, 1862, against France. Ethnic dancing, music, crafts, and food.
(520) 292–9326

JUNE

Diá de San Juan Fiesta
Tucson
A celebration of the "Season of Monsoon Rains" complete with a traditional procession and blessing, charros (cowboys) and escaramuzas (trick horseback riders), food, and live entertainment.
(520) 792–4806

AUGUST

Southwest Wings Birding Festival
Sierra Vista
Field trips, displays, lectures, bat stalks, owl prowls, displays, arts, and crafts.
(866) 224–7233

Vigilante Day
Tombstone
Shoot-outs, hangings, concert, chili cook-off, saloon girls.
(520) 457–9317 or (888) 457–3929

Peach Mania Festival
Willcox
"U-pick" peaches
(520) 384–2084

SEPTEMBER

Annual Labor Day Rodeo
Sonoita
Western rodeo complete with barrel racing, a wild horse race, team roping events, and mutton busting at the Sonoita Fairgrounds.
(520) 455–5553

Brewery Gulch Days
Bisbee
Horseshoe and waterball tournament, kiddie carnival, live music, bed races, pet parade, Miz Ol' Biz contest, mining games, cake walk.
(520) 432–5421 or (877) 424–7234

Rendezvous of Gunfighters
Tombstone
Shows in the O.K. Corral by the best western groups from around the United States.
(520) 457–9317 or (888) 457–3929).

Santa Cruz County Fair
Sonoita
Old-fashioned carnival, exhibits, and live entertainment.
(520) 287–3685

OCTOBER

Butterfield Overland Stage Days
Benson
Celebration of overland mail route from St. Louis to San Francisco, reenactments, stage rides, arts and crafts, entertainment, dances, car show.
(520) 586–2842

(Continued on page 126)

TOP ANNUAL EVENTS IN SOUTHERN ARIZONA

Gem and Mineral Show
Bisbee
Dealers, display of rare minerals, outdoor show, field trips.
(520) 432–5421 or (877) 424–7234

Fiber Arts Festival
Bisbee
Fashion show, fiber animals such as sheep and llamas, displays, demonstrations, workshops, guest speakers.
(520) 432–5421

Bisbee 1000—The Great Stairclimb
Bisbee
A fun and popular physical fitness challenge for all ages and levels of fitness. Held in October.
(520) 432–5421 or (877) 424–7234

Fall Festival
Patagonia
Juried arts and crafts, country western, bluegrass, folk, mariachi, Latin jazz, rock & roll, Saturday night dance, western events. Second weekend in October.
(520) 394–0060 or (888) 794–0060

Festival of Color
Sierra Vista
Annual hot-air balloon rally.
(520) 417–6960

Helldorado Days
Tombstone
Oldest celebration, with shoot-outs, fashion show, and street entertainment. Third weekend in October.
(520) 457–2550 or (888) 457–3929

La Fiesta de los Chiles
Tucson
International cuisine, entertainment, music, artisans and crafts people.
(520) 326–9686

Rex Allen Days
Willcox
Celebration of singing cowboy star Rex Allen. First weekend in October.
(520) 384–2272 or (800) 200–2272

left stranded, straddling only desert. The structure, which resembled a scaled-down version of the Golden Gate bridge, is named after Harry McPhaul, a former territorial prison guard who ventured into the mining industry and once had claims in this area.

See Yuma County by train by boarding the *Yuma Valley Railway* (928–783–3456) at the end of Madison Avenue. A diesel engine pulls a restored 1922 Pullman Coach along the banks of the Colorado while a historian/guide tells passengers about the area. The railroad operates from October through June.

Explore the Colorado River with *Yuma River Tours* (928–783–4400; www.yumarivertours.com). Group tours and day trips on a small cruiser are offered. Lunch is included. A more leisurely method of seeing the western edge of Yuma is aboard a paddleboat. *The Colorado King I Paddleboat* (928–782–2412), which is also owned and operated by Yuma River Tours, is a replica of the craft that used to cruise the Colorado River in Mark Twain's time. Dining tours are available. The paddleboat tours operate October through June.

NOVEMBER

Festival of Lights
Bisbee
Live nativity in historic Bisbee.
(520) 432–6000

Historic Home Tour
Bisbee
(520) 432–5421 or (520) 432–5446

**Colorado River Crossing
Balloon Festival**
Yuma
Sunrise balloon liftoffs, sunset balloon
glow and fireworks, entertainment.
(928) 343–1715

DECEMBER

Luminaria Nights
Tucson
Holiday lights, music by local groups
and choirs at the Tucson Botanical
Gardens.
(520) 326–9686

Fourth Avenue Street Fair
Tucson
Arts and crafters, community stage,
entertainers, and "Kidstreat."
(520) 624–5004 or (800) 933–2477

La Fiesta de Tumacácori
Tumacácori
Entertainment and crafts, folklorico and
Native American dancing, Mexican,
Indian, old-time Arizona music.
(520) 398–2341

Christmas Apple Festival
Willcox
Judged arts and craft show, bazaar, craft
demos, Santa Claus, tree lighting ceremony, entertainment, raffles, door prizes.
(520) 384–2272 or (800) 200–2272

Numerous restaurant chains populate Yuma, but so do longtime family-operated businesses. One of these is **Lutes Casino** (928–782–2192) at 221 Main Street, which is the oldest continuing pool hall and domino parlor in the state. Lutes offers sandwiches and other fast-food items in a somewhat wacky atmosphere.

Another is the **Yuma Landing Restaurant** (928–782–7427) at 195 South Fourth Avenue. Along with serving up a hearty menu of homemade meals, this landmark restaurant is decorated with historical photographs and is located near the site of the monument marking the landing site of Robert G. Fowler, who touched down at this location on October 25, 1911, with his Wright model B biplane—the first airplane to land on Arizona soil.

Many national chains are on standby to house road warriors visiting Yuma. Among the top choices are **Best Western Coronado Motor Hotel** (928–783–4453 or 800–780–7234; www.bestwestern.com) at 233 4th Avenue, which offers rooms with a refrigerator and microwave. The **Best Western Inn Suites Hotel**

Sand Dune Stand-ins

Arizona's deserts are among the world's most verdant, so visitors looking for a Sahara-like landscape will find more vegetation than bargained for. However, a sandier setting exists west of Yuma. Travel west on Interstate 8 to Gray's Well exit and follow the frontage road. You'll wind up surrounded by sand dunes that have served as stand-ins for Middle Eastern dunes in many TV shows and films, dating back to about 1921 when Valentino's *The Sheik* was filmed here. All three versions of *Beau Geste* were at least partially lensed in these dunes, as well as the Jimmy Stewart movie *The Flight of the Phoenix*. (At the very end of the film, a patched-together plane heads over these dunes and disappears from sight. In real life it crashed just out of camera range, killing the pilot.) The tremendously popular George Lucas film *Star Wars* was partially filmed here, as was the science fiction hit *Stargate*. There are no real markers or landmarks here to photograph—just miles of sand—so bring your imagination and maybe a few props like a light saber or your pet Ewok.

(928–783–8341) at 1450 Castle Dome Avenue features complimentary continental breakfast. Nearby the ***Shilo Inn*** (928–782–9511 or 800–222–2244; www.shilo inns.com) at 1550 South Castle Dome Avenue has a free buffet breakfast.

Head east on Interstate 8 to ***Gila Bend*** (928–683–2002; www.gilabendaz.org). The town got its name from the sharp bend in the Gila River that used to occur at this point before the river was diverted for agricultural purposes.

Today visitors to Gila Bend can step back into history in a variety of ways. Just west of town is petroglyph-covered ***Painted Rocks.*** You can reach this wildlife area by taking I–8 to exit 102. The exact meaning of these 1,000-year-old Hohokam etchings is unknown. People, reptiles, and geometric doodles cover the black basalt rocks. There's a recreational lake and a picnic area here, so if you have the time, pack a lunch, bring a sketch pad, and try to decode all the combinations of the primitive alphabet depicted on Painted Rocks. The ***Agua Caliente Hotel and Hot Springs*** ruins are also located just west of town. To reach them, exit from I–8 onto Sentinel Road. The former hotel and surrounding adobe buildings—constructed to take advantage of the area's status as a stage stop as well as the supposed therapeutic values of the water—are still partially standing. You can pose by a crumbling adobe wall and then send copies of the picture to your friends and family. Tell them you've picked out your retirement home. You won't be able to relax in the hot springs, however; they dried up years ago.

In downtown Gila Bend is the ***Gila Bend Historical Museum*** (928–683–2002) at 644 West Pima Street. Dedicated to the preservation of archaeological and historical finds, it includes information gathered from the Hohokam Ceremonial Platform that's near town. The platform dates from A.D. 800; there are plans to re-excavate and open up some of the area as a state park. The museum is open daily from 8:00 A.M. to 4:00 P.M.; donations accepted. The museum is also the visitor information center.

Gila Bend is home to several unusual dwellings. The former **Stout Hotel,** at the corner of Pima and Capitol Streets, is a poured concrete building constructed around 1929 as a first-rate hotel for railroad and automobile travelers. It had air conditioning and steam heat and an ice plant in the basement. In its heyday its many famous guests included Clark Gable and Carole Lombard. Incidentally, the pair appears to have been quite fond of Arizona, having been on the guest lists of several other hotels statewide, including the Monte Vista in Flagstaff and Phoenix's San Carlos Hotel and Arizona Biltmore Resort. Now part of the hotel is being used as a general store. The rest is awaiting restoration, but no date has been set to begin yet.

Across an *arroyo* (a streambed to non-Southwesterners), just west of the town's ice plant, is a curious-looking structure built of railroad ties. Constructed in the midst of the Great Depression by **Harvey Brown** (aka "Jungle Jim" because of the pith helmet he wore), this once was a store that sold everything from sandwiches to luggage. Brown's customers were vagrants like himself, and, ironically, the building—whose exact ownership is in question—is now being used by squatters. If you're interested in twentieth-century U.S. history, this unusual building is worth a visit because it represents a typical American's boot-strap response to hard times.

The Oatman Massacre

South of the hotel ruins on Sentinel Road is the site of the *Oatman Massacre.* A large, white cross on a nearby plateau stands as a monument to the Oatman family. On March 19, 1851, Royce and Mary Ann Oatman and their seven children were part of a Mormon pilgrimage to the Arizona/California border area. They were camped on this spot when a group of Yavapai Indians approached and asked for food and tobacco. Royce complied but, fearful that he wouldn't have enough for his family, refused the Yavapais' request for seconds. The family, with the exception of fifteen-year-old Lorenzo, fourteen-year-old Olive, and her younger sister Mary Ann, was brutally slain. Lorenzo survived by playing dead, while the two girls were taken as captives. Mary Ann died soon after, and Olive was sold to the Mohave Indians and later ransomed back into white society (in a bizarre twist, she became a celebrity as a result of her ordeal, though her story was largely used as anti–Native American propaganda). The actual site of the killings is just east of the roadway, but it can only be reached by a four-wheel-drive vehicle.

Only a handful of restaurants operate in Gila Bend. A safe bet is a stop at one of the fast-food eateries that beckon hungry travelers or the twenty-four-hour coffee shop at the **Best Western Space Age Lodge** (928–683–2273 or 800–780–7234; www.bestwestern.com) at 401 East Pima Street. Whether you're hungry or not, you have to stop by the kitschy roadside inn. This priceless piece of Americana was built in the early 1960s and for years had a Sputnik-style satellite attached to the roof. It was remodeled in 2000, and a brand new spacecraft now sits atop the roof.

Less than an hour south of Gila Bend on Highway 85 is the tiny town of **Ajo** (520–387–7742). Though the word ajo (*ahh-ho*) is Spanish for garlic and also is used as a mild expletive, some historians believe the town's name actually originated from a similar-sounding Tohono O'Odham word for paint (ore from this area was used for making pigment). In any case Ajo was the oldest-known mine site in the state, and until the 1980s Phelps Dodge ran a sizable copper-mining operation out of here. The mines originally were made profitable during World War I by John C. Greenway, who also gets the credit for building the town's palm tree–shaded **Spanish Colonial Plaza** in Ajo's center. The plaza is a traditional town square created in a Spanish Colonial revival style. In the midst of the plaza is a large, green park and surrounding it are shops, restaurants, and two churches. To the south of the plaza is a Federated church built in 1926. Just north of that structure sits a mission-style Catholic church constructed in 1924.

A number of buildings from the 1920s and before are still standing. **Curley School,** southwest of the plaza on Vanand, was constructed in 1919. The **Train Depot,** directly northeast of the plaza, dates from 1915. **New Cornelia Hotel,** just east of Curley School, was constructed in 1916. The exteriors of these buildings, most done in Spanish Colonial revival, are easily incorporated into a walking tour. Stop by the Ajo Chamber of Commerce on Highway 85 just south of the Plaza and ask for a self-guided tour map.

A building that has been restored is now a charming bed-and-breakfast inn. The **Guest House Inn** (520–387–6133; www.guesthouseinn.biz) at 700 Guest House Road was built in 1925 by Phelps Dodge Corporation as a guest house for its visitors. The inn offers four rooms with private baths. The rooms are furnished in Southwestern style, some with Victorian antiques. Breakfast is hearty, and from the patio you can watch a variety of native birds, including quail and cactus wrens. Rates are $89 for double occupancy. Breakfast is included.

Ajo today is one part retirement community, one part snowbird haven, and one part bedroom community for people who don't mind the two-hour commute to Phoenix or Tucson.

Ajo's gorgeous mountain views and charming Old World architecture are certainly enchanting. For some, however, Ajo is merely a stopping-off point on the way to **Organ Pipe Cactus National Monument** (520–387–6849; www .nps.gov/orpi), located south off Highway 85. If you were to take a giant octopus, turn it upside down, and plant it in the dirt, you would have a rough idea of what an organ pipe cactus looks like. In color and form these cacti resemble saguaros, but unlike saguaros, they have a half-dozen or more long arms reaching out from a center point. They are quite spectacular, especially during their blooming season. This fantastic show typically occurs at dusk from May through July.

The monument, by the way, is the starting point for notorious **El Camino del Diablo**—"the Devil's Highway." Over the years this stretch of godforsaken road has claimed numerous lives (more than 400 during the California gold rush). If you've got a four-wheel-drive vehicle, you may want to attempt this hot, bumpy, desolate trek that ends near Yuma. Because there are no road services along the way, plan on taking plenty of supplies (especially water) for you and your car. A safer, easier drive over a graded dirt road can be taken from near the Organ Pipe National Monument Visitor Center. Called the **Ajo Mountain Drive,** this 21-mile loop will take you through the Diablo Mountain Range to Mount Ajo and back to the visitors center. Along the way you'll see many varieties of cacti and desert creatures. In early spring you may see wildflowers, and in the late spring and early summer months, cactus blossoms dot the landscape.

After the monument take Highway 86 east toward Tucson. Just past the town of Sells, turn south onto Highway 386. This route will lead you 6,900 feet above sea level to the top of Kitt Peak in the Quinlan Mountains. The view, which takes in the neighboring Baboquivari Mountains and long stretches of Sonoran desert, is not only quite spectacular, but this is the site of **NOAO Kitt Peak National Observatory** (520–318–8726; www.noao.edu/kpno). The observatory is home to the world's largest solar telescope and the world's largest collection of telescopes. Though the climb up a paved road to the observatory is a bit steep, if you're interested in astronomy, it's worth the effort. The observatory's McMath solar telescope is the largest aperture solar telescope in the world. The visitors center gives one-hour-long guided tours to either the 4-meter or the 2.1-meter telescope as well as the solar telescope. Picnic grounds with barbecue grills also share space on the peak, and many tourists to Kitt Peak bring lunch. The observatory is located at 950 North Cherry, Tucson, and is open daily from 9:00 A.M. to 4:00 P.M. Tours are held at 10:00 A.M., 11:30 A.M., and 1:30 P.M. and cost $2.00 per person.

Downtown and East Tucson

From Kitt Peak, **Tucson** (520–624–1817 or 800–638–8350; www.visittucson.org) is the next major stop. Known as the Old Pueblo by locals, Tucson was founded in 1775 and is one of the oldest continually inhabited sites in the United States. Archeologists have discovered Hohokam artifacts that date back thousands of years. The community is an eclectic meld of Native American, Mexican, Spanish, Asian, and European cultures. Consider the fact that the town was founded on the site of an ancient Indian settlement by an Irishman serving in the Spanish Army!

You can reach Tucson from Kitt Peak by taking Highway 86 east. Once you reach the Tucson city limits, Highway 86 turns into Ajo Way. This puts you on the southwest side of the city. Take the Interstate 10 west freeway entrance from Ajo Way, and follow I–10 to the Broadway Boulevard exit. As you exit onto Broadway Boulevard, you'll be driving into downtown Tucson.

While you're cruising on I–10, you'll notice that Tucson is surrounded by mountains. To the west are the Tucson Mountains; to the east, the Rincons. Directly north are the Santa Catalinas, and down south are the Santa Ritas. Some of the peaks are snow-capped in winter, and **Mount Lemmon** in the Catalinas is known for being the southernmost skiable peak in the United States. The community of **Summerhaven** near the top of the mountain is renowned as a cool summer getaway only an hour's drive from the city. Unfortunately, a devastating forest fire burned down most of Summerhaven in June 2003. The town has since been undergoing construction. Despite the ravages of the Aspen Fire, the Mount Lemmon Ski Valley is open and offers a full season of snow sports. In the off-season the ski lift still runs, providing visitors with great views of the Catalinas (520–576–1400).

You can reach Mount Lemmon by taking I–10 north to Grant Road. Follow Grant Road until it reaches the far east side of Tucson. The road will become Tanque Verde Road. Stay on Tanque Verde Road until you reach the Catalina Highway. Turn left onto the Catalina Highway and drive north. The road will take you all the way up Mount Lemmon.

Mountains are very important to Tucsonans. For one thing, they provide landmarks. While you're traveling anywhere on the northwest side of Tucson, glance to the west and you'll notice a small peak with an "A"

trivia

Mount Lemmon, in the Santa Catalina Mountains north of Tucson, is the southernmost ski area in the continental United States and is the only mountain in the state named after the first woman who climbed it—Sara Plummer Lemmon.

whitewashed onto the rocks. **Sentinel Peak** ("A" Mountain to locals) is where the community called *Chukson* ("spring at the foot of the black mountain") began. The "A"—whitewashed every year by University of Arizona freshmen—has been a prominent monument

since 1914. There is a narrow, paved road that takes you all the way up Sentinel Peak. The view of the city from the peak, especially as the sun sets and lights begin to twinkle on, is quite spectacular. To reach Sentinel Peak take the Congress Street exit from I–10 and head west toward the peak. One note of caution: You probably don't want to linger on the peak after dark; Sentinel Peak at night becomes a favorite "parking" and hangout spot for high schoolers and others.

From Sentinel Peak you can reach the downtown by simply driving east on Congress Street. Less than two decades ago, downtown Tucson was dead: mortally wounded by new, centrally located shopping malls that forced the downtown department stores to close up. Downtown—roughly bounded by Fourth Avenue on the east, Church Street on the west, Council on the south, and Twelfth Street on the north—became a graveyard that no one wanted to whistle past after dark.

Today the once-silent area, together with neighboring districts such as the university area, is as vibrant and exciting as a jazz sax solo. The backbeat of the new downtown comes from the **Tucson Arts District,** (520–624–9977; www.tusconartsdistrict.org) which regularly holds **Downtown Nights** on Saturday evenings. During these events the cafes, art galleries, and boutique shops that line both sides of Congress Street, Broadway Boulevard, and other downtown routes stay open late. Street musicians play in the square, and you'll see everything from strolling Shakespearean actors to aging hippies selling tie-dyed T-shirts. For example, members of the Tucson Symphony Orchestra sometimes play short concerts aimed at getting kids interested in music. Seasonal **Art Walks,** held every Thursday from October through May, are another project aimed at getting locals and tourists into the downtown area. During the cooler winter months, from October through December, a local historian takes visitors on guided walking tours through the historic downtown neighborhoods on the second and fourth Saturdays of each month. You don't have to wait for a special day, however, to enjoy the galleries, performance venues, and cafes. The following paragraphs direct you to some of the area's most unique and interesting attractions.

Dinnerware Gallery (520–792–4503; www.dinnerwarearts.com) at 210 North Fourth Street always has interesting exhibits. One month the gallery might pair a sculptor who creates realistic images of people with an installation by a performance artist who will display a dining room set wrapped in newspaper. You'll discover as you visit these and the other downtown galleries that art in Tucson is very diverse. Some of it is heavily influenced by the Southwest. Much of it, however, is cosmopolitan. You'll see abstract and impressionist and pop art that would look right at home in a New York high-rise apartment as well as pieces that portray coyotes, Native Americans, Spanish missions, and other classic symbols of Tucson's history.

trivia

The sun shines 340 days a year in Tucson.

Within walking distance of the downtown galleries is the newly renovated and expanded *Tucson Museum of Art and Historic Block* (520–624–2333; www.tucsonarts.com) at 140 North Main Avenue. The museum, considered to be a mini-Guggenheim in its interior design, houses numerous permanent collections, including a large exhibit of pre-Columbian art. The courtyard in front of the museum is often used for events, including blues and jazz concerts as well as block-party-style fund-raisers for the museum. The museum is open Tuesday through Saturday from 10:00 A.M. to 4:00 P.M. and Sunday from noon to 4:00 P.M. Admission is $8.00 for adults, $6.00 for seniors, and $3.00 for children ages 13 and up. The museum offers free admission on the first Sunday of each month.

Across the courtyard from the Tucson Museum of Art is the historic *Stevens/Duffield House* at 150 North Main Avenue.

On the *Presidio* square are other historic houses—the *Romero House* from the 1860s, the *Corbett House* built in 1907, and *La Casa Cordova* built in the pre–and post–Civil War years. The *Fish House* (aka Goodman Pavilion) built in 1867 now houses a collection of Western art.

Tucson has truly emerged as a hot spot for haute cuisine. Great choices include *Barrio Bar & Grill* (520–629–0191) at 135 South Sixth Avenue, a down- town bistro, and *Anthony's in the Catalinas* at 6440 North Campbell (520–299–1771; www.anthonysinthecatalinas.com), which features more than 1,700 wines and a Continental menu.

As you might suspect of a town located smack-dab in the heart of Old West territory, quite a few rough-and-tumble incidents took place in the downtown area. At the corner of Church and Pennington Streets, a couple of blocks south of North Main Avenue, a bizarre shooting involving two prominent members of the community occurred in 1891. C. Handy, the chief surgeon for the Southern Pacific Railroad (and one-time chancellor for the nascent University of Arizona) shot and killed Francis J. Heney, the lawyer representing Handy's wife in their divorce.

A few blocks farther south on Main Avenue and Simpson Street beyond the Convention Center, in the neighborhood known as **Barrio Historico,** stands an adobe wall with a plaque dedicated to **El Tiradito** ("the little castaway"). One version of the story goes that many years ago, a young sheepherder who lived with his wife and his in-laws on a ranch outside of town fell in love with his wife's mother. While meeting in town for an adulterous liaison, they were caught by the sheepherder's father-in-law, who killed the young man and buried him. Because the sheepherder was buried in unconsecrated ground, he was forever doomed as a sinner—a castaway. Today, locals light candles and leave hand-printed prayers at this wishing shrine. It is said that if your candle burns the whole night through, your dream will come true.

Next to El Tiradito is **El Minuto Cafe** (520–882–4145; www.elminuto cafe.com) at 354 South Main Avenue. It's a very popular Mexican restaurant featuring authentic versions of Sonoran cuisine. During weekdays it's difficult to get a table at lunch. It's equally busy in the evening if there's an event at the nearby Tucson Convention Center or the Arizona Theatre Company Temple of Music and Art.

A brief jog to the north is **Old Town Artisans** (520–623–6024 or 800–782–8072; www.oldtownartisans.com) at 201 North Court Avenue. It's a collection of fine art, jewelry, and crafts shops that sits in the area of the original Spanish presidio. Two front rooms contain adobe blocks dating back to the 1860s. The complex also includes **La Cocina** (520–622–0351), with indoor and outdoor dining, and a java joint known as **Presidio Coffee Company.**

On Congress Avenue there's lots to see and do. You might want to peruse the many antiques and secondhand shops. At the end of the street is the historic **Hotel Congress** (520–622–8848 or 800–722–8848; www.hotelcongress .com) at 311 East Congress Street. A funky sort of place, the hotel provides basic accommodations and houses the **Club Congress,** which features live music on weekends (i.e., current alternative). The **Cup Cafe,** where you can get gourmet coffee and a bite to eat, is also within the hotel complex. The club and cafe are considered the "be-seen" hot spots in downtown Tucson.

At 330 South Scott Avenue is the **Arizona Theatre Company Temple of Music and Art** (520–622–2823; www.arizonatheater.org), a beautiful complex that includes a cabaret theater, a main auditorium, a cafe, and an art gallery. Performances by the Arizona Theatre Company are held here, as are concerts and other cultural events. The Arizona Theatre Company's season is usually September through May. Tickets may be purchased online.

About a three-minute drive east of downtown is **Fourth Avenue** (Merchants Association; 520–624–5004; www.fourthavenue.org), a lively strip of real estate that has the atmosphere (and the history) of San Francisco's Haight-Ashbury neighborhood. In the 1960s and 1970s, the businesses in this sleepy residential area were dominated by head shops and smoky bars where (nearly) free love and illegal drugs flowed. Today 4th Avenue has really cleaned up its act. The eclectic mix of shops includes *Bison Witches Bar and Deli* (520–740–1541), a restaurant and bar; *Native Seed Search* (520–622–5561; www.nativeseeds .org); and *Arroyo Design* (520–884–1012), a shop featuring custom furniture made from desert wood including mesquite and ironwood. Other shops specialize in antique clothing, such as *How Sweet It Was* (520–623–9845; www.howsweetitwas.com) at 419 North Fourth Avenue and *Desert Vintage & Costume* (520–620–1570) at 636 North Fourth Avenue.

Lots of restaurants to choose from guarantee that you won't go hungry. *Carusos Restaurant* (520–624–5765) at 434 North Fourth Avenue has been serving Italian food to Tucsonans for about fifty years. Across the street, *Delectables* (520–884–9289; www.delectables.com) at 533 North Fourth Avenue offers a variety of gourmet items, including fruit and cheese plates. If your sweet tooth gets the better of you, stop at the corner of Sixth Street and Fourth Avenue to find the *Chocolate Iguana* on Fourth Avenue (520–798–1211) at 500 North Fourth Avenue. It sells all sorts of candy, baked goods, and coffee drinks. It also has an interesting selection of greeting cards.

Fourth Avenue is best known locally for its two annual weekend street fairs—one usually runs in early December, and one is in late March or early April. Besides arts, crafts, and food booths (where you can sample some wonderful Tohono O'Odham frybread), the fairs feature street entertainers and representatives from all sorts of worthy human rights/animal rights groups. During a typical street fair, Fourth Avenue is blocked off between University Boulevard and Ninth Street, and exhibitors' booths are set up down the center of the avenue. Additionally, the sidewalks are taken over by people doing face painting and hair weaving and musicians playing everything from folk standards to doo-wop ballads. These events are extremely popular and draw Tucsonans of every background and visitors from every state. Expect to park at least four or five blocks away from Fourth Avenue—and to part with a few bucks for a spot. The fairs usually start Friday afternoon.

trivia

Tucson has thrived under four flags—the Spanish, Mexican, Confederate, and United States—and is the oldest continually inhabited site in the United States, with artifacts found in the area dating back to before Christ.

To leave Fourth Avenue you can simply drive out of the neighborhood via University Boulevard, or you can take the trolley. The *Old Pueblo Trolley*

(520–792–1802; www.oldpueblotrolley.org), reinstalled just a few years ago (it originally ran from 1906 to 1930), takes riders down University Boulevard past shops and restaurants to the main gate of the University of Arizona. On Tucson's fairly flat urban streets, it isn't quite the hair-raising, white-knuckle trip that San Francisco's streetcars take up Powell Street, but it is a lot of fun. The all-day fare lets you get on and off.

Known internationally for its optical sciences department, the **University of Arizona** (520–621–2211; www.arizona.edu) also has a number of other outstanding programs, including its basketball team, the Wildcats, which have had the nation's highest winning percentage since 1987. The school has produced such NBA stars as Sean Elliott, Brian Williams, and Steve Kerr. The older part of the campus, just through the main gate on University Boulevard, contains a number of interesting buildings and museums. Among them are **Centennial Hall**, which is a performing arts venue, **Old Main**, which is the school's first classroom, and the **Center for Creative Photography** (520–621–7968), which holds an archive of photographs from Ansel Adams and Alfred Steiglitz and features rotating and traveling exhibits.

The University of Arizona Museum of Art (520–621–7567; http://art museum.arizona.edu) at 1031 North Olive Road on the University of Arizona campus has an impressive collection that ranges from pre-Renaissance to twentieth century, including works by Dürer, Rembrandt, Matisse, Picasso, O'Keeffe, and Audubon. The museum is open weekdays from 9:00 A.M. to 5:00 P.M. and Sunday from noon to 4:00 P.M. Call for summer hours. Closed on holidays. Founded in 1893, the **Arizona State Museum** (520–621–6302, 1013 East University Boulevard; www.statemuseum.arizona.edu) is also part of the university. It specializes in American Indian cultures of the Southwest and northern Mexico and is recognized as one of the world's finest resources for artifacts (100,000 plus). More than 25,000 ethnographic objects also make up the collection. The museum is open Monday through Saturday from 10:00 A.M. to 5:00 P.M., and Sunday from noon to 5:00 P.M. Closed on holidays.

Just west of campus is the **Arizona Historical Society** (520–628–5774; www.arizonahistoricalsociety.org) at 949 East Second Street. Permanent and rotating exhibits display the state's past, and user-friendly archives are available for those who want to look up any arcane lore about Tucson. The historical society also holds annual events such as La Fiesta de San Agustin, a two-day celebration of Tucson's patron saint. The fiesta, held in fall, features Mexican and Native American music and entertainment, games for adults and kids, and food. The museum is open Monday through Saturday from 10:00 A.M. to 4:00 P.M. Admission is $5.00 for adults, $4.00 for seniors, and $4.00 for students ages 12 to 18. Admission is free on the first Saturday of each month.

East of campus is the ***Arizona Inn*** (520–325–1541 or 800–933–1093; www.arizonainn.com), which is on the National Register of Historic Places, across Campbell Avenue at 2200 East Elm Street. This 1930 hacienda-style hotel not only exudes charm but has the dual advantages of being near the center of town yet isolated enough to provide peace and quiet to its guests. It's a good place to visit in spring and fall just to stroll through the flower-bedecked inner courtyard. The inn is a popular spot for weddings and formal dinners. Visiting celebrities who want to eschew the big resorts often bunk here.

If you seek not celebrities but celebrated food with a Spanish accent, take a quick trip to ***South Tucson,*** a separate 1-square-mile city within Tucson's borders. Head south on Tucson Avenue until you can exit onto 22nd Street, then go west on 22nd Street until you reach South 4th Avenue and head south.

There are several Mexican restaurants and cafes in this area, including ***Guillermo's Double L Restaurant*** (520–792–1585) at 1830 South Fourth Avenue. This establishment features Sonoran cuisine, a hybrid created by the indigenous peoples of Northern Mexico using Native American and Spanish influences. If you're bored with bland, fast-food-style tacos, enchiladas, and the like, you'll be pleasantly surprised at the variety of flavors Sonoran cuisine employs. One caveat for diners: Expect crowds on weekends. Hosts or hostesses may tell you there is a twenty-minute wait—it may actually be closer to forty minutes. You can spend your wait watching the colorful low-riding cruisers out on the boulevard.

The east side of Tucson has its own ***Saguaro National Park Rincon Mountain District*** (520–733–5153; www.nps.gov/sagu). To reach Saguaro National Park, take Broadway east to Old Spanish Trail and follow the signs. It doesn't offer the dramatic sunset views of Saguaro National Park Tucson Mountain District, but it's nearly 50,000 acres larger than the west side park. Stop at the Saguaro National Park Rincon Mountain District visitors center (open from 9:00 A.M. to 5:00 P.M. daily) and ask about the condition and difficulty of the trails before doing any hiking here. There are some easy loop trails, but others are quite difficult. Restrooms and picnic areas are available at both the east side and west side parks. During times of drought when the desert brush is especially dry, you may be asked not to use the barbecue grills.

The east side also has a wonderful, hidden arboreal getaway called ***Sabino Canyon*** (520–749–2327 or 520–749–2861; www.sabinocanyon.com). Drive east on Tanque Verde Road to Sabino Canyon Road, go north and keep driving, and you'll wind up in the parking lot. Sabino Canyon has roadrunners that are so tame they eat out of your hand and tram rides that can take you through the canyon (no other vehicles are allowed). The tram also runs in the moonlight on certain days of the year. Experienced hikers who visit Sabino Canyon often choose to make the trek to Seven Falls—occasionally quite a spectacular swimming hole, depending on the rain. It's only about a 5-mile hike, but the ground can be quite rocky and the underbrush treacherous. A quicker way to get there is to ride the tram to the start of Bear Canyon Trail and then hike the last 2 miles.

Incidentally, Tanque Verde Road could probably win an award as one of the strangest-looking streets in Arizona. It has a variety of weird statuary along its route: a life-size Tyrannosaurus rex at the Kolb intersection; an ersatz castle at Golf 'n' Stuff; a sculpted metal fish jumping out of the dry Tanque Verde wash (river) onto the street; and a wagon sitting on top of boulders at Trail Dust Town (home to the **Dakota Cafe** (520–298–7188) at 6541 East Tanque Verde Road—a great place to get nouvelle cuisine with a Southwestern flair). Not far from the Tanque Verde strip is the **Tanque Verde Guest Ranch** (520–296–6275 or 800–234–3833; www.tanqueverderanch.com) at 14301 East Speedway. It's an authentic, Old West–style dude ranch that was even used as the location for the Nickelodeon series *Hey Dude*. It has stables, tennis courts, and gourmet dining. Accommodations here are surprisingly luxurious, and the foothills setting is incomparable.

Tucson's West Side

From south Tucson, backtrack to Speedway Boulevard and head west. Pretty soon you'll notice that the cacti begin to outnumber the houses. Speedway becomes Gates Pass Road, and suddenly you're in the heart of **Saguaro National Park Tucson Mountain District** (928–733–5158; www.nps.gov/sagu), a terrific place to watch sunsets and take pictures, especially in the spring when the saguaro's white blossoms open. The park was created to preserve the majestic saguaro cactus, which only grows in the Sonoran Desert. It can take a saguaro ten years to reach an inch in height and fifty-plus years before it grows arms. It's not unusual for a saguaro to be more than one hundred years old, although they're frequently killed off by frost, fire, and bacterial infection. State laws protect these mighty cacti from damage or theft. Several hiking or biking trails run through the park. They range from easy to moderately difficult. Before you start off on any of them, stop by the visitors center and talk to a park ranger. If you've never hiked in the desert before, it presents its own set of challenges.

An interesting attraction on this side of the city is the **Arizona-Sonora Desert Museum** (520–883–2702; www.desertmuseum.org) at 2021 North Kinney Road. It features only plants and animals native to the Sonoran Desert. You can see everything from mountain lions and javelinas to bark scorpions. The museum also has an extensive mineral collection. During summer the museum

often holds special evening events so
that visitors can get a look at bats, night-
blooming cacti, and other nocturnal
phenomena. Museum hours vary; call
for information. Tucson is also brim-
ming with entertaining options for expe-
riencing the best of the Old West. *Old Tucson Studios* (520–883–0100;
www.oldtucson.com), located just down the road from the Desert Museum,
underwent an extensive $13-million reconstruction necessitated by a devastat-
ing 1995 fire. More than 250 movies have been filmed at this 1880s frontier
town set, also known as "Hollywood in the Desert." Cowpokes and wannabes
will find western-themed buildings, rides, and shows.

If casino gambling is your sort of amusement, you're in luck—and you're
also adhering to a Tucson tradition. Wyatt Earp and Doc Holliday used to play
faro here in the 1880s. Take Valencia Road west, and turn south onto Camino
de Oeste. You're now on the *San Xavier* (depending upon your facility with
Spanish, you can try to pronounce the first syllable or simply say "Hah-veer")
Indian Reservation. This is Pascua Yaqui land, and the tribe operates the
Casino of the Sun (800–344–9435; www.casinosun.com) at 7406 South
Camino de Oeste, an enterprise that includes 500 gaming machines, high stakes
bingo, and live keno, poker, and blackjack. And if you're hungry, the casino
offers an all-you-can-eat prime rib buffet.

The reservation also is the location of *Mission San Xavier del Bac*
(520–294–2624; www.sanxaviermission.org) at 1950 West San Xavier Road. The
fabled "White Dove of the Desert" is one part museum (containing artifacts and
paintings that are several hundred years old) and one part Jesuit church, with
regular services and many weddings. It's common to run into a wedding party
while you're visiting the mission. You can take a self-guided tour of the church
if there isn't a mass or other service going on. Also venture across the courtyard,
and you'll find shops selling Native American crafts and vendors offering frybread and other goodies. The Mission is open daily from 8:00 A.M. to 5:00 P.M.

On the east side of the reservation, on land deeded to the Tohono
O'Odham Indians, sits the *Desert Diamond Casino* (520–393–2700 or 866–
332–9467; www.desertdiamond.com) at 7350 Old Nogales Highway. It has
nearly everything the Casino of the Sun has including blackjack and poker.
Both casinos have slots with progressive jackpots and opportunities to win
vehicles. Both have fast-food eateries.

Closer to town, off Oracle and Ina Roads, is *Tohono Chul Park* (520–
742–6455; www.tohonochulpark.org) at 7366 North Paseo del Norte. This preserved site of natural Sonoran Desert has an easy-to-follow trail through forty-

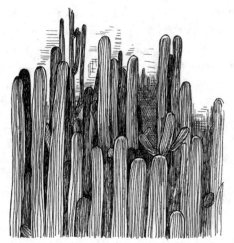

Saguaro National Park

nine acres that contain about 500 species of plants and animals. Wrens, quails, roadrunners, and other birds frequent the park, and you may see a black-tailed jackrabbit or two. Year-round the park hosts demonstrations on low-water landscaping, lectures on Southwestern history, and seasonal events. Tohono Chul also has an art gallery that shows Southwestern artists and a tearoom in a hacienda-style home with a plant-filled courtyard. The park is open from 8:00 A.M. to sunset, with occasional after-hours events.

Santa Cruz County

Mexico is only about an hour's drive south from Tucson, and to get there you pass through the tail end of Pima County into *Santa Cruz County* (520–287–3685; www.nogaleschamber.com), an area with an oxcart load of history and rustic charm. The state's name actually originated in this region, where the Tohono O'Odham Indians called the land Arizonac, meaning "place of little springs."

Take the Nogales Highway off-ramp from I–10, and you'll merge onto Interstate 19. For part of the next 20-mile stretch—where signs begin to show both miles and kilometers—there isn't much to see out the window: shrubs, sand, and an occasional patch of intense greenness where palo verde and mesquite have taken root. The scenery, however, zips by quite quickly, delivering motorists to the town of *Green Valley* (520–625–7575 or 800–858–5872; www.greenvalleychamber.com). As the name implies, Green Valley is as verdant as a garden show. Set into a valley created by the Santa Rita Mountains, this Pima County community of about 20,000 was started some three decades ago as a retirement haven. The close-knit nature of Green Valley is in evidence everywhere. You won't find graffiti, litter, or abandoned buildings. The streets are clean, and the people are friendly. Lots of shops for groceries, restaurants—such as **Manuel Mexican Restaurant** (520–648–6068) at 75 West Calle de Las Tiendas and the long-established **Arizona Family Restaurant** (520–625–3680) at 80 West Esperanza Boulevard—and a half-dozen golf courses make the town appealing to vacationers.

Just north of Green Valley is also the site for the **Titan Missile Museum** (520–625–7736; www.pimaair.org), a National Historic Landmark on DuVal Mine Road. In the early 1980s, when the Titan II missile silos were deactivated, all but this one were destroyed. Green Valley's silo is the same today (minus the warhead, of course) as it was when it was part of America's defense program. Guided tours are available of the control room, the crew living quarters, and the missile launch area. The museum contains aircraft and mockups of early space capsules. Tours cost $8.50 for adults, $7.50 for seniors, and $5.00 for children ages 7 to 13, and begin at 9:00 A.M.; the last one leaves at 4:00 P.M.

About 10 miles south on I–19 is Santa Cruz County and the tiny town of **Amado,** a ranching community with a few shops and restaurants.

A favorite restaurant in the area is **Cantina Romantica** (520–398–2914 or 800–547–2696; www.rexranch.com) at the Rex Ranch, which is located at 131 Amado Montosa Road. Chef Misko whips up an extraordinary menu of creative cuisine, all served up in the gorgeous restaurant at this historic landmark. The restaurant is open for dinner Wednesday through Sunday. Reservations are required.

Another five minutes or so away on I–19 is **Tubac** (520–398–2704; www .tubacaz.com), the oldest city in the state—established in 1752 as a Spanish settlement and, today, sort of Arizona's answer to the artists' colony of Santa Fe, New Mexico. The attractions in this community are close together, and walking or bicycling is the best way to get around. Park your car in one of the lots just off I–19, and stroll down Tubac's narrow streets. Shops and art galleries like **C. Curry Studio & Gallery** (520–398–3304) and **Lee Blackwell Studio** (520–398–2268) offer handcrafted jewelry and crafts items. The community has a yearly arts festival in winter and a fall historic reenactment of the trek of Juan Bautista de Anza, the Spanish officer who passed through the area before he founded what would later become San Francisco. Be sure to see the **Tubac Presidio State Historic Park** (520–398–2252) on Burruel Street on the east

trivia

In the film *Tin Cup*, Kevin Costner was shown teeing off at the Tubac Golf Resort in southern Arizona.

side of town. The crumbling adobe remains of the original presidio wall (before the fort was relocated to Tucson) are here, along with an 1885 schoolhouse and a museum with exhibits detailing Spain's influence in this area. Also stop by *St. Ann's Church,* built in 1920 by a Bavarian carpenter.

When hunger pangs strike check out *Wisdoms Cafe* (520–398–2397) at 1931 East Frontage Road. This Mexican restaurant, established in 1944, is a favorite among visiting celebrities.

And if you need a cozy place to rest your head, try the *Tubac Secret Garden Inn* (520–398–9371; www.tubacsecretgarden.com), a Spanish Colonial B&B located in Tubac's historic area.

Heading south on I–19 takes you to another historic spot: *Tumacácori National Historic Park* (520–398–2341; www.nps.gov/tuma), a collection of three Spanish colonial missions, including the *Tumacácori Mission.* Many visitors stop off just to photograph the mission, built by Franciscan friars and Native Americans in the early 1800s. Standing inside the weathered adobe rooms, you can see that the people who built this mission, which was an integral part of life in the Santa Cruz Valley during the 1800s, put a tremendous effort into the construction. To see the historic mission under a different light, stop by from January through April for the scheduled *Tumacácori Under the Full Moon.* Rangers take nighttime visitors on guided tours of the national park for the nominal price of the park's regular $3.00 admission. Tumacácori National Historic Park also offers guided tours of the nearby *Missions San Cayetano de Calabazas and Los Santos Ángeles de Guevavi* every Wednesday from October through March. Reservations (520–398–2341) for the $10 tour are required and are limited to six people per tour.

The best cultural experience of this trip may be 15 miles down the road in the city of *Nogales* (520–287–3685; www.nogaleschamber.com). Nogales (the word means "walnut") is a town with a split personality. On the American side of the border, it seems like a sleepy bedroom community tucked into rolling hillsides. Here and there are spots of industry or commerce, especially along Grand Avenue, the city's main drag. The town has had more than its share of problems in recent years: political squabbles, pollution problems, and an economy that's especially dependent on the Mexican peso. Yet Nogales keeps plugging along, partly because many of the residents have family, friends, and business partners on the other side of the border.

It's what's south of the border that some visitors come to see. It is possible to cross over into Nogales, Mexico, without a visa, passport, or birth certificate if you stay within the border zone. Be advised, however, that if you want to go farther south into Mexico, you will need some documentation, and you may have to put up a bond to take a vehicle or boat into the country. The situation is changing because of new Homeland Security regulations, so check with the chamber of commerce before traveling. You should also be aware that American auto insurance is not honored in Mexico. You should purchase relatively inexpensive Mexican insurance if you are taking your car across the border. There are a number of clearly marked insurance agencies on the American side where you can buy the necessary policy before taking your vehicle into Mexico. You may also consider parking your vehicle on the American side (you may have to pay a few dollars for a space) and walking across the border.

Nogales, in the Mexican state of Sonora, is definitely another world. The streets are narrow, and often the paving bricks are cracked or uneven. Much of the city isn't accessible to people in wheelchairs. Throughout the city you'll see many vendors clustered together under one awning. Everything is for sale here: jewelry, blankets, leather goods, electronics, arts and crafts, and liquor—especially the ever-popular Mexican specialties like tequila (made from the root of the agave cactus), kahlua (coffee liqueur), and cerveza (beer to you gringos and gringas). Luxury items like Cartier watches also are available here at duty-free rates. You can fill prescriptions here quickly and cheaply, and many Arizonans drive to Nogales to stock up on allergy medications and other drugs that are significantly pricier in the States. American currency is readily accepted and is often preferred over pesos.

Some of the products for sale are illegal in the States. Fireworks, switchblades (most made in Germany or Italy), and illegal drugs are among the most notable contraband. Mexican customs officials will detain and search you if they think your behavior is suspicious. If you get into trouble on the Mexican side, don't expect the American guards to help you. Buyer (smuggler) beware!

Although you'll find a lot of friendly people (and some great bargains on glassware and silver jewelry if you're willing to haggle a little), you should be aware that shopkeepers eschew subtle sales tactics for the direct approach. They can be a bit forward at times, and some of the merchants think nothing of touching female customers in a manner considered inappropriate in the United States. There is also a dark side to Nogales. In recent years the problem of street kids mugging tourists has reared its ugly head. To play it safe, stay on well-traveled avenues and don't display any signs of wealth such as flashy jewelry, rolls of bills, expensive clothes, and camcorders. Keep away from the kids who approach you offering to do favors. Recently Nogales began using bilingual students to provide guidance to tourists, and the city has also beefed up police patrols in an effort to keep muggers away from the border area.

As for dining south of the border, it's wise to follow the standard rules for *touristas:* Don't drink the water unless it's in a restaurant advertising purified water, don't eat anything that's been undercooked, and don't purchase food from street vendors. You'll find Sonoran cuisine a little different from the Americanized version of Mexican food. Cheese is often goat cheese; the chili peppers tend to be hotter (even the innocent-looking habanéro, also known as "the gringo killer"); and a lot of seafood entrees are flavored with fresh lime juice. Prices at the better Nogales restaurants are about the same as in Arizona.

Did you know that Arizona has a *wine country?* Actually the history of grape growing in southeastern Arizona dates back to the Spanish missionaries who planted vines here in the seventeenth century. After you've visited south of the border, you may want to explore a different side of the Grand Canyon State. Instead of taking I–19 back toward Tucson, take the freeway

trivia

Arizona Wines have complemented meals served at the White House since 1989.

entrance to Highway 82 east. You'll head north toward the town of *Patagonia* (520–394–0060 or 888–794–0060; www.patagoniaaz.com). For nature lovers, this area is in itself a delight. The Nature Conservancy's *Patagonia-Sonoita Creek Preserve* (520–394–2400; www.nature.org) is a cottonwood-willow riparian forest with trees as old as 130 years and as tall as 100 feet. More than 260 species of birds call the preserve home, including the gray hawk, green kingfisher, and violet-crowned hummingbird. There are also white-tail deer, javelina, and coyote. Many species of fish inhabit a perennial stream that runs through the preserve. Guided tours are held at 9:00 A.M. every Saturday. Admission is $5.00 for adults.

Continuing north on Highway 82, you'll find that while the state doesn't yet have the number of wineries and vineyards you'll find in California's wine country (www.arizonawine.org), the former ranch lands of *Sonoita* and *Elgin* are doing quite nicely in their current incarnations as grapefields. The vineyards that dot the hillsides of this gently rolling terrain include Callaghan, Charron, Sonoita, and Village of Elgin. Among the wineries, Callaghan is known for its Buena Suerte Cuvees. Many different varieties of table wine grapes are grown here. Approximately 20,000 cases of wine are produced annually by the winemakers in this region.

Depending on the time of year you visit, you may be able to watch a crush (usually in August), where you can see the grapes being stomped. April is the month for the Annual Wine Festival, when the fields are blessed by a coalition of clergy members. Whatever the month, you can drop by the *Chapel of Santa Maria,* an adobe territorial-style nondenominational shrine located in Elgin, just a tiny detour off Highway 82.

This entire region was the site for many mines (copper, lead, silver, and gold), some of them in operation until the 1930s. Surrounding these mines were small communities, which sprang up in the 1850s to the 1880s. All long abandoned, these towns are little but crumbling adobe, not even worth the trouble to try to find. Many are on private property, so check with the Nogales/ Santa Cruz Chamber of Commerce (520–287–3685) before wandering off. They can provide you with information on road conditions and which sites might still be worth visiting. One final word of caution if you do set off on your own: If you happen to come across a mine shaft, under no circumstances should you enter. Cave-ins are common; snakes and other creatures often take up residence in these locations; and caches of old, unstable dynamite have been found in shaft corridors.

Tombstone Area

Just east of Santa Cruz County is **Cochise County,** once the stomping ground (and I mean that in the most literal sense) of Johnny Ringo, Wyatt Earp, and Doc Holliday. If your base of operations is Tucson, you can reach the historic towns of Benson, St. David, Tombstone, Sierra Vista, Bisbee, and Douglas by taking I–10 east until you reach Highway 80, then heading south. You can also reach them from Santa Cruz County by taking Highway 82 (which runs through Patagonia and Elgin) east to Highway 80. Depending upon which direction you come from, you either arrive at Benson first (coming from Tucson) or Tombstone (from Sonoita).

For the sake of simplicity, let's assume you've driven down from Tucson.

Just before the Benson turnoff, you'll see a sign marked J–SIX RANCH ROAD/ MESCAL. **Mescal,** to the north toward the mountains, is a dream factory. Since 1968 this make-believe town—a series of dirt streets and wooden buildings— has been the location for countless Western movies, TV shows, and commercials. Originally built for the Lee Marvin film *Monte Walsh,* it has since been used for the features *High Plains Drifter, Tom Horn, Tombstone,* and *The Quick and the Dead,* as well as the series *The Young Riders.* Unfortunately Mescal is strictly a closed set. Uninvited visitors are not allowed, and guards are posted to see to it that none show up. However, you can drive up the access road to the KEEP-OUT sign and with a good pair of binoculars you can easily make out many of the buildings. For a look at a western movie town that you can walk through, head north to the ***Gammons Gulch Ghost Town Movie Set*** (520–212–2831; www.gammonsgulch.com). This set of a 1890s mining town is open for tours from 9:00 A.M. to 4:00 P.M., Wednesday through Sunday, from September to May.

Just down the road a bit is ***Benson*** (520–586–2842; www.bensonchamber

az.com), situated in the San Pedro Valley. The scenery here is sporadically lush, with vistas that often include snowcapped mountains.

Fourteen miles east of Benson on I–10, you'll come to the turn-off to scenic **Texas Canyon,** which is known for its strange and spectacular rock formations. If you want to explore the canyon by foot or on horseback, you may want to check into the **Triangle T Guest Ranch** (520–586–7533; www.triangle guestranch.com). The ranch offers your choice of casitas and has cabins and also a restaurant and saloon. Rates start at $125.

trivia

The San Pedro River in southeastern Arizona's Cochise County actually flows northward into the United States from Mexico.

South on Highway 90, between Bisbee and Sierra Vista, you'll find another natural jewel at the **San Pedro Riparian National Conservation Area** (520–586–3467). This area protects 40 miles of riparian habitat of the San Pedro River, which supports more than 350 species of birds—making this a prime bird-watching destination.

If you head south towards Sierra Vista from Benson, you'll come to **Kartchner Caverns** (520–586–2283). These pristine caves are considered to be some of the most beautiful and unusual "living" cave formations in the world. The crystalline underground garden takes shape in an array of unusual formations or "speleothems"—shields, stalactites, stalagmites, columns, cave pearls, soda straws, flowstone, popcorn, rimstone dams, and cave cotton. One of the reasons that Kartchner Caverns is world-renowned is that it is a living cave, where all of the glorious speleothems are still growing. The Throne Room and Rotunda Room, the first rooms open for tours, feature the longest soda straw formation in the United States at 21 feet and 2 inches, and the largest column in the state reaching to an impressive height of 58 feet. The Big Room, which opened for tours in November 2003, also has some notable features— the world's most extensive formation of brushite moonmilk, the first reported occurrence of turnip shields, and the first noted occurrence of birdsnest needle formations. The Big Room is also the nursery roost for female cave myotis bats from April through September, during which time the Big Room is closed in an effort to foster the cave's unique ecosystem.

Bibliophiles may want to take a slight detour to the **Singing Wind Ranch Bookshop** (520–586–2425), north of I–10 via Ocotillo Road (turn at Singing Wind Road and look for the green gate with a chain). The bookshop's numerous offerings are grouped helter-skelter within a Southwestern ranch house, where hunting for buried treasures is as much fun as finding them. A treat for Benson's visitors is a stop at Lorene Whaley's **Horseshoe Cafe** (520–586– 3303),

154 East Fourth Street. This two-story landmark has been in Whaley's family for decades, and, as a child, Whaley even lived upstairs in an apartment above the cafe. Burgers are mouthwatering, and the Mexican fare is good. The Horseshoe's giant cinnamon rolls are killer. It's a great spot for watching the trains go by and enjoying some down-home cooking.

Heading south on Highway 80 takes you through more riparian areas to the tucked-away town of *St. David*. Like much of southeastern Arizona, this peaceful little village was booming when nearby mines were open. Today, you can enjoy browsing in antiques shops or visiting the *Holy Trinity Monastery* (520–720–4642; www.holytrinitymonastery.org). The monastery has a gift shop, library, meditation garden, museum, and other areas that are open to the public.

Tombstone (888–457–3929; www.tombstone.org), "the town too tough to die," is only a few miles away from St. David on Highway 80. The story goes that the burg's founder (a prospector) was told that the only thing he would find in southern Arizona would be his tombstone—and the name stuck. The town had a much harder time sticking around than did the name. It was a prosperous mining community in the early 1880s, but by 1909 the community had fallen on hard times. It became prohibitively expensive to pull ore out of the nearby mines, which had flooded after miners had struck underground streams.

Driving into town, high on a hill to your left, you'll see the grave sites of infamous *Boot Hill* (520–457–3300), where the victims of the gunfight at OK Corral were buried. This wasn't, however, the original location for the cemetery; it was moved when the road was built. You can take a self-guided tour of the cemetery, photograph the sometimes comical markers (HERE LIES LESTER MOORE / FOUR SHOTS FROM A .44 / NO LES, NO MORE), and shop in the gift shop.

The community of Tombstone is rightfully proud of its place in American history. About $37 million in various ores was removed from the mines in its environs before they ceased operation. Even in the wild and woolly 1880s, the town of nearly 10,000 residents (now 1,500) had cultural activities, including literary societies, theater, and musical groups. Important mine-related events that occurred here were reported all over the country. Today Tombstone survives primarily because tourists who are fascinated with the Old West want to (as one sign puts it) WALK WHERE THEY [Western outlaws like the Clantons] FELL.

Allen Street in the heart of the historic section of Tombstone actually looks very much like a movie location, and this effect is heightened by staged gunfights that occur at regular times during *Helldorado Days* (usually October), *Nellie Cashman Rose Festival* (usually April), and other popular celebrations the town holds. Both sides of the boardwalk get crammed with camcorder-wielding tourists, as actors in 1880s attire shoot it out with black-powder firearms. Ironically the town has had a few problems with visitors brandishing real guns on the streets. So, as was the case in the days of Wyatt Earp, wearing firearms in town has been banned. Reenactors are exempt.

A number of souvenir shops line Allen Street, selling everything from T-shirts to Navajo jewelry.

On Allen and Sixth Streets sits the ***Bird Cage Theatre*** (520–457–3421 or 800–457–3423), a notorious gambling hall, saloon, and cathouse that operated from 1881 until 1889. The atmosphere was so wild in here that there are 140 bullet holes in the walls from gun battles. The Bird Cage Theatre is open daily for tours, and it's worth seeing as a good example of the type of place where frontier men entertained themselves. Hours are from 8:00 A.M. to 6:00 P.M. Theater tours cost $6.00 for adults, and there are discounts for children, seniors, and groups.

While you're on Allen Street, you may be tempted to pay the fee to walk around in the ***OK Corral*** (520–457–3456; www.ok-corral.com) at 308 Allen Street. The live daily show is at 2:00 P.M. In all fairness it's worth a peek. You can tour exhibits of photographs of early Tombstone and read original newspaper accounts of the famous gunfight between the Clantons and the Earps. Inside the corral you can see life-size statues of the Earps and the Clantons arranged to represent the real participants of the shoot-out. The corral wasn't, however, the actual site of their armed altercation. The gunfight took place in 1881, in a vacant lot around the corner, across the street from where Fly's Boarding House once stood. The shooting lasted about a minute and occurred at nearly point-blank range. The final score: Morgan and Virgil Earp were seriously wounded; Doc Holliday was grazed by a round (he allegedly ran away in hysterics—a vicious killer, he was neither a good shot nor a brave man); Billy Clanton and Tom and Frank McLaury were shot dead. An excellent book on the subject is Paula Mitchell Marks's *And Die in the West,* which is available in bookstores on Allen Street.

On a happier note, Tombstone is also home to the ***world's largest rose tree*** (planted in 1885), located at the ***Rose Tree Museum*** (520–457–3326), just a short walk from Allen Street on Fourth and Toughnut Streets. The Lady Banksia rose tree is in the courtyard of a home that once belonged to Amelia Adamson, grown from a shoot given to her by the wife of a Scottish immigrant. The roses bloom from mid-March to mid-April, and even when the bush is dormant, you can enjoy the museum displays within the converted home. The displays recount life in early Tombstone. The museum is open daily from 9:00 A.M. to 5:00 P.M.

If hunger pangs get the better of you, try ***Nellie Cashman's*** (520–457–2212) at Fifth and Toughnut Streets. Located in a historic building and named after one of the town's leading citizens of the 1880s, this traditional American restaurant has Western memorabilia on the walls and a menu that includes salads, sandwiches, steaks, chicken, hamburgers, and homemade pie. The

Longhorn Restaurant (520–457–3405) at Fifth and Allen Streets also offers American cuisine in addition to a little peek at history: Virgil Earp was shot and killed by a gunman firing from one of the Longhorn's second-story windows.

If you decide to stay in Tombstone, try the *Tombstone Boarding House* (520–457–3716 or 877–225–1319) at 108 North Fourth Street. This B&B is a restored Victorian home that's been decorated in period splendor. Likewise, the *Tombstone Bordello Boarding House* (520–457–2394) on Allen Street is a historic adobe home that reflects a time when the West was wilder. One of the town's newspapers is the *Tombstone Epitaph* (the other one is the *Tombstone Tumbleweed*), considered Arizona's oldest newspaper. Featured prominently in TV series like *Wyatt Earp* and *Bat Masterson,* the more than one-hundred-year-old paper is published by the University of Arizona's journalism department. However, if you want to take a different look at frontier life and the Old West, you can pick up a map of the area's ghost towns at the *Tombstone Chamber of Commerce* (888–457–3929).

Bisbee, Douglas, and Sierra Vista

Continuing south on Highway 80 takes you to another historic place: *Bisbee* (520–432–5421 or 866–2–BISBEE; www.bisbeearizona.com), formerly a mining town and now best known as an artists' community and a retreat for celebrities. It has been heralded by *Travel and Leisure* magazine as one of the "Best New American Destinations," comparing the century-old town with such world-renowned arts destinations as Aspen and Santa Fe. Set in the Mule Mountains, the older section of Bisbee (which can easily be covered on foot but is not particularly accessible for wheelchairs) may remind you a bit of San Francisco. The wooden Victorian buildings that dot the hillside and line the narrow main street have maintained their quaint charm. To find your way around, park in the first lot you come to as you enter town on Highway 80, and walk across the street to the *Chamber of Commerce* office. They can give you maps of the area, as well as information on any events—poetry readings, music festivals, art openings—that may be taking place that day.

Next, you may want to wander into the *Bisbee Mining and Historical Museum* (520–432–7071; www.bisbeemuseum.org) on Main Street (just look for the train out front). The museum, situated in the 1897 Copper Queen Consolidated Mining Offices, details Bisbee's mining history and has displays of minerals that were found in and around the Mule Mountains. It also offers a glimpse into the town's past by describing its transition from boom to bust. The museum is open daily from 10:00 A.M. to 4:00 P.M. Admission is $5.00 for adults, $4.50 for seniors, and $2.00 for children.

While in the older section of Bisbee, you may want to take the underground tour of the **Queen Mine** (520–432–2071 or 866–432–2071; www.cityof bisbee.com/queenminetours.htm) on Arizona Street. The tour guides are former Queen Mine workers who take visitors deep into the defunct mine aboard original miniature train cars. Be sure to stop by the grand **Copper Queen Hotel** (520–432–2216; www.copperqueen.com) on Howell Avenue, where Theodore Roosevelt once stayed and which continues to operate as a hotel and a restaurant. Rumor has it that a few friendly spirits inhabit the rooms of this classic hotel. For that matter, walking through the antiques shops lining Main Street is a trip back in time.

Antiques buffs and visitors looking for one-of-a-kind treasures will find Bisbee's winding streets a virtual paradise. Galleries, boutiques, gem shops, and antiques stores are plentiful, offering everything from locally mined Bisbee Blue turquoise to original art—much of it is created by local artisans.

Christina Plascencia's **55 Main Gallery** (520–432–4694) displays original art, clothing, and handcrafted jewelry. She even brings in psychics to entertain browsers in the gallery she describes as "a holistic venue for showing the essence of Bisbee . . . something for mind, body, and spirit." **Jane Hamilton Fine Art** (520–529–4886) showcases paintings, raku, and glass at 29 Main Street. **Óptimo Custom Hatworks** (520–432–4544 or 888–FINE–HAT; www .optimohatworks.com) sells Panama straw hats from Ecuador. While walking the main drag, you might want to stop and sample the eclectic mix of honey products at **The Killer Bee Guy** (520–432–2938 or 877–2–B–SWEET). In addition to the fabulous array of honey butters, you'll also find the spicy "Smooth Horseradish Honey Mustard," which won the 2005 Napa Valley World Mustard Competition bronze award.

Dining is equally eclectic in this historic hillside burg. **Cafe Roka** (520–432–5153; www.caferoka.com) is gaining a well-deserved reputation for its gourmet fare presented in a historic storefront along the main drag. Another historic spot, the **Brewery Steakhouse** (520–432–3317), fires up mesquite-grilled steaks and ribs, fresh seafood, and pasta seven days a week at 15 Brewery Gulch. Upstairs Bisbee's old stock exchange is the site for the **Stock Exchange Bar,** which attracts a diverse crowd and is prominently adorned with the original 1914 stock board that covers an entire wall.

Besides the aforementioned Copper Queen, there are several comfortable, unique places to stay in town. The **School House Inn** (520–432–2996 or 800–537–4333) at 818 Tombstone Canyon Road is, as the name implies, a former school house. It has airy yet cozy rooms with private bathrooms. The **Oliver House** (520–432–1900) at 24 Sowles Road is a bit of a hike from the main drag but has a lot of Victorian charm.

For nostalgia fanatics perhaps the only logical lodging choice would be the **Shady Dell Vintage Trailer and RV Park** (520–432–3567; www.theshady dell.com). This cluster of restored vintage Airstream trailers ranges from a 1949 Airstream to a 1951 Royal Mansion and is located near the town's traffic circle. Each RV is furnished with period artifacts, chenille bedspreads, and radios tuned to swing music. Rates are from the past, as well, with accommodations available for $40 to $90. Adjacent to the Shady Dell is another period treasure, an actual refurbished diner that serves up the standard diner grub.

From Bisbee you can either continue along Highway 80 to Douglas (520–364–2477), almost on the Mexican border, or you can backtrack north on Highway 80 and take Highway 90 west to Sierra Vista.

Let's consider **Douglas** (520–364–2477) first. One reason for making the drive to Douglas is to cross the border for a shopping trip in Agua Prieta (*ah-wah pree-etta,* meaning "dark water"); others are to romp in the surrounding Coronado National Forest or to visit the Gadsden Hotel.

Agua Prieta, a city of about 100,000, is headquarters to many *maquiladras* (Mexican factories built by American companies) and features the same sort of Old World shopping you'll find in Nogales. If you're suffering from buyer's remorse because you passed up a *gonga* (bargain), you have a second shot at it.

On the north side of the border, the **Coronado National Forest** (520–388–8300; www.fs.fed.us/r3/coronado) is an area ringed with mountain ranges, most notably the Dragoons to the northwest, the Peloncillo mountains to the east, and the Chiricahuas to the northeast. The Dragoons are the location of the fabled Cochise Stronghold, the last battle site for the legendary Native American leader. The Chiricahuas are known for being a bird-watcher's paradise, providing haven for varieties like the elegant trogon.

History buffs can take a detour on the Geronimo Trail to the restored **Slaughter Ranch** (520–558–2474), about 16 miles east of Douglas—and truly off the beaten path! John Slaughter, a former Texas ranger, was the sheriff of Cochise County during the late 1880s. He is credited with running a lot of the riffraff out of the area. The **Slaughter Ranch Museum** is open Wednesday through Sunday from 10:00 A.M. to 3:00 P.M.

If comfort and a certain early twentieth-century elegance are what you're looking for in lodgings, check into **The Gadsden Hotel** (520–364–4481; www.hotelgadsden.com) on G Avenue. The Gadsden was built in 1907 as a grand hotel for cattle barons and other well-heeled travelers, including Wilford Brimley, Paul Newman, Eleanor Roosevelt, Amelia Earhart, Johnny Depp, Faye Dunaway, Lee Marvin, and Jerry Lewis. Natasia Kinsski and Charlie Sheen called the Gadsden home during the filming of *Terminal Velocity*. It, too, is rumored to be inhabited by a few friendly ghosts! It boasts a lobby with an Italian marble staircase and four marble columns decorated in fourteen-karat gold leaf. This hotel, listed on the National Register of Historic Places, is a completely modern facility with air-conditioned rooms, apartments, and executive suites with kitchenettes, and convention facilities. Rates range from $50 to $100.

Church Square on East E Avenue is believed to be the only place in the world with four churches on four corners in the same block. Once you've seen Douglas, you can either head west to Sierra Vista or north up to Willcox.

The city of *Sierra Vista* (520–417–6960 or 800–288–3861; www.vistasierra vista.com) can be reached by taking I–10 east from Tucson to Highway 90, or by taking Highway 80 west to Highway 90. Those who think of southeastern Arizona as vast stretches of vacant desert are in for a shock when they near Sierra Vista. The area around the town has not only the mountain views its name promises but also long expanses of paloverde, mesquite, and grasslands. A short distance from Sierra Vista are Garden Canyon and Ramsey Canyon Preserve. *Garden Canyon,* on the nearby Fort Huachuca property, is usually open for visitors and is a good place for bird-watchers to spot elegant

trivia

Dueling deities: Church Square in the city of Douglas is believed to be the only place in the world with four churches on four corners in the same block.

trogons, Montezuma quail, and even northern pygmy owls. *Ramsey Canyon Preserve* (520–378–2785; www.nature.org), which is protected by the Nature Conservancy, is a great place for hummingbird watching and just one of the many reasons Sierra Vista is known as the "Hummingbird Capital of the World." This proliferation of winged wonders (fourteen species) is the cornerstone of the annual Southwest Wings birding festival that takes place every August in Sierra Vista and surrounding habitats. It's even possible on occasion to take part in banding the tiny, colorful creatures. For more information about hummingbird banding, write to Ramsey Canyon Preserve, 27 Ramsey Canyon Road, Hereford, AZ 85615. At the preserve's entrance, the *Ramsey Canyon B&B* (520–378–3010; www.ramseycanyoninn.com) has modern accommodations and freshly baked pies. Space in these facilities books fast! Just outside the preserve is a new addition to the county, the nonprofit *Arizona Folklore Preserve* (520–378–6165; www.arizonafolklore.com). There Arizona's Official Balladeer, Dolan Ellis, entertains visitors with the songs, legends, and poetry of the Old West, accompanied by stunning photographic images he has collected. The Arizona Folklore Preserve is open on weekends for performances by Ellis (a former member of the New Christy Minstrels) and other folk artists and is dedicated to the collection, presentation, and preservation of Arizona folklore.

Fort Huachuca (520–533–5736) is just a few minutes west of Sierra Vista. An Army base that today serves as headquarters for the U.S. Army's Intelligence Center and Information Systems Command, the fort's history stretches back to the 1870s, when it was established as a camp to protect settlers against Apache raiders. It has had an interesting history as a base for the soldiers who tracked down Geronimo and the troops who battled Pancho Villa, as well as home for the African-American cavalry units that came to be known as the "buffalo soldiers." The fort had its ups and downs after World War II. It even closed for a while. In 1954 it was turned into the Army's electronic proving ground. One former soldier who served at the fort in the 1950s is a well-known speaker on the UFO circuit. He claims that he saw the Army test extraterrestrial aircraft there, though no proof of his claims exists. A history museum is dedicated to the various incarnations of Fort Huachuca.

Modern accommodations and charming bed-and-breakfast inns are plentiful in Sierra Vista, with nearly 900 rooms available. The nicest full-service hotel is the 148-room *Windermere Hotel & Conference Center* (520–459–5900 or 800–825–4656; www.windermerehotel.com) at 2047 South Highway 92, located a few miles from the turnoff for Ramsey Canyon.

Northern Cochise County

You can reach historic sites like the Chiricahua National Monument and the adobe ruins of *Fort Bowie* by taking Highway 90 from Sierra Vista; take I–10 to Willcox, and then follow Highway 186 to *Chiricahua National Monument* (520–824–3560; www.nps.gov/chir). Here are many hoodoos (huge stone towers) surrounded by pine and juniper forests. Take the Bonita Canyon Drive through the monument, and you'll reach the top of Massai Point. You can park here and get a terrific view of the Chiricahua Mountain range, known as the "Wonderland of Rocks." Picnic tables and restrooms are available at marked areas within the monument. North of the monument is *Fort Bowie National Historic Site* (520–847–2500; ww.nps.gov/fobo/). It was established in 1862 to protect travelers from Apache raids. Today all that remains of the fort are crumbling adobe walls. A museum on the grounds displays exhibits illustrating the fort's history. An easy 1½-mile walk from the parking lot to the fort travels past the ruins of a Butterfield Stage Coach Station and a cemetery where the son of Apache leader Geronimo is buried.

If you take Highway 181 heading northwest, the next town you reach is *Willcox* (800–200–2272 or 520–384–2272; www.willcoxchamber.com), located in the Sulphur Springs Valley, an agricultural paradise. More than two dozen farms grow everything from apples to chilis to pecans. Harvest seasons vary, but many range from late July through late September or early October. Some of these farms allow you to pick your own produce, and you can write for or pick up a brochure with a list of the farms and a map from Willcox Chamber of Commerce, 1500 North Circle I Road, Willcox, AZ 85643. For a historic look at the area, stop by the **Chiricahua Regional Museum** (520–384–3971), which chronicles the area's rich history and agriculture-based economy. The museum is at 127 East Maley Street and is open Monday through Saturday from 10:00 A.M. to 4:00 P.M.

If you'd prefer to sample nature's bounty without risking throwing your back out, you may want to drop by the nearby **Stout's Cider Mill** (520–384–3696; www.cidermill.com) at 1510 North Circle I Road. It can be reached by taking exit 340 from I–10. The mill offers apple cider, ice cream, a variety of condiments and snacks, and several very tempting types of apple pie, including one with no added sugar or artificial sweeteners. Stout's Cider Mill is open daily year-round.

West of Willcox just off I–10 resides the museum housing the infamous *Thing.* This "Thing" isn't the hand from the *Addams Family* series or the creature from either the John Carpenter or the Howard Hawks science fiction films. It's the *other* thing. The one advertised on the giant yellow billboards you can't help but see unless you drive through southeastern Arizona with your eyes closed. The "museum" (for want of a better description) housing "The Thing?? Mysteries of the Ages" is a barnlike building that for about three-and-a-half decades also has contained a variety of antiques. Its proud centerpiece is a mummylike figure encased in glass. No one knows for certain if this is a genuine mummy. (It's possible: Some cliff-dwelling Native American tribes, including the Anasazi, tucked their dead away in places out of reach of scavengers, and more than a few of these bodies have been recovered.) In any case, you can get in for less than a buck, and I recommend the museum to Stephen King

Cowboy Singer Rex Allen

Willcox's favorite son unquestionably is cowboy singer Rex Allen, whose film, television, and recording career is celebrated at the **Rex Allen Arizona Cowboy Museum** (520–384–4583) at 150 North Historic Railroad Avenue. The museum also contains exhibits about frontier settlers and the cowboy way of life. The museum is open daily from 10:00 A.M. to 4:00 P.M. Willcox hosts an annual Rex Allen Days festival the first weekend in October. Featured events include a rodeo, a parade, and stage shows.

aficionados, lovers of roadside Americana, and anyone who grew up in the 1950s or 1960s who read EC or Warren horror comics ("Look, Johnny—that thing is moving! EEYYYIII!").

Even if you're not wrapped up in mummies, you'll find that the scenery around Willcox is quite lovely. In places this high-desert community barely resembles the Southwest. Nowhere is this more apparent than on the marsh-like *Willcox Playa Wildlife Refuge,* just south of town. Bird-watchers may want to plan a visit to occur between late October and mid-February to catch a glimpse of the sandhill cranes that nest in the playa. Sandhill cranes are believed to be one of the oldest species of birds. Standing four feet tall with a five-to-seven-feet wingspan, they are quite spectacular. Each January, Willcox stages a major celebration of the cranes' arrival (by the thousands) during the *Wings over Willcox* event.

Also south of Willcox on Forest Route 84 is *Cochise Stronghold* (520–826–3593). This national monument is the site where the legendary chief of the Chiricahua Apaches made his final stand against the U.S. Army. He is buried within the monument, though no one knows the exact location. The area, both rugged and serene, is home to a variety of wildlife and offers a number of picnic areas and campsites. Hiking trails are well marked but can be quite difficult because of the elevation and the rocky nature of the terrain.

Places to Stay in Southern Arizona

GREEN VALLEY

Viscount Suite Hotel,
4855 East Broadway;
(520) 745–6500.
Microwaves and refrigerators in all suites; three restaurants. Inexpensive.

PEARCE

Grapevine Canyon Ranch,
P.O. Box 302,
Pearce AZ; 85625;
(520) 826–3185 or
(800) 245–9202;

www.gcranch.com
Open year-round. Eleven rooms nestled in a picturesque canyon in rugged Dragoon Mountains 80 miles southeast of Tucson. Moderate to expensive.

TUBAC

Tubac Country Inn,
13 Burruel Street;
(520) 398–3178;
www.tubaccountryinn.com
Five suites with private entrances in historic downtown Tubac. No children under 12. Moderate.

TUCSON

Arizona Inn,
2200 East Elm Street;
(520) 325–1541 or

(800) 933–1093;
www.arizonainn.com
Centrally located, historic, charming, extensive gardens. Moderate to expensive.

Hampton Inn Tucson,
1375 West Grant Road;
(520) 206–0602.
All rooms have microwaves and refrigerators, breakfast bar, heated pool. Inexpensive.

The Hilton Tucson East,
7600 East Broadway Boulevard;
(520) 721–5600.
Full-service atrium hotel with spacious rooms offering mountain views. Inexpensive.

Westin La Paloma,
3800 East Sunrise Drive;
(520) 742–6000 or
(800) 677–6338;
www.westinlapaloma
resort.com
487 rooms, spa, water slide,
five restaurants, stunning
views. Moderate.

YUMA

Clarion Suites,
2600 South Fourth Avenue;
(928) 726–4830 or
(800) 333–3333;
www.choicehotels.com
Hotel-motel with pool and
spa, plus laundry. Moderate.

Places to Eat in Southern Arizona

BISBEE

The Bisbee Grill,
#2 Copper Queen Plaza;
(520) 432–6788.
This dining room has a reputation for having the best
burgers in town. Other menu
items include salads, sandwiches, Mexican specialties,
pasta, salmon, and steaks.
Reservations are recom-
mended. Inexpensive to
moderate.

Cafe Cornucopia,
14 Main Street;
(520) 432–4820.
This local favorite serves
homemade soups, salads,
and sandwiches in a casual
setting until 5:00 P.M.
Inexpensive.

TOMBSTONE

Lamplight Room,
108 North Fourth Street;
(520) 457–3716 or
(877) 225–1319;
www.tombstoneboarding
house.com
Located in the Tombstone
Boarding House, this fine-
dining establishment serves
up French and Mexican cuisine for dinner. Reservations
are recommended.
Moderate.

WEB SITES FOR SOUTHERN ARIZONA

Arizona Department of Tourism
www.arizonaguide.com

**Benson-San Pedro Valley
Chamber of Commerce**
www.bensonchamberaz.com

**Bisbee Chamber of Commerce
and Visitor Center**
www.bisbeearizona.com

**Greater Sierra Vista Area
Chamber of Commerce**
www.sierravistachamber.org

Green Valley Chamber of Commerce
www.greenvalleychamber.com

**Metropolitan Tucson
Convention & Visitors Bureau**
www.visittucson.org

**Nogales-Santa Cruz
Chamber of Commerce**
www.nogaleschamber.com

**Northern Pima County
Chamber of Commerce**
www.the-chamber.com

Patagonia Area Business Association
www.patagoniaaz.com

Tombstone Chamber of Commerce
www.tombstone.org

Tubac Chamber of Commerce
www.tubacaz.com

Yuma Convention and Visitors Bureau
www.visityuma.com

Longhorn Restaurant,
Fifth and Allen Streets
(across from Crystal Palace);
(520) 457–3405.
For good steaks in Old West
ambience. Inexpensive to
moderate.

TUBAC

The Artist's Palate,
40 Avenida Goya, Plaza de
Anza;
(520) 398–3333.
Soup, salads, sandwiches,
pasta, pizza, steak, and
seafood. Open from 6:00
A.M. to 10:00 P.M. daily. Moderate to expensive.

Melio's Trattoria,
2261 East Frontage Road;
(520) 398–8494.
Italian food created in the
Roman tradition. Moderate.

TUCSON

**El Charro Mexican
Cafe & Gift Shop,**
311 North Court Avenue;
(520) 622–1922;
www.elcharrocafe.com
Oldest family-operated Mexican restaurant in the United
States, with a long tradition
of spicing things up! Inexpensive to moderate.

Sweet Tomatoes,
6202 East Broadway
Boulevard;
(520) 747–4137 or
4420 North Stone Avenue;
(520) 293–3343.
All you care to eat from a
buffet of fresh salads, from-
scratch soups, and hot
muffins. Inexpensive.

YUMA

Bella Vita,
2755 South Fourth Avenue;
(928) 344–3989.
This family-owned Italian
spot is known locally for its
huge portions and delicious,
authentic fare. Don't let its
"hole-in-the-wall" location
fool you. It's worth a stop for
a modestly priced meal.
Hours are 6:00 A.M. to 9:00
P.M. Monday through Saturday and 7:00 A.M. to 3:00
P.M. Sunday. Inexpensive.

The Crossing,
2680 South Fourth Avenue;
(928) 726–5551.
Talk about selection!
From steak and prime rib to
burgers, seafood, and pasta,
the Crossing has a little
something for everyone at
prices that won't break

the bank. Hours are from
11:00 A.M. to 9:30 P.M.
Monday to Saturday and
11:00 A.M. to 8:30 P.M.
Sunday. Inexpensive.

**Martinez Lake Restaurant
and Cantina,**
West end of Martinez
Lake Road;
(928) 783–0253.
Overlooking the water with a
full menu and live music
twice a week. Worth the
thirty-minute drive from
downtown Yuma. Inexpen-
sive to moderate.

River City Grill,
600 West Third Street;
(928) 782–7988.
Caribbean and South American cuisine with a focus on
trendy fish dishes. Moderate
to expensive.

Indexes

Entries for museums, accommodations, and restaurants appear in the special indexes on pages 165–169.

GENERAL INDEX

Adventures Out West, 91

Agate Bridge, 73

Agua Caliente Hotel and Hot Springs, 128

Agua Prieta, 152

Air Grand Canyon, 20

Air Star Airlines, 20

Airport Mesa, 24

Ajo, 130

Ajo Mountain Drive, 131

Allen Street, 148

all-steel dam, 41

Alpine, 79

Amado, 142

AMC Arizona Center 24 Theatres, 95

American Fine Art Editions, Inc., 105

Antelope House, 68

Apache Junction, 113

Apache Leap, 115

Apache Sitgreaves National Forest, 76

Apache Stables, 20

Apache Tears Caves, 114

Apache Trail, 114

Arcosanti, 28

Arizona Center, The, 95

Arizona Desert Mountain Jeep Tours, 92

Arizona Folklore Preserve, 153

Arizona Highland Celtic Festival,

Arizona Historical Society, 137

Arizona Office of Tourism, xi

Arizona Science Center, 98

Arizona Snowbowl, 13

Arizona Soaring/Estrella Sailport, 90

Arizona State University, 111

Arizona Temple Visitors Center, The, 112

Arizona Theatre Company Temple of Music and Art, 135

Arizona Wing of the Confederate Air Force, The, 112

Arroyo Design, 136

Art Walks, 133

Ash Fork, 41

Ash Fork Cemetery, 41

Avondale, 108

Barrio Historico, 135

Bell Rock, 24

Benson, 146

Besh-Ba-Gowah Archaeological Park, 81

Betatakin Ruins, 69

Biltmore Fashion Park, 104

Biosphere II, 115

Bird Cage Theatre, 149

Bisbee, 150

Bisbee Chamber of Commerce, 150

Black Hills Rockhound Area, 83

Blue Sky Street Eagle, 89

Bonita, 83

Boot Hill, 148

Borgata, 105

Boyce Thompson Arboretum, 114

Boynton Canyon Vortex, 24

Brigham City, 74

Bright Angel Trail, 22

Bullhead City, 45

C. Curry Studio & Gallery, 142

Cameron Trading Post, Motel, and Restaurant, 65

Camp Verde, 28

Canyon de Chelly, 67

Canyon del Muerto, 68

Canyon View Information Plaza, 19

Carefree, 106

Carl Hayden Visitors Center, 9
Casa Grande National
    Monument, 117
Casa Malpais Pueblo Archeological
    Park, 79
Casino of the Sun, 140
Cathedral Rock, 24
Catlin Court Historic District, 111
Cave Creek, 106
Centennial Hall, 137
Center for Creative Photography, 137
Center for the New Age, 24
Cerreta Candy Company, 111
Chandler, 113
Chapel of Santa Maria, 145
Chapel of the Holy Cross, 27
Chase Field, 94
Chinle, 67
Chino Valley, 55
Chiricahua National Monument, 154
Chloride, 37
Chloride Fire Department, 37
Christmas trees at the Swiss
    Village, 80
Church Square, 153
Cimarron River Rafting Co., 113
City Jail, 51
Clarkdale, 50
Club Congress, 135
Cobre Valley Center for the
    Arts, 81
Cochise County, 145
Cochise Stronghold, 156
Colorado City, 1
Colorado King I Paddleboat,
    The, 126
Colorado River Indian Tribes
    Reservation, 48
Colors of the West, 18
Copper Rose, 52
Corbett House, 134
Corner, The, 75
Coronado National Forest, 152
Cosanti, 105
Cottonwood, 50
Cowboy Artists of America, 25

Cricket Pavilion, 96
Crook's Trail, 28
Curley School, 130

Dante's Descent, 42
DASH (Downtown Area Shuttle), 98
Desert Botanical Garden, 102
Desert Diamond Casino, 140
Desert Storm Hummer Tours, 92
Desert Vintage & Costume, 136
Desert Voyagers Guided Raft
    Trips, 113
Devil's Highway, The, 130
Dinnerware Gallery, 133
Dolan Springs, 35
Dolly Steamboat, 114
Douglas, 152
Downtown Area Shuttle (DASH), 98
Downtown Nights, 133
Downtown Phoenix, 99

Eagar, 79
East Rim (Grand Canyon), 20
El Camino del Diablo, 131
el Pedregal, 106
El Tiradito, 135
Elgin, 145
English Village, 47
Equestrian Center, 77

Faust Gallery, 105
Federal Penitentiary, 83
Festival of Lights, 25
Fiddler's Contest, 80
Fiesta del Tlaquepaque, 25
55 Main Gallery, 151
fine arts festival, 80
First Christian Church, The, 97
First Interstate Bank (Clarkdale), 51
Fish House, 134
Flagstaff, 12
Flagstaff SummerFest, 15
flagstone quarries, 41
Florence, 116
Fool Hollow Lake Recreation Area, 77
Fort Apache Historic Park, 78

Fort Bowie, 154
Fort Bowie National Historic Site, 154
Fort Grant, 83
Fort Huachuca, 154
Fort McDowell Casino, 107
Fort Verde State Park, 28
Fountain Hills, 107
Four Corners National Monument, 71
Fourth Avenue, 135
Fred Harvey Transportation
    Company, 20
Fredonia, 6

Gammons Gulch Ghost Town
    Movie Set, 146
Ganado, 64
Garden Canyon, 153
Gila Bend, 128
Glen Canyon Dam, 9
Glen Canyon National Recreation
    Area, 9
Glendale, 111
Glendale Arena, 111
Globe, 80
Gold Road Mine Tour, 45
Goldfield Ghost Town, 113
Goldfield Ghost Town and Mine
    Tours, 114
Gouldings Trading Post, Lodge, and
    Museum, 70
Grady Gammage Memorial
    Auditorium, 97
Graham County Historical Society, 84
Grand Canyon, 8
Grand Canyon (East Rim), 20
Grand Canyon (North Rim), 8
Grand Canyon (South Rim), 19
Grand Canyon (West Rim), 33, 36
Grand Canyon Field Institute, 22
Grand Canyon Railway, 18
Grand Canyon West, 36
Granny's Attic Antique Market, 80
Gray's Petrified Wood Co., 74
Greater Phoenix Convention &
    Visitors Bureau, xi, 87–88
Green Valley, 141

Greer, 79

Hackberry, 42
Harvey Brown store, 128
Hart Prairie Preserve, 15
Hashknife Pony Express Riders, 72
Hassayampa Building, 109
Hassayampa River Preserve, 110
Havasu National Wildlife Refuge, 48
Havasupai Indian Reservation, 37
Helldorado Days, 148
Herberger Theater Center, 99
Heritage Square (Flagstaff), 15
Heritage Square, The (Phoenix), 99
Hi Jolly Monument, 49
Historic Route 66 Association of
    Arizona, 43
Holbrook, 72
Holy Trinity Monastery, 148
Homolovi State Park, 74
Hon-Dah Resort Casino, 77
Hoover Dam, 33
Hopi Cultural Center, 72
Hopi Festival of Arts and Culture, 15
Hopi Reservation, 71
Hot Air Expeditions Inc., 90–91
House Rock Ranch, 7
How Sweet It Was, 136
Hualapai Indian Reservation, 36
Hualapai Mountain Park, 42
Hualapai River Runners, 36
Hubbell Building, 74
Hubbell Trading Post, 64
Hunt Ranch, 42
Hyder's Livery Stable, 109

Indian country, 59
Inscription Rock, 72

J. Russell and Bonita Nelson Fine
    Arts Center, 112
Jane Hamilton Fine Art, 151
Jazz on the Rocks Benefits
    Festival, 27
Jerome, 51
Jerome State Historic Park, 52

Joshua trees, 35

Kartchner Caverns, 147
Kayenta, 66
Kayenta Trading Post, 66
Keepers of the Wild Nature Park, 42
Keet Seel, 69
Killer Bee Guy, The, 151
Kingman, 43
Kitt Peak National Observatory, 131

La Casa Cordova, 134
Lake Havasu, 46
Lake Havasu City, 46
Lake Mead, 33
Lake Mead Visitors Center, The, 35
Lake Mohave, 45
Lake Powell, 9
Lake Powell Resorts & Marinas, 10
Lee Blackwell Studio, 142
Litchfield Park, 107
London Bridge, 46
London Bridge Watercraft Tours, 48
Lookout Studio, 21
Lost Dutchman Days, 113
Lowell Observatory, 13
Lower Salt River Recreation Area,
    The, 113
Lutes Casino, 127

Madonna of the Trail Statue, 78
Mammoth, 115
Marble Canyon, 7
McFarland Historical State
    Park, 116
McPhaul Bridge, 123
Mesa, 112
Mescal, 146
mesquite tree, 108
Meteor Crater, 17
Metrocenter, 104
Metropolitan Tucson Convention and
    Visitors Bureau, xi
Minnetonka Trading Post, 74
Mission San Xavier del Bac, 140

Missions San Cayetano de Calabazas
    and Los Santos Ángeles
    de Guevavi, 143
Mogollon Rim Overlook, 77
Montezuma Castle National
    Monument, 27
Montezuma Well, 27
Monument Valley, 70
Monument Valley National Navajo
    Tribal Park Headquarters and
    Visitor Center, 70
Mount Graham, 83
Mount Lemmon, 132
Mule trips, 20
Mummy Cave, 68
Museum Club, The, 15
Mystery Castle, 103

Native Seed Search, 136
Navajo Arts & Crafts
    Enterprise, 67
Navajo County Courthouse, 72
Navajo Festival of Arts and
    Culture, 15
Navajo Nation, 59
Navajo National Monument, 68
Navajoland, 59
Nellie Bly, 52
Nellie Cashman Rose Festival, 148
Nelson Fine Arts Center, 112
New Cornelia Hotel, 130
Newspaper Rock, 74
NFL Arizona Cardinals Stadium, 42
NOAO Kitt Peak National
    Observatory, 131
Nogales (Arizona), 143
Nogales (Sonora, Mexico), 144
North Rim (Grand Canyon), 8
Northern Arizona University, 12
Northern Light Balloon
    Expeditions, 26

O'Odham Tash, 118
Oak Creek Canyon, 23
Oatman, 44

Oatman Massacre site, 129
OK Corral, 149
Old County Courthouse, 99
Old Jail, 37
Old Main, 137
Old Pueblo Trolley, 136
Old Town Artisans, 135
Old Town Glendale, 111
Old Tucson Studios, 140
Óptimo Custom Hatworks, 151
Oracle, 116
Oracle Festival of Fine Art, 116
Oraibi, 71
Organ Pipe Cactus National
    Monument, 131
Orpheum Theatre, 100
Out of Africa Wildlife Park, 50

Painted Desert, 73
Painted Rocks, 128
Papillon Grand Canyon
    Helicopters, 20
Parker, 48
Past Time Antiques, 82
Patagonia, 145
Patagonia-Sonoita Creek
    Preserve, 145
Payson, 80
Peach Springs, 36
Petrified Forest, 73
Petrified Forest National Park, 73
Petroglyphs, 41
Phoenix, 87
Phoenix Convention and Visitors
    Bureau, 87
Phoenix International Raceway, 108
Phoenix Public Library, 103
Phoenix Zoo, The, 102
Picacho Peak, 118
Picket Post Mountain, 114
Pinal County Courthouse (first), 117
Pinal County Courthouse
    (second), 117
Pine, 80
Pink Jeep Tours, 26

Pipe Spring National Monument, 6
Pony Express, 72
Poston, 48
Prescott, 53
Presidio, 134
Pueblo Indian Gallery, 18

Quartzsite, 49
Queen Mine, 151

Rainbow Bridge, 11
Ramsey Canyon Preserve, 153
Rawhide Wild West Town, 113
Red Rock Fantasy, 25
Red Rock State Park, 24
Red Sands Bar, 75
Renaissance Festival, 113
Riordan Mansion State Historic
    Park, 16
Romero House, 134
Round Valley Ensphere, 79
Route 66, 40
Roy Purcell's murals, 37
Rustic Raspberry, 18

Sabino Canyon, 138
Safford, 82
Saguaro Lake, 107
Saguaro National Park Rincon
    Mountain District, 138
Saguaro National Park Tucson
    Mountain District, 139
Salt River Recreation, Inc., 113
San Manuel, 115
San Pedro Riparian National
    Conservation Area, 147
San Xavier Indian Reservation, 140
Santa Cruz County, 141
Scottsdale, 104
Sedona, 24
Sedona Annual International Film
    Festival, 27
Sedona Art and Sculpture Walk, 27
Sedona Arts Festival, 27
Seligman, 42

Sentinel Peak, 133
Shambles Village, 47
Show Low, 77
Sierra Vista, 153
Singing Wind Ranch Bookshop, 147
Skull Valley, 55
Sky Harbor International Airport, 87
Slaughter Ranch, 152
Slide Rock State Park, 23
SMOR (San Manuel, Mammoth, Oracle Region), 115
Snowflake, 76
Soap Creek, 20
Sonoita, 145
Sonoran Desert, 87
South Rim (Grand Canyon), 19
South Tucson, 138
Spanish Colonial Plaza, 130
Spider Rock Overlook, 68
Springerville, 78
St. Ann's Church, 143
St. David, 148
St. Johns, 77
St. Mary's Basilica, 99
State Capitol, 97
Steamboat Mountain, 6
Stevens/Duffield House, 134
Stout Hotel, 129
Strawberry, 80
Strawberry Schoolhouse, 80
Summerhaven, 132
Sun Devil Stadium, 112
Sunrise Park Resort, 77
Sunrise Ski Resort, 77
Sunset Crater Volcano National Monument, 11
Superior, 114
Swiss Village Shopping Plaza, 80

Taliesen West, 96
Tallest Fountain in the World, 107
Teamshop Chase Field, 95
Teamshop (US Airways Center), 94
Tempe, 111
Temple Bar Marina, 35

Texas Canyon, 147
Thing, 155
Thumb Butte, 54
Tlaquepaque Arts and Crafts Village, 25
Tohono Chul Park, 140
Tom Mix Monument, 115
Tombstone, 148
Tombstone Chamber of Commerce, 150
Tonto National Forest, 113
Tonto Natural Bridge State Park, 80
Toroweap Point, 6
Tortilla Flat, Arizona, 114
Train Depot, 130
Tseghahodzani, 67
Tsegi Canyon, 69
Tuba City, 66
Tubac, 142
Tubac Presidio State Historic Park, 142
Tucson, 132
Tucson Arts District, 133
Tumacácori Mission, 143
Tumacácori National Historic Park, 143
Tumacácori Under the Full Moon, 143
Turf Soaring School, 90
Tuzigoot National Monument, 50

Unicorn Balloon Company, 90
University of Arizona, 137
Upton House, 109
US Airways Center, 94

Valentine, 42
Valley Center for the Arts, 81
Valley of the Sun, 87
Verde Canyon Railroad, 50
Verkamp's, 22
Vermillion Cliffs, 7
Victorian Treasures, 52
Vulcan's Throne, 20
Vultee Arch, 26

Vulture Mine, 108

Wahweap Lodge and Marina, 9
Walnut Canyon National
    Monument, 17
Watchtower, 20
Whiskey Row, 54
White House Ruin, 68
White Mountain Apache Cultural
    Center, 78
White Mountains Apache
    Reservation, 77
Wickenburg, 108
Wilderness River Adventures, 10
Willcox, 154
Willcox Playa Wildlife Refuge, 156
Williams, 18
Window Rock, 66
Window Rock Tribal Park and

Veterans' Memorial, 67
wine country, 145
Wings over Willcox, 156
Winslow, 74
Winslow-Lindbergh Airport, 75
Winterfest, 14
World Jet-Ski Racing Finals, 48
world's largest rose tree, 149
World's Oldest Rodeo, The, 80
Wupatki National Monument, 11

Yuma, 121
Yuma Crossing State Historic
    Park, 123
Yuma River Tours, 126
Yuma Territorial Prison State Park,
    The, 123
Yuma Valley Railway, 126

MUSEUMS AND SIGHTS

Apache County Museum, 77
Arizona Doll and Toy Museum, 98
Arizona Historical Society/Pioneer
    Museum, 13
Arizona Mining & Mineral
    Museum, 99
Arizona-Sonora Desert Museum, 139
Arizona State Museum, 137
Astronauts Hall of Fame, 17
Bead Museum, The, 111
Bisbee Mining and Historical
    Museum, 150
Bonelli House, 44
Chiricahua Regional Museum, 155
Colorado River Indian Tribes
    Museum, 48
Colorado River Museum, The, 45
Desert Caballeros Western Museum
    and Park, 109
Douglas Mansion, 52
Fray Marcos Hotel, 18
Gila Bend Historical Museum, 128
Gila County Historical Museum, 81

Gouldings Trading Post, Lodge, and
    Museum, 70
Gray's Petrified Wood Co., 74
Hall of Flame, 100
Heard Museum, 100, 106
Lake Havasu Museum of
    History, 48
Mesa Southwest Museum, 113
Mohave Museum of History and
    Arts, 43
Museum of Astrogeology, 17
Museum of Northern Arizona, 13
Navajo Tribal Museum and Gift
    Shop, 67
Old Trails Museum, 74
Phippen Western Art Museum, 54
Phoenix Art Museum, 102
Phoenix Museum of History, 98
Pinal County Historical
    Museum, 117
Pioneer Arizona Living History
    Museum, 103
Pioneer Museum, 13

Pueblo Grande Museum, 103
Rex Allen Arizona Cowboy
Museum, 155
Rose Tree Museum, 149
Sharlot Hall Museum, 54
Silva House, 98
Slaughter Ranch Museum, 152
St. Michaels Historical Museum, 66
State Capitol, 97

Superstition Mountain Lost Dutchman
Museum, 113
Titan Missile Museum, 142
Tucson Museum of Art and Historic
Block, 134
University of Arizona Museum of Art,
The, 137
Victorian Rosson House, 98

BED-AND-BREAKFAST INNS, LODGES, MOTELS, AND GUEST RANCHES

Anasazi Inn at Tsegi Canyon, 71
Arizona Biltmore Resort and
Spa, 96
Arizona Inn, 138, 156
Best Western Adobe Inn, 76
Best Western Arizonian Inn, The, 73
Best Western Coronado Motor
Hotel, 126
Best Western Inn Suites Hotel
(Yuma), 127
Best Western Payson Inn, 80
Best Western Phoenix/Glendale, 119
Best Western Space Age Lodge (Gila
Bend), 130
Best Western Wetherill Inn, 71
Blue Water Resort and Casino, 56
Bridgeview Motel, 47
Bright Angel Lodge, 21
BW Grand Canyon Squire Inn, 29
Caleo Resort and Spa, 120
Cameron Trading Post, Motel, and
Restaurant, 65
Canyon Motel and Railroad RV
Park, 30
Canyon Wren, Cabins for Two,
The, 23
Cedar Hill B&B, 82
Clarion Suites, 156
Cliff Dwellers Lodge, 7
Connor Hotel, 56
Comfort Inn, 56

Copper Queen Hotel, 150
Days Inn (Winslow), 86
Days Inn (Show Low), 86
Days Inn & Suites (Payson), 85
Days Inn West, 56
El Tovar, 21
Embassy Suites (Flagstaff), 16, 29
Enchantment Resort, 30
Flying E Ranch, 110
Flying Eagle Bed and Breakfast, 51
Gadsden Hotel, The, 152
Garland's Oak Creek Lodge, 23
Ghost City Inn, 52
Gouldings Trading Post, Lodge, and
Museum, 70
Grand Canyon Lodge, 8
Grand Hotel, The, 29
Grapevine Canyon Ranch, 156
Greer Lodge and Cabins, 85
Guest House Inn, 130
Hampton Inn Tucson, 156
Hassayampa Inn, 53, 56
Hilton Tucson East, The, 156
Hidden Meadow Ranch, 85
Historic Hotel Brunswick, 56
Holiday Inn (Kayenta), 85
Hotel Congress, 135
Hotel Vendome, 53, 56
Howard Johnson Lodge/Suites, 56
Hualapai Lodge, 36
Hualapai Mountain Resort, 42

Hyatt Regency Phoenix, 119
Imperial Motel, 44
Inn at 410, 16
Inn at Rancho Sonora, 117
Jacob Lake Inn, 29
Jerome Grand Hotel, 56
Kay El Bar Ranch, 110
La Posada, 75
Lake Mohave Resort and
    Marina, 46
Linda's Lake Powell Condos, 30
Little America Hotel, 16
Lodge at Sedona, The, 30
London Bridge Resort, 47
Los Abrigados Resort and
    Spa, 25
Marble Canyon Lodge, 7
Marriot Phoenix Mesa Hotel and
    Convention Center, 119
Motel 6 (Holbrook), 85
Mountain Meadows Cabins, 85
Nautical Inn Resort, 56
Noftsger Hill Inn, 82
Oak Creek Terrace Resort, 23
Oakwood Inn B&B, 79
Oatman Hotel, 44
Oliver House, 151
Olney House Bed and Breakfast, 85
Phantom Ranch, 9, 22
Phoenician, The, 120
Pointe South Mountain Resort, 120
Quality Inn (Tuba City), 85
Quality Inn Navajo Nation Capital, 67
Rainbow's End Resort, 85

Ramsey Canyon B&B, 153
Rancho Casitas, 110
Rancho de los Caballeros, 110
Red Garter, 30
River Queen Resort Motel, 46
School House Inn, 151
Sedona Super 8 Motel, 30
Shady Dell Vintage Trailer and RV
    Park, 152
Shilo Inn, 128
Silver Queen Motel, 44
Sled Dog Inn, 29
Sunrise Resort Hotel, 78
Surgeon's House, 52
Tal Wi-Wi Lodge, 79
Tanque Verde Guest Ranch, 139
Tempe Ramada, 120
Thunderbird Lodge Motel, 71
Tombstone Boarding House, 150
Tombstone Bordello Boarding
    House, 150
Triangle T Guest Ranch, 147
Tubac Country Inn, 156
Tubac Secret Garden Inn, 143
Viscount Suite Hotel, 156
Wahweap Lodge and Marina, 9
Westin La Paloma, 157
Wigwam Motel, 73
Wigwam Resort, The, 107
Williams Family Ranch, 110
Windermere Hotel & Conference
    Center, 154
Woodland Inn and Suites, 85

RESTAURANTS, CAFES, AND OTHER EATERIES

Alice Coopers'town Phoenix, 95
Amigo Cafe, 71
Anthony's in the Catalinas, 134
Arizona Family Restaurant, 142
Artist's Palate, The, 158
Barrio Bar & Grill, 134
Beaver Street Brewery and Whistle
    Stop Cafe, 15

Bella Vita, 158
Best Western Adobe Inn, 76
Bisbee Grill, The, 157
Bison Witches Bar and Deli, 136
Black Bart's Steakhouse and Musical
    Revue, 30
Black Rock Ranch Wilderness
    Retreat, 85

Blue Moon Cafe, 31
Booga Reds, 79
Brewery Steakhouse, 151
Bright Angel Fountain, 21
Brown Mug, 75
Buster's Restaurant and Bar, 31
Cafe Cornucopia, 157
Cafe Roka, 151
Cafe Terra Cotta, 105
Cameron Trading Post, Motel, and
    Restaurant, 65
Cantina Romantica, 142
Carusos Restaurant, 136
Casa Blanca Cafe, 86
Chalet Restaurant and Bar, 86
Charlie Clark's Steak House, 86
Charly's, 31
Chocolate Iguana, 136
Christmas Tree Restaurant, 86
Coffee Pot Restaurant, 31
Cold Stone Creamery, 96
Cookery, The, 57
Copper Queen Hotel, 150
Cracker Barrel Restaurant, 57
Crossing, The, 158
Cucina Paradiso, 86
Cup Cafe, 135
Dakota Cafe, 139
Dara Thai, 31
Delectables, 136
DJ's Cafe and Saloon, 40
El Charro Mexican Cafe & Gift
    Shop, 158
El Coronado, 86
El Minuto Cafe, 135
El Rancho Mexican Restaurant, 86
El Tovar, 21
5 & Diner, 120
Flatiron Cafe, 52–53
Friday's Front Row, 94
Fry Bread House, 120
Grand Canyon Lodge, 8
Guillermo's Double L Restaurant, 138
Gurley Street Grill, 57
Hard Rock Cafe, 95

Haunted Hamburger, 53
Haus Murphy's (Glendale), 120
Hooters, 96
Horseshoe Cafe (Benson), 147
Horseshoe Cafe, The
    (Wickenburg), 110
Iguana's Mexican River Cantina, 46
il Palazzetto, 94
Jackson's on Third, 95
Jerry's, 86
Johnny Angel's Diner, 78
Judy's Cook House, 82
Kingman Airport Cafe, 57
Kricket's, 100
Krystal's Steak and Seafood
    Restaurant, 57
L'Auberge, 27
La Cocina, 135
Lamplight Room, 157
Lexus Club, The, 94
Little America Hotel, 16
Lombardi's, 96
Longhorn Restaurant, 150, 158
Macky's Grill, 86
Majerle's Sports Grill, 94
Mango's Mexican Cafe (Mesa), 120
Manor House Restaurant and Rock'n
    Horse Saloon, 86
Manuel Mexican Restaurant, 142
March Hare, 110
Martinez Lake Restaurant and
    Cantina, 158
Melio's Trattoria, 158
Mi Amigo Mexican Grill, 96
Mine Shaft Market, The, 37
Miss Kitty's Steakhouse and
    Saloon, 31
Mr. D'z Route 66 Diner, 44
Mudshark Brewing Company, 57
Murphy's, 53
Nellie Cashman's, 149
Oatman Hotel, 44
Oaxaca Restaurant & Cantina, 27
Palace (Jerome), 53
Palace (Prescott), 55

Pancho McGillicuddy's, 31
Pasto, 31
Pine Country Restaurant, 31
Pizzeria Bianco, 98
Prescott Brewing Company, 57
Presidio Coffee Company, 135
Que Bueno, 107
Red Devil Italian Restuarant, 120
Red Rooster Cafe, 53
River City Grill, 158
Rod's Steakhouse, 18
Romo's Cafe, 73
Sam's Cafe, 96
Screamers, 110
Seamus McCaffrey's Irish Pub &
   Restaurant, 102
Sliders American Grill, 95

Starbucks, 96
Steaks & Sticks, 26
Stock Exchange Bar, 151
Stout's Cider Mill, 155
Sweet Tomatoes, 158
Teeter House, 98
Tennessee Saloon, 37
Tom's Tavern, 100
Tuquoise Room at La Posada, 86
Twisters, 18
Uno's Chicago Grill, 96
Vermillion Cliffs Candy
   Shop & Deli, 3
Wayside Cafe, 73
Wisdoms Cafe, 143
Yuma Landing Restaurant, 127

About the Author

In between outings with her twin sons, Carrie Miner writes regularly for *Arizona Highways, Phoenix Magazine,* and other publications. She is a member of the Society of American Travel Writers.